SECOND EDITION

Life

ADVANCED

PAUL DUMMETT

Australia • Brazil • Mexico • Singapore • United Kingdom • United States

Life Advanced Workbook
Paul Dummett

Vice President, Editorial Director: John McHugh

Executive Editor: Sian Mavor

Publishing Consultant: Karen Spiller

Development Editor: Stephanie Parker

Editorial Managers: Sarah Ratcliff and Laura Brant

Contributing Writer: Nick Kenny (IELTS practice test)

Head of Strategic Marketing ELT: Charlotte Ellis

Editorial Manager: Claire Merchant

Senior Content Project Manager: Nick Ventullo

Manufacturing Buyer: Elaine Bevan

IP Analyst: Michelle McKenna

IP Project Manager: Carissa Poweleit

Cover: Lisa Trager

Text design: Vasiliki Christoforidou

Compositor: Lumina Datamatics Ltd

Audio: Prolingua Productions and Tom Dick and Debbie Productions Ltd

© 2019 National Geographic Learning, a Cengage Learning Company

ALL RIGHTS RESERVED. No part of this work covered by the copyright herein may be reproduced or distributed in any form or by any means, except as permitted by U.S. copyright law, without the prior written permission of the copyright owner.

"National Geographic", "National Geographic Society" and the Yellow Border Design are registered trademarks of the National Geographic Society ® Marcas Registradas

For product information and technology assistance, contact us at
Cengage Learning Customer & Sales Support, cengage.com/contact

For permission to use material from this text or product,
submit all requests online at **cengage.com/permissions**
Further permissions questions can be emailed to
permissionrequest@cengage.com

ISBN: 978-1-337-28649-7

National Geographic Learning
Cheriton House, North Way,
Andover, Hampshire, SP10 5BE
United Kingdom

National Geographic Learning, a Cengage Learning Company, has a mission to bring the world to the classroom and the classroom to life. With our English language programs, students learn about their world by experiencing it. Through our partnerships with National Geographic and TED Talks, they develop the language and skills they need to be successful global citizens and leaders.

Locate your local office at **international.cengage.com/region**

Visit National Geographic Learning online at **NGL.Cengage.com/ELT**
Visit our corporate website at **www.cengage.com**

CREDITS

Text:
We are grateful to the following for permission to reproduce copyright material:

Extract from *Dumbing Down Our Kids: Why American Children feel good about themselves but can't read, write or add*, copyright © 1995 by Charles J. Sykes. Reprinted by permission of St. Martin's Press. All rights reserved; National Geographic for extracts adapted from 'Tibet's Golden 'Worm'' by Michael Finkel, August 2012, http://ngm.nationalgeographic.com; Interview with Daniel Raven-Ellison http://www.nationalgeographic.com; 'Sky caves of Nepal' by, Michael Finkel, October 2012, http://ngm.nationalgeographic.com; 'The City Solution' by Robert Kunzig, NG Magazine, December 2011http://ngm.nationalgeographic.com; 'Here comes the sun' by Peter McBride, National Geographic Traveler, October 2012, http://travel.nationalgeographic.com/travel/countries/india-yoga-traveler/; 'I Found the Bones of the *Bounty*' by Luis Marden, December 1957, http://ngm.nationalgeographic.com/1957/12/pitcairn-island/marden-text; http://www.nationalgeographic.com/explorers/bios/albert-lin/; 'Interview with Jake Shimabakuro' by Amina Ragheb, 22 March 2011, http://worldmusic.nationalgeographic.com; 'Interview with Marie Arana' by Melissa Wiley, 2007. http://ngm.nationalgeographic.com; and 'The New Oil Landscape The fracking frenzy in North Dakota has boosted the U.S. fuel supply—but at what cost?' by Edwin Dobb, NGM, March 2013, http://ngm.nationalgeographic.com, copyright © National Geographic. Reproduced with permission; Daniel Raven-Ellison for an interview adapted from text on www.nationalgeographic.com. Reproduced with kind permission; Chimurenga Magzine for an extract from http://www.pilgrimages.org.za. Reproduced with permission; Jake Shimabakuro for an interview adapted from text on http://worldmusic.nationalgeographic.com. Reproduced with kind permission; Interview with Marie Arana by Melissa Wiley. Reproduced by kind permission of Marie Arana, author of the memoir 'American Chica,' the novel 'Cellophane', and the biography 'Bolívar: American Liberator'; Perseus Books Group for an extract from *Mighty Be Our Powers* by Leymah Gbowee, p.102, Beast Books, September 2011. Reproduced with permission; ACE - African Conservation Experience for an extract based on details on Phinda Game Reserve, www.conservationafrica.net/projects/phinda-wildlife-research-project. Reproduced with kind permission; Guardian News & Media Ltd for an extract adapted from 'Why the Scottish wildcat is staring extinction in the face' by Robin McKie in *The Observer* 16 September 2012, copyright © Guardian News & Media Ltd, 2012; pp110–111 sources: Identically Different: Why you can change your genes by Tim Spector, 2012, pages 7–24; 'The Nature of Nurture' by Rebecca Priestley, New Zealand Listener, November 2013; 'Gene Genie' by Mark Broatch, New Zealand Listener, September 2013.

Cover: © Subir Basak/Getty Images.

Photos: 4 © Halfpoint/Shutterstock.com; 6 © Dan Westergren/National Geographic Creative; 8 Mike Booth/Alamy Stock Photo; 9 Tony Tallec/Alamy Stock Photo; 10 © Andrey_Popov/Shutterstock.com; 12 © Kevin Frayer/Stringer/Getty Images; 14 © Gary John Norman/Getty Images; 16 © Daniel Raven-Ellison; 17 © aslysun/Shutterstock.com; 19 (l) © Sasha Leahovcenco; 19 (m) Hemis/Alamy Stock Photo; 19 (r) © Tim Matsui/Liaison/Getty Images; 20 (t) Kumar Sriskandan/Alamy Stock Photo; 20 (b) david sanger photography/Alamy Stock Photo; 22 © Richard l'Anson/Getty Images; 24 (l) © funkyfrogstock/Shutterstock.com; 24 (m) © mambo6435/Shutterstock.com; 24 (r) © EcoPrint/Shutterstock.com; 25 imageBROKER/Alamy Stock Photo; 26 © oblong1/Shutterstock.com; 28 © Gene Blevins/AFP/Getty Images; 30 © Bill Pugliano/Stringer/Getty Images; 32 Asia Images Group Pte Ltd/Alamy Stock Photo; 33 © Fuse/Getty Images; 36 Justin Kase zsixz/Alamy Stock Photo; 40 Sergey Uryadnikov/Alamy Stock Photo; 41 © Peter Kim/Dreamstime.com; 42 © Luciano Mortula/Shutterstock.com; 43 © Fred Derwal/Getty Images; 44 © Peter McBride/National Geographic Creative; 45 MediaWorldImages/Alamy Stock Photo; 46 © Ljupco Smokovski/Shutterstock.com; 48 GoGo Images Corporation/Alamy Stock Photo; 49 © ArtmannWitte/Shutterstock.com; 50 © Mike Flippo/Shutterstock.com; 52 © Hans Verleur Photo & Film/Getty Images; 53 © Luciano Mortula/Shutterstock.com; 54 UniversalPhotography/Alamy Stock Photo; 55 Paul Price/Alamy Stock Photo; 56 Niels van Kampenhout/Alamy Stock Photo; 57 © Tino Soriano/National Geographic Creative; 58 (t) Joern Koehler/dpa picture alliance archive/Alamy Stock Photo; 58 (b) © Tim Laman/National Geographic Creative; 59 © http://selfiecity.net, Dr. Lev Manovich, Noritz Stefaner, Dr. Mehrdad Yazdani, Dr. Dominikus Baur, Jay Chow, Daniel Goddemeyer, Alise Tifentale, Nadav Hochman, 2014; 60 Craig Lovell/Eagle Visions Photography/Alamy Stock Photo; 62 © Joe Klamar/AFP/Getty Images; 63 © Ronald Sumners/Shutterstock.com; 64 © Jan Persson/Redferns/Getty Images; 65 © Pavel L Photo and Video/Shutterstock.com; 66 © William Albert Allard/National Geographic Creative; 68 Juice Images/Alamy Stock Photo; 70 Juergen Hasenkopf/Alamy Stock Photo; 71 Huw Jones/Alamy Stock Photo; 72 © Luis Marden/National Geographic Creative; 73 Ken Welsh/Alamy Stock Photo; 74 (t) INTERFOTO/Alamy Stock Photo; 74 (b) GL Archive/Alamy Stock Photo; 75 (tl) © Jim Richardson/National Geographic Creative; 75 (tr) Science History Images/Alamy Stock Photo; 75 (bl) © Jules Gervais Courtellemont/National Geographic Creative; 75 (br) © Amy Toensing/National Geographic Creative; 76 © Peter Betts/Shutterstock.com; 78 World History Archive/Alamy Stock Photo; 80 © Amanda Schwab/StarPix/REX/Shutterstock; 81 Jeff Morgan 16/Alamy Stock Photo; 82 © Toshiyuki Aizawa/Bloomberg/Getty Images; 83 (t) Michel Loiselle/Alamy Stock Photo; 83 (ml) © John McEvoy; 83 (mr) © B. Yen; 83 (bl) © Jason Edwards/National Geographic Creative; 83 (br) © Matthieu Paley/National Geographic Creative; 84 © Holly Harris/Getty Images; 86 © Rob Wilson/Shutterstock.com; 88 © Eliza Grinnell, Harvard SEAS Communications/Harvard School of Engineering and Applied Sciences; 89 © icyimage/Shutterstock.com; 92 (tl) © steve estvanik/Shutterstock.com; 92 (tr) © Frans Lanting/National Geographic Creative; 92 (bl) © Elizabeth C. Zurek/Shutterstock.com; 92 (br) © Boris Stroujko/Shutterstock.com; 94 © karrapavan/Shutterstock.com; 96 © Frans Lanting Studio/National Geographic Creative; 97 © Karin Hildebrand Lau/Shutterstock.com; 98 Mircea Costina/Alamy Stock Photo.

Illustrations: 14, 38 David Russell.

Printed in China by RR Donnelley
Print Number: 01   Print Year: 2018

Contents

Unit 1	Lessons for life	page 4
Unit 2	More than a job	page 12
Unit 3	Design for life	page 20
Unit 4	Innovation	page 28
Unit 5	The magic of travel	page 36
Unit 6	Body matters	page 44
Unit 7	Digital media	page 52
Unit 8	The music in us	page 60
Unit 9	Window on the past	page 68
Unit 10	Social living	page 76
Unit 11	Reason and emotion	page 84
Unit 12	Mother nature	page 92
IELTS practice test		page 100
Audioscripts		page 114
Answer key		page 135

Unit 1 Lessons for life

1a Things they never taught you

Listening eight rules for life

1 🔊 1 Listen to a talk given to a group of college graduates and answer these questions.

1 What was the speaker going to talk about originally?

2 What does he actually talk about?

Glossary
entitled (adj) /ɪnˈtaɪt(ə)ld/ believing you deserve to get what you want
flipping burgers (exp) /ˈflɪpɪŋ ˈbɜː(r)ɡə(ə)z/ a job that involves cooking hamburgers in a fast-food restaurant
nerd (n) *colloquial* /nɜː(r)d/ a person skilled at something technical but lacking in social skills

2 🔊 1 Listen again and choose the correct options to complete the rules that the speaker mentions.

1 What you get in life is *just / unjust*.
2 You *must aim for / can't expect* great job conditions from the start.
3 Employers are generally *more strict / less strict* than teachers.
4 Flipping burgers is *a beginning / not a job you should do*.
5 Things will go wrong in your life and most probably it will be *your / someone else's* fault.
6 The boring chores in life *can be left to others / have to be done by everyone*.
7 In the real world, you will *often / seldom* get a second chance to get things right.
8 Don't underestimate people with good *technical expertise / social skills*.

Grammar time phrases

3 🔊 1 Complete the sentences with these time phrases. Then listen to the talk again and check your answers.

> about fifteen years ago   at the time   before that
> currently   many years ago   next year
> over the last twenty years   rarely   sooner or later

1 _____, I'm writing a book about scientific inventions.
2 I'm going to give you some rules of life that I read _____ in a book.
3 _____, I had believed myself to be – as you probably do now – one entitled individual.
4 You will not make eighty thousand dollars _____.
5 _____, your grandparents had a different word for burger flipping.
6 But they were like that because _____ they were paying your bills.
7 _____, schools have abolished the idea of winners and losers.
8 That _____ happens in real life.
9 _____, you'll end up working for one.

4 Look at the time phrases in these sentences spoken by a student who is about to graduate. Complete the sentences with the correct form of the verbs in brackets.

1 At the moment, I _____ (take) a break from my studies.
2 Last week, I _____ (attend) a lecture on a career in the diplomatic service.
3 Before that, I _____ (never / be) to a careers advice talk.
4 Nowadays, most graduates _____ (seem) to think that the world owes them a living.
5 I _____ (wonder) for some time what I'm going to do with my life.
6 But I _____ (have) to make a decision in the coming weeks whether to continue studying or apply for a job.

Vocabulary life lessons

5 Complete these sentences. You have been given the first letter of the missing words.

1 My father told me: 'Be kind to people and, as much as possible, forgive them when they do wrong. Because in the end anger and bitterness will just eat you up.' He was right, but it's easier s_____ than d_____.
2 I think the most v_____ lesson anyone has ever taught me was my English teacher, who said: 'Keep an open mind and you will learn a lot.'
3 'Do things that take you out of your comfort zone' is a g_____ principle in my life. Because no one has ever managed to progress by playing safe.
4 I always make a p_____ of listening to what older people have to say – not just dismissing them as out of touch.
5 I try to learn f_____ my m_____ in life. One thing I've learned is that it's much better to travel light than take loads of stuff with you that you'll never use, which is what I always used to do.
6 I think to remain humble and to try to live as simple a life as possible is a good rule of t_____.

6 Dictation the problem with advice

🔊 2 Listen to someone describing how advice and wisdom can be misinterpreted. Complete the paragraph.

One _____
_____.
An example _____
_____.
One of his main ideas was _____
_____,
they will _____.
He called _____.
People _____
_____,
but _____,
_____.
Unfortunately, _____
_____,
which _____.

1b What's in a name?

Reading the importance of names

1 Read the article. Which of these statements (a, b or c) best represents the author's view?

   a Our names should help describe our character.
   b Names are useful in giving a person a sense of identity.
   c Native American names are useful because they identify social status.

2 Read the article again. Are the sentences true (T) or false (F)?

   1 Native American Indians share a belief in the significance of names.
   2 It is common for Native Americans to name people after things in the natural world.
   3 Native American names can evolve as people go through life.
   4 Names usually reflect something the parents saw at the time of the child's birth.
   5 Many cultures still use names to indicate the place people were born in.
   6 In the West, nicknames are always used to identify someone's social status.

What's in a name?

Do you feel that your name is an essential part of who you are? What factors did your parents consider when they named you? Had they already been thinking about the name before you were born? Have you changed your name at any time in your life because you thought it did not suit you?

For some, names mean little. For others, such as Native American Indians, who have been following the same naming traditions for generations, it is a critical part of one's identity. Although traditions differ from one Native American tribe to another, all tribes attach great importance to the name or names that each individual is given.

You are probably familiar with Native American names taken from nature, such as Laughing Water, Rolling Thunder, White Feather, etc. (NB the belief that such names derive from what their parents were looking at when the child was born is false.) You are probably less aware that their names can also describe certain attributes, such as character (e.g. Independent) or physical appearance (e.g. Broad Shoulders) or social status (e.g. Wife). Among some tribes, these names are continually changing according to people's achievements or life experiences. In some cases, a person will change names three or four times during their life.

Names in Native American Indian culture are descriptive, reminding the bearer of their place in nature or of their reputation in society. In other cultures, surnames often denoted where a person came from or what their family profession was: 'Julie London', 'James Carpenter' are examples in English. But even if such names still exist, they are no longer an indication of a person's identity.

Perhaps the most similar thing to the Native American tradition in modern western society is the nickname. My given name is Sarah, but my parents and childhood friends know me as 'Sally', a derivative name which has no particular meaning. The people I met at university nicknamed me 'Starah' (i.e. 'starer') because I have a bad habit of staring at people. Since I have been with my husband, my name has returned to Sarah. Such nicknames may not have the descriptive power of Native American names, but they do serve as important markers of the stages in our lives. Who knows what name people will be calling me in another ten years?

Unit 1 Lessons for life

Grammar the continuous aspect

3 Find and name five different continuous tenses used in the article.

4 Look at these pairs of sentences with simple and continuous verb forms. What is the difference in meaning – if any – in the pairs of sentences?

1. a The name Lucas **is** very popular.
   b The name Lucas **is getting** very popular.
2. a People always **pronounce** my name wrong.
   b People **are** always **pronouncing** my name wrong.
3. a They**'ve made** a list of names for their baby, who is due in May.
   b They**'ve been making** a list of names for their baby, who is due in May.
4. a At one time they **had thought** of giving all their children names beginning with 'M'.
   b At one time they **had been thinking** of giving all their children names beginning with 'M'.
5. a When I **got** married, I decided to change my surname to 'Romano'.
   b When I **was getting** married, I decided to change my surname to 'Romano'.
6. a They've had five boys, so they **hope** the next baby is a girl.
   b They've had five boys, so they**'ll be hoping** the next baby is a girl.

5 Complete these sentences with the correct tense. Use six continuous forms and two simple forms.

1. Sorry I was late picking you up. _____ (you / wait) there long?
2. I can smell cigarettes. _____ (someone / smoke) in here?
3. I heard a scream and ran towards the river. A boy _____ (play) too close to the bank and (fall) _____ in.
4. Sorry I can't meet you later. I'm afraid I _____ (work) late tonight.
5. We _____ (live) in one room for the last three months because builders _____ (repair) our roof.
6. I _____ (hear) a lot of strange stories in my time, but that is probably the strangest.

Vocabulary personality and identity

6 Match the personality types (1–6) with the descriptions (a–f).

1. a control freak
2. a driven person
3. a family person
4. a free spirit
5. a larger-than-life character
6. the life and soul of the party

a is very lively and sociable
b is independent and does not follow conventions
c wants to manage every aspect of a situation
d has a strong and forceful presence
e puts home life before other things
f is motivated and ambitious

Wordbuilding binomial pairs

7 Choose the correct options to complete the sentences.

1. Can I have some *quiet and peace / peace and quiet*, please? I'm trying to concentrate.
2. I do exercise *as and when / when and as* I can, which is not often enough!
3. As far as business trips go, it was great – *sweet and short / short and sweet*.
4. That was my first marathon. I've got a few *pains and aches / aches and pains* now, but no injuries.
5. *Then and now / Now and then*, I wonder if I should have gone to college.
6. The event is not all *fun and games / games and fun*. There is a serious side to it too.
7. *First and foremost / Foremost and first*, we choose a name that we hope is not too common.
8. *Large and by / By and large*, it's a pretty good place to live.

8 Pronunciation linking in word pairs

a 🔊 3 Listen to how these binomial words pairs are linked with *and* as a weak form.

1. I hear you **loud and clear**.
2. He'll be **up and about** in no time.
3. It's a game of **cat and mouse**.
4. She's **sick and tired** of people asking what she's going to do with her life.
5. The job has been a bit **up and down** lately.
6. It's **part and parcel** of being a parent.

b Practise saying the sentences in Exercise 8a in the same way.

9 Match the binomial word pairs (1–6) from Exercise 8a with the correct definitions (a–f).

a changeable
b out of one's sick bed
c an integral element
d clearly
e fed up (with)
f one trying to catch the other

7

1c The English we speak

Listening the evolution of English

1 🎵 4 Look at these statements about the English language. Do you think the statements are true (T) or false (F)? Then listen to a lecture on the evolution of English and check your answers.

1. Throughout its history, the English language has been subject to outside influences.
2. English is principally a Germanic language.
3. The language of Shakespeare is very different from modern English.
4. People living in the colonies tried to preserve the integrity of British English.
5. Many people around the world speak a very simplified, functional form of English.
6. The constant adaptation of English has been a negative thing.

2 🎵 4 Listen again and choose the correct option (a or b) according to the speaker. Pause the CD each time before moving onto the next question.

1. The English language has:
   a influenced other cultures.
   b both influenced and been influenced by other cultures.
2. The fact that Anglo-Saxon, not Latin, was the dominant influence on English is:
   a unlike other countries in Western Europe.
   b because the Romans were hated in Britain.
3. The language stopped changing so fast after the 16th century because:
   a books became more common.
   b no one invaded Britain after that date.
4. The speaker implies that compared to British English, the language used by Americans is:
   a more open.
   b more refined.
5. The author suggests that English is now a global language because:
   a it is such an adaptable language.
   b it became the language of international trade.
6. Non-native speakers who want to speak English:
   a must choose for themselves what kind of English they want to speak.
   b must be careful not to learn the wrong version of English.

3 Choose the correct definition (a or b) for the words in bold from the lecture.

1. The **legacy** of the Romans is evident in the Romance languages.
   a great achievement
   b gift to future generations
2. Instead of replacing English, French was **assimilated** into it.
   a incorporated   b transformed
3. The language continued to remain quite **organic**.
   a basic   b in a state of evolution
4. From this point in history, British colonialism **thrived**.
   a did well   b began to diminish
5. English was successful in its global reach because it was a **versatile** language.
   a simple to use   b easy to adapt

Word focus *life*

4 Complete the sentences with *life* using these words.

brings	fact	larger	lifelike
saver	story	time	walks

1. Jenny is a _____-than-life character; you know when she's in the room!
2. Thanks for covering my shift yesterday. It was a real **life-**_____.
3. Teaching is a profession that attracts people from **all** _____ **of life**.
4. The way he reads the stories really _____ **them to life**.
5. It's **a** _____ **of life** that you won't get anywhere without effort.
6. Making the wrong career move has been **the** _____ **of my life**.
7. That statue of a cat in your garden is incredibly _____.
8. My daughter loves university. She's **having the** _____ **of her life**.

Unit 1 Lessons for life

1d How did you get into that?

Real life getting to know people

1 🔊 5 Listen to the conversations. Note down where each conversation takes place and what details you learn about each person.

Conversation 1
Place: ___
Teresa: ___
Ana: ___
Conversation 2
Place: ___
Jeff: ___
Khalid: ___

2 🔊 5 Complete these questions and statements using ONE word in each space. Then listen to the conversations again and check your answers.

Conversation 1
1 What did you _____ the talk?
2 Sorry, I _____ introduced myself. I'm Teresa.
3 _____ in Spain is it?
4 Do you _____ joining me?

Conversation 2
1 Where are you _____?
2 I'm Jeff, _____ the _____.
3 What are you _____ to be _____?
4 Wow, that sounds _____.

3 What do you think the speakers meant (a or b) when they used the phrases in bold?

1 a lot of **food for thought**
   a things that need serious consideration
   b unanswered questions
2 it's **not a million miles from** there
   a not so far from
   b not so different from
3 let me just **get rid of** all these papers
   a throw away
   b find somewhere to put
4 your **best bet** would be …
   a best chance
   b best route
5 **way above my head**, I'm afraid
   a too stressful for me
   b too difficult for me

4 Pronunciation merged words in everyday phrases

a 🔊 6 Listen to the sentences with merged words. Complete the sentences.

1 _____ the exhibition?
2 _____ going out for some fresh air?
3 _____ company is it, exactly?
4 _____ being the only boy in a family of girls?
5 Sorry, _____ that before.
6 _____ the course?
7 _____ coffee or something?
8 So, _____ before?

b Listen again and repeat each sentence.

5 Listen and respond meeting a stranger

🔊 7 You have been invited to dinner by an old friend, Nicola, in a foreign town you are visiting. Someone at the dinner who you don't know comes up to speak to you. Respond with your own words. Then compare your response with the model answer that follows.

Hi there, I don't think we've met. I'm Antony.

Hi, Antony. Good to meet you. I'm José.

1e Holiday policy

Writing taking notes

1 🔊 8 Look at these notes that an employee made during a short talk about leave (i.e. time off work) and sabbaticals (i.e. a long period of leave given every few years in some jobs, e.g. universities). Listen and complete the notes.

Sabbaticals and unpaid leave

- formal document in 2 wks

- sabbaticals, i.e. paid leave: 3 mths for every 6 yrs worked if on [1] .... or above; only for full-time staff; part-time staff arrangements tbc

- unpaid leave: [2] ....
  decides on each case, e.g. sick parents; no unpaid leave for people who have worked for less than [3] ....

---

2 Writing skill using abbreviations

🔊 8 What do you think these abbreviations from the notes mean? Write the words in full. Then listen again and check the words the speaker actually uses.

1. wks ....
2. i.e. ....
3. mths ....
4. yrs ....
5. tbc ....
6. e.g. ....

3 Write abbreviations for these words.

1. approximately ....
2. with reference to ....
3. including ....
4. and so on ....
5. ten in the morning ....
6. hours ....
7. please note ....
8. per cent ....
9. second ....
10. per week ....

4 Write this message in full sentences.

> Jeff rang 11 a.m. Wants you to go to London to discuss contract details, i.e. commission, quantities, etc. Time of mtg tbc. NB not in office til Thurs.

5 🔊 9 You are going to take notes on a talk to company employees about holiday policy. First look at the guidelines for taking notes. Then listen and complete the notes.

1. Only include important information.
2. Reduce the number of words by omitting articles, auxiliary verbs, unnecessary pronouns.
3. Use abbreviations.

New policy

....
....
....

Reasons for policy

....
....
....

Employee responsibilities

....
....
....

Details

....
....
....

10

Unit 1 **Lessons for life**

Wordbuilding binomial pairs

1 Underline the correct word to complete each binomial pair.

1 more *and / or* less
2 take it *and / or* leave it
3 cut *and / but* dried
4 out *and / or* about
5 slowly *and / but* surely
6 live *and / but* learn
7 wear *and / to* tear
8 sink *and / or* swim
9 give *and / but* take
10 back *and / to* front

2 Complete these sentences using the pairs in Exercise 1.

1 I think you've got your jumper on _____.
2 There's _____ in any relationship. You can't have everything your own way.
3 The sofa looks almost new. There's a little bit of _____ on the cushion covers, but that's all.
4 My grandmother's 89 now and _____ stuck at home. She doesn't get _____ as she used to.
5 In my first job, no-one showed me what I had to do at all – it was just _____.
6 The negotiation is pretty _____, as I see it. I've said what I want and, frankly, they can _____.
7 We're making progress _____. It hasn't been an enjoyable experience, but you _____, I suppose.

Learning skills using idioms

3 Try to answer these questions about idioms. Then compare your answers with those on page 136.

1 What are the benefits of using idioms in your English?
2 What is the effect on the listener if you get the idiom wrong?
3 Are these statements true (T) or false (F)?
   a Choosing whether to use an idiom or not depends on the context (your audience, whether you're writing or speaking, etc.).
   b Even if you don't speak the language well, including a few idioms can give a better impression.
   c Idioms change more quickly than other aspects of the language.
   d Only use idioms that are new and current.
   e Idioms and slang are pretty much the same thing.

4 Look at the options in these sentences. Do you think it is appropriate to use the idiom or not in each case?

1 A job interview

A: So tell me a little about yourself, Mr Barton.
B: Well, I'm 34 years old and *a real go-getter / very ambitious*.

2 A letter advising a friend about investing money in shares

A good *rule of thumb / principle* is always to spread your investments between different sectors.

5 Try some of the idioms that you learned in Unit 1 in context. Ask your teacher if your use of them is correct and appropriate.

Check!

6 Do the quiz. All the answers are in Student's Book Unit 1.

1 Complete these quotes.
   a 'Better to walk without knowing where than to _____ doing nothing.' (Tuareg proverb)
   b 'If you want to make peace with your enemy, you have to _____ with your enemy.' (Nelson Mandela)
   c 'Learn from the mistakes of others. You can't live long enough to make them all _____.' (Eleanor Roosevelt)
   d 'But love is _____, and lovers cannot see.' (Shakespeare)

2 What are the opposites of these types of people? You have been given the first letter.
   a a realist ≠ a d_____
   b a serious person ≠ a j_____
   c a shy type ≠ an o_____ type

3 Rearrange the letters to make time phrases.
   a present simple
      n a y d o w a s _____
      l e g a r e n l y _____
   b present perfect
      o s f r a _____
      c l e r e n t y _____
   c future
      r o o n e s   r o   t e l a r _____
   d past perfect
      r o r i p   o t   t a t h _____

11

Unit 2 More than a job

2a Golden worm diggers

Listening *yartsa gunbu*

1 🔊 10 Look at the photo and then listen to a news report. Answer the questions.

1 Where are these people?

2 What are the people looking for, and why?

3 What would they normally be doing for a living?

2 🔊 10 Read this summary. Then listen again and complete the summary using one word in each space.

In May and June, on the Tibetan Plateau, you can see people ¹_____ the grass for a small ²_____ called *yartsa gunbu*. *Yartsa gunbu* is highly valued for its ³_____ properties. It grows inside the body of a ⁴_____ and then sends a small ⁵_____ above the ground. The Chinese believe it improves your life ⁶_____ and so demand for it has ⁷_____ in recent years. The local people, who in the past made a living by herding ⁸_____ and sheep, now make much more money from *yartsa gunbu*. But ecologists are worried about the ⁹_____ of *yartsa gunbu* and think it may die out.

Wordbuilding phrasal verb *get*

3 Choose the correct option.

1 I'm the only one in the family earning at the moment, but we *get by / get through*.

2 I'm really not in the mood for a party, but I can't *get away with / get out of* it. I promised Sheree I'd go.

3 Well, thanks for all your advice. I'll *get back / get through* to you if I need anything else.

4 I think Jake will go a long way. He's very positive. If he has a disappointment, he *gets over / gets round* it very quickly.

5 I wish she had said what was on her mind. I couldn't understand what she was *getting at / getting to*.

6 I'm sorry I haven't fixed the catch on the window yet. I'll try to *get round to / get away with* it later today.

Grammar perfect forms

4 🔊 **10** Look at these sentences from the report. Which verb did the speaker use? Listen to the report again and check your answers.

1 It's as if someone *had dropped / had been dropping* a valuable ring and then asked their friends to help search for it.
2 What they *have looked for / are looking for* is a small fungus called *yartsa gunbu*.
3 It's so prized in China that half a kilo *has been known / was known* to sell for up to $50,000.
4 One couple I talked to *had searched / had been searching* all day and *has found / found* only thirty specimens.
5 For centuries, herbal doctors *have prescribed / had prescribed yartsa gunbu* for all sorts of medical problems.
6 Zhaxicaiji *has started / started* her own *yartsa* company in 1998.
7 Since then, the business *has grown / grew* year on year.
8 These communities *thrive / are thriving* on *yartsa gunbu*'s rarity.
9 The cycle will stop, because the fungus that infects the larvae *will be disappearing / will have disappeared*.
10 Perhaps the next generation of golden worm diggers *will be searching / will have searched* harder than ever.

5 Complete these sentences by putting the verbs in the correct tense. Use simple or perfect forms.

Does *yartsa gunbu* actually work? Recent research ¹ _____ (show) that it helps the blood absorb more oxygen, which in turn, ² _____ (help) the user to feel more energetic.

People in the West ³ _____ (criticize) the use of herbs in Chinese medicine for being unscientific, but in fact, it is a practice which ⁴ _____ (be based) on thousands of years of practice. Moreover, many of the ingredients are the same as those in western medicines. An American study in 2002 ⁵ _____ (show) that in nearly fifty per cent of the new drugs produced in the previous twenty years, scientists ⁶ _____ (use) natural plants as a starting point.

So far, western medicine ⁷ _____ (not / exploit) Chinese knowledge of herbs. One drug, however, that ⁸ _____ (be) very successful in treating malaria, comes from the plant artemisinin. But there is no sign that more drugs like this ⁹ _____ (be developed) any time soon. This is a shame as, without a doubt, there ¹⁰ _____ (be) a lot that the West can learn from Chinese medicine.

Vocabulary work and life

6 Complete these sentences. You have been given the first letter of the missing words.

1 The animals are our l_____ . Without them we couldn't survive.
2 When we interview new applicants, we always give them a simple t_____ to perform.
3 Some students go on to university, but many opt to learn a t_____ like interior decorating or plumbing or building.
4 Medicine is more than just a job; it's a v_____ .
5 It's difficult to make a decent l_____ as an artist, unless you become very well known.

7 Pronunciation extra /ɪ/, /iː/ or /aɪ/

🔊 **11** Look at the underlined syllables in these words and put the words into categories according to the vowel sound each contains: /ɪ/ as in *bit*, /iː/ as in *beat* or /aɪ/ as in *bite*. Then listen and check your answers.

me<u>di</u>cinal	sur<u>vi</u>ve	spe<u>ci</u>fic	<u>ti</u>ny	fi<u>nan</u>cial
<u>pri</u>vate	<u>pre</u>vious	<u>pre</u>scribe	re<u>vi</u>talize	<u>vi</u>sa
un<u>sci</u>entific	spe<u>ci</u>men	<u>ca</u>terpillar	<u>ki</u>lo	<u>ar</u>tist

8 Dictation interview with a journalist

🔊 **12** Listen to an interview with the journalist who reported the story of the golden worm diggers and complete his answers.

I: So, John, how did you come across this story?
J: ¹ I _____ .

I: And what was it that interested you this time?
J: ² Well, _____ .

I: And what was that in this case?
J: ³ I _____ .

    ⁴ So I _____ .

13

2b Deep-sea line fishers

Reading a game of cat and mouse

1 Read the article about an expedition to catch a bluefin tuna and answer the questions.
   1 What is difficult about catching these fish?
   2 What method do the people in the article use?

Glossary
bait (n) /beɪt/
hook (n) /hʊk/
line (n) /laɪn/
reel (n) /riːl/
rod (n) /rɒd/

2 Read the article again. Are these sentences true (T) or false (F)? Or is there not enough information (N) to say if the sentences are true or false?
   1 The narrator is new to sea fishing.
   2 If the fish weren't so heavy, they'd be easy to catch.
   3 Numbers of bluefin tuna have declined because of the high number of line fishers.
   4 Bluefin tuna generally feed on other smaller fish.
   5 Troy used his instinct to know where the fish were.
   6 It's necessary to leave the line a little loose to make the fish think you are not interested.

Deep-sea line fishers

Some people have compared catching a bluefin tuna to trying to catch a car going at eighty kilometres per hour. So, not having done any line fishing at sea before, I was pretty apprehensive – but also excited – about the trip that my friend, a professional line fisher called Troy had organized.

At the same time, my hopes were not high. 95 per cent of the time, bluefin tuna line fishers come back empty-handed and a few hundred dollars worse off in the attempt. Just finding the fish is difficult enough, but once you've found them, you are then faced with the task of landing a fish that can weigh in excess of 300 kilos.

Of course, tracking them down has become more difficult in recent years because of overfishing. Because demand for tuna is so high, fishing companies employ an intensive form of fishing called 'purse seine,' where they use big circular nets to trap the tuna. This has devastated the Atlantic tuna population, reducing it by over eighty per cent in the last thirty years.

Three days before we were due to set off, Troy got a call from a friend who informed him of a secret fishing spot about forty miles off the coast. Since we had nothing else to do, we headed there that evening, and the following morning, just as he had said, thousands of bluefin tuna showed up.

In order to keep our prey interested, we dropped chunks of fish into the water and then baited our lines and let them out. Tuna feed at depths of fifty to a hundred metres, so you need a lot of line. For about two hours, we sat there waiting for something to happen, and then suddenly Troy's rod bent dramatically and the reel started spinning furiously, casting line out at an incredible rate.

Knowing the fish like to swim towards the boat to make you think they are off the line, Troy jumped on the rod so that he could keep the line tight. Then we followed the fish, steering the boat in the same direction, while Troy slowly reeled it in. After about an hour of this, the fish started to get tired of us chasing it and it came closer to the surface, where we could see it. 'Grab the harpoon gun,' Troy shouted and I knew that my moment had come.

Unit 2 More than a job

Idioms safety

3 Match the two parts to make idioms connected with safety.

1. second
2. cut
3. be on the safe
4. follow
5. do things by
6. better to be safe
7. wrap someone in
8. err on the

a. side
b. the book
c. side of caution
d. nature
e. cotton wool
f. corners
g. than sorry
h. the correct procedure

4 Complete these sentences using idioms from Exercise 3.

1. I always wear a bicycle helmet, even if I am riding a short distance – just to _____.
2. You can't _____ your children _____ all the time. You have to allow them to take some risks.
3. Safety is actually _____ to me because I used to have a job repairing electricity lines.
4. It's very tempting to _____ when you think you can do something more quickly by not observing all the safety rules.
5. If you _____ rather than thinking you know better, you will be fine.

Grammar passive forms

5 Rewrite the sentences transforming one verb in each sentence to make a passive construction.

1. My friend, Troy, had organized the trip.
2. Once you've found the fish, that's only the beginning of your task.
3. In 'purse seine' fishing, people use big circular nets to trap the tuna.
4. Purse seine fishing has devastated the Atlantic tuna population in the last thirty years.
5. Troy jumped on the rod so that he could keep the line tight.
6. The fish started to get tired of us chasing it.

6 Complete these sentences with passive constructions using the verbs in brackets. Use *be* or *get* to form each passive verb as you think appropriate.

1. Did you hear about poor Esty? She _____ (call) in to work at the weekend on her birthday!
2. I wish they would just let me get on with the job. I'm tired of _____ (tell) what to do.
3. Please be careful using that axe. You _____ (injure).
4. I don't mind driving, but it's more relaxing _____ (drive) – depending on who the driver is, of course!
5. I submit my photos to the newspaper, but if they don't like them, I _____ (not / pay).
6. _____ (you / invite) to the opening of the exhibition? It's next Friday.

7 Read the passage and underline the best options (active or passive) to complete the text. Where you think either could work, underline both.

If you had to say what the most dangerous professions in the world were, probably ¹*you would not include fishing / fishing would not be included* on your list. Yet, statistically, deep-sea fishing is the world's riskiest job. In the UK, fishermen have a one in twenty chance of ²*fishing killing them / being killed* during their working lives. When you consider the conditions that ³*fishing forces them / they are forced* to work in, it is not surprising: rough seas, freezing temperatures, long hours and lots of heavy, moving equipment. Another industry that has a similarly high injury rate is logging (cutting down trees for wood). ⁴*Loggers also work long hours / Long hours are also worked by loggers* and they, too, use heavy, dangerous equipment. They are also at risk of injury from heavy tree trunks slipping or falling. One job that might have been on your list is mining. Although ⁵*they employ fewer people / fewer people are employed* in mines these days, it remains a dangerous professions. This is not just because of the obvious risks of mines collapsing but also because of the long-term effects of ⁶*breathing in poor air / poor air being breathed in*.

15

2c Guerrilla geographer

Listening Daniel Raven-Ellison

1 🎵 13 Listen to part of a radio programme about Daniel Raven-Ellison's new approach to geography. Which of these statements (a, b or c) best summarizes this new approach?

a a critical approach that challenges people to question traditional geography teaching

b an inclusive approach that encourages communities to redesign their neighbourhoods

c a practical and fun approach that promotes social and environmental awareness

2 🎵 13 Listen again and complete these sentences and questions.

1 What does one of Daniel Raven-Ellison's challenges ask participants to find?

2 What was Raven-Ellison's job before?

3 For Raven-Ellison geography is more than just _____.

4 What kind of exploration does he want to promote among children?

5 Guerrilla geography is all about having _____.

6 He says most city guides are selective in what they show, but his films show the _____.

7 What is the best way to appreciate your neighbourhood properly?

8 The fun nature of *Mission: Explore*'s tasks disguise the fact that you need to _____.

9 What is one children's survey of the community designed to measure?

10 For Raven-Ellison, education should encourage people to be _____.

3 Look at the words in bold from the programme. Choose the correct synonym (a or b).

1 Outdoor exploration **spurs** innovative problem solving …
   a encourages   b involves

2 Walking gives you a different, more **tangible** perspective …
   a enjoyable   b real

3 It's a **hands-on** format that's very accessible.
   a lively   b practical

4 … moments that will be **crucial** to tackling issues like climate change …
   a essential   b helpful

Word focus *foot/feet*

4 Match the idioms (1–4) with their definitions (a–d).

1 I **got off on the wrong foot** with my boss when I told him I didn't like using computers.

2 He offered to give the talk with me, but then at the last minute he **got cold feet**.

3 The company **shot itself in the foot** by not investing in new technology when it had the chance.

4 Don't worry if it all seems strange at first. You'll soon **find your feet**.

a have a bad start

b start to feel more confident in a new situation

c withdraw from doing something because you feel anxious

d do something that damages your own situation or prospects

5 The idioms in bold are in the wrong sentences. Replace the idioms with the correct ones.

1 She **found her feet**, but relations with her colleagues are much better now.

2 I hope I didn't **have two left feet** when I told her how like her sister she was.

3 I've never been good at dancing – I **get off on the wrong foot**.

4 She really **followed in her father's footsteps** by not taking the promotion when she was offered it.

5 People often ask me why I didn't **get my foot in the door** and become a doctor like him.

6 Hannah **got cold feet** very quickly at university and made some good friends.

7 I'm now working for Google. I was very lucky to **put my foot in it** because so many people want to work there.

8 She was going to jump from the ten-metre board but she **shot herself in the foot**.

16

Unit 2 More than a job

2d Tell me a bit about yourself

Vocabulary personal qualities

1 Look at the statements and write the adjective that sums up this quality. You have been given the first letter.

My strengths? Well, …

1 I care about doing a good job. c
2 I will always get the job done. r
3 I love my work. e
4 I want to do well. m
5 I don't get distracted from my work. f
6 I'm willing to do anything I'm asked to do. f
7 I keep things in order so as to be efficient. w   -o
8 If I don't have the tools to do something, I'll find another way. r

Real life presenting yourself

2 🎧 14 Listen to a man, Hiroki, presenting himself at an interview for a graduate training programme. Answer the questions.

1 What kind of work does the company do?

2 What relevant experience does Hiroki have?

3 🎧 14 Listen again. Write the five qualities from the list in Exercise 1 that you think Hiroki possesses. Give reasons for your answers.

1 c
Reason:

2 w   -o
Reason:

3 r
Reason:

4 e   and m
Reason:

4 Pronunciation word stress

a 🎧 15 Look at these words used in the interview and underline the stressed syllable(s) in each word. Then listen and check.

1 experience   6 particular
2 commendation   7 relevant
3 infrastructure   8 important
4 authorities   9 enthusiastic
5 suitability

b 🎧 15 Listen again and practise saying each word with the same stress.

5 Listen and respond a suitable candidate

🎧 16 You are at an interview for a job working as a trainee hotel manager at a top London hotel. The interviewer asks you some questions. Respond with your own words. Then compare your response with the model answer that follows.

1
So can you tell me a little about yourself and what attracted you to this job?

Yes, my name is Eduardo Torres and I'm a graduate in Hotel Management. I have been working for the last year at a country hotel and I would like to get a job with a bigger chain of hotels.

17

2e A letter of application

Writing a covering letter or email

1 Writing skill fixed expressions

a Complete these phrases from a covering letter. You have been given the first letter of the missing words.

a The job a_____ me because I know of your company's reputation for …

b I am a_____ for interview any time.

c I am writing in r_____ to your advertisement for …

d C_____, I am working for …

e A_____ someone who has worked in this field previously, I think I am a s_____ candidate.

f Please find a_____ my CV.

g Thank you for t_____ the time to c_____ this application.

h Regarding the specific r_____ you mention, I also have: …

b Look at the key elements of a covering letter and match 1–8 with the phrases (a–h) from Exercise 1a.

1 State the job applied for and where and when it was advertised.
2 Refer to your CV.
3 Mention your present situation.
4 Explain why you are suited to the job.
5 Show that you know something about their organization.
6 Respond to any key qualifications that you have that are needed for this job.
7 Thank them for their time.
8 Explain where and when you can be contacted.
9 Give the letter a personal touch.

2 Read the covering letter. Which of the key elements (1–9) from Exercise 1b are missing?

Dear Ms Newman

I am writing in response to your advertisement on the Jobsonline website for a fundraiser at Harmon Adult College. I enclose my CV, which details my qualifications and relevant experience.

The job attracted me because I know several people who have studied at Harmon College and I am aware of the good work that you do in helping the long-term unemployed get retrained to enter the world of work again.

Regarding the specific requirements that you mention:

• I have a Master's degree in Economics.

• I am a resident in the London area.

• I have my own car.

I am available for interview at any time, given reasonable notice. Many thanks for considering this application.

I look forward to hearing from you.

Yours sincerely

Jane Knowles

Jane Knowles

3 Write extra text for each missing element. Use your own or invented information. Mark on the letter in Exercise 2 where the extra text should go.

Unit 2 More than a job

Wordbuilding *get*

1 The verb *get* has multiple meanings (when used alone as well as in phrasal verbs). Try to guess what *get* means in these sentences. (Note that the last two are phrasal verbs.)

1 Sorry, I just don't *get* what you're trying to say.
2 Don't *get* too excited about it. It's not certain yet that we'll move to Canada.
3 I'm going to try to *get* some time off work next week so that I can revise for my exams.
4 You go and have your shower and I'll *get* us some supper.
5 Put your wallet away. I'll *get* this.
6 I'll try to *get* her to change her mind, but I'm not optimistic.
7 Can you *get* me a glass of water if you're going to the kitchen?
8 Don't worry about giving me a lift. I can easily *get* the bus.
9 It really *gets to* me that he can make jokes about other people, but he can't take a joke himself.
10 To *get on* in this profession, you have to keep constantly up-to-date with new technology.

2 Match the meanings (a–j) with the verb *get* in 1–10 in Exercise 1.

a fetch
b pay for
c progress
d go (on/in)
e understand
f obtain or be given
g annoy
h make or persuade
i prepare
j become

Learning skills listening: top-down strategies

3 Before listening to an extract in English, try to use the same strategies that help you understand content when listening in your own language. Ask yourself these questions.

1 What is the context for this listening (an everyday conversation, a lecture, a scientific report, an interview, etc.)?
2 What is the probable attitude of the speaker (e.g. are they trying to persuade/inform/complain, etc.)?
3 Am I listening just for gist or for some specific information (dates, times, names, etc.)?
4 What do I know already about this subject/situation and what questions would I like to have answered by what I am about to hear?

4 Look at these contexts (1–3). Ask yourself questions 2–4 from Exercise 3. Decide a) the probable attitude of the speaker; b) whether you are listening for gist or specific information; and c) what questions you want answered.

1 a news report about a new electric car
   a ....
   b ....
   c ....
2 an interview with a sociologist about her new book on attitudes to childhood
   a ....
   b ....
   c ....
3 a discussion between three friends about a recently released film
   a ....
   b ....
   c ....

Check!

5 Do this quiz. All the answers are in Student's Book Unit 2.

1 Complete the descriptions of these people from Unit 2.

   a   b   c

   a Kazakh ....
   b M........................ people
   c S........................ ....

2 Look at the attributes (a–c) of each person in Exercise 1 and say what each enables them to do.
   a great patience
   b extraordinary vision
   c being the right weight

3 Complete these grammar explanations.
   a Perfect forms are used to look .... at an event that has an impact on a .... time.
   b We sometimes use .... + past participle, rather than *be* + past participle, to form the passive.

4 Complete the sentences. Then rearrange the first letters of each word to make the name of a character in this unit.
   a Please do .... hesitate to .... me if you have any questions.
   b Oh dear! I hope I didn't put .... foot .... it.
   c .... look forward to .... from .... soon.
   d Female smokejumpers do the same .... as .... smokejumpers.

   Name: J........................ C........................

19

Unit 3 Design for life

3a My town

Listening my town

1 🔊 **17** You will hear two people talking about towns they live or have lived in. Listen and complete the table. If no information is given, write NM (not mentioned).

	Glastonbury	Ghent
Location		
Size of town		
Type of town		
Reasons for liking		

2 🔊 **17** Listen again and choose the correct option (a, b or c) to complete each statement.

1 Glastonbury Festival takes place:
  a in the town of Glastonbury.
  b in some fields near Glastonbury.
  c at a world heritage site.

2 Glastonbury town changed when:
  a some festival-goers began to settle there.
  b the first festival was held in 1970.
  c people realized what a magical place it was.

3 Now the town has an unusual mixture of:
  a ethnic groups.
  b people with different lifestyles.
  c commercial activities.

4 The speaker suggests that not many people visit Ghent because:
  a it's a long way from Brussels and Bruges.
  b they don't know how attractive it is.
  c they think it's just a small provincial town.

5 Ghent is home to a lot of:
  a traditional industries.
  b shipping industries.
  c large industries.

6 The variety of activities in Ghent means that people are:
  a quite tolerant.
  b quite educated.
  c quite socially active.

3 Look at these expressions used by the speakers. Match the words in bold in 1–8 with their definitions (a–h).

1 pleasant **period** houses
2 a **transformative** experience
3 an **alternative** lifestyle
4 it's all a bit **wacky**
5 my **adopted** town for a while
6 part of its **charm**
7 around the old **docks**
8 The other **drawback**

a life-changing
b attraction
c disadvantage
d unconventional
e area where ships are loaded
f strange and funny
g belonging to a past time
h that you have chosen to live in

Vocabulary describing towns

4 Complete the definitions. You have been given the first two letters of the missing words.

1. A town which is deserted is a gh_____ town.
2. A town which is pleasantly old-fashioned is qu_____.
3. An area of very poor housing on the edge of a city is called a sh_____ town.
4. A part of a city that grows without any planning we call a sp_____ suburb.
5. Another word for *untidy* is sc_____.
6. Buildings which are boring and unimaginatively designed are ch_____.
7. A village where very little ever happens we call a sl_____ village.
8. Another word for a holiday town by the sea is a seaside re_____.
9. An area which has not been looked after or renovated is r_____-d_____.

Grammar qualifiers

5 🔊 17 Look at these sentences from the descriptions you heard. Underline the most appropriate form. Then listen again and check your answers.

1. Glastonbury is *fairly / rather* well-known around the world for its music festival.
2. All in all, it was *a bit sleepy / quite a sleepy*, traditional kind of English town.
3. Well, now the town is a *quite / rather* odd mix of older, more conservative residents and younger people.
4. … shops selling healing crystals … it's all *a bit / quite* wacky, really.
5. But actually I *like it quite / quite like it*!
6. Actually, it might be *cheating slightly / rather cheating* to call it a town.
7. One of the benefits of having that kind of mix is that people tend to be *a little / quite* open-minded.
8. There's also masses to do but going out isn't *particularly / rather* cheap.
9. The other drawback is the weather, which is *a bit / pretty* terrible most of the time – grey and rainy.
10. I'm from Italy and, I have to say, it got me down *a bit / fairly* at times.

6 Complete this conversation using an appropriate qualifier in each space.

A: Where were you brought up?
B: Not ¹_____ far from here, actually. In Bourneville.
A: Where's that? I'm not ²_____ familiar with this area.
B: It's ³_____ near the centre of Birmingham. I suppose you'd call it a suburb.
A: So what was that like? I imagine it was still ⁴_____ an urban area, wasn't it?
B: Well, no, actually. Bourneville is a very pleasant, leafy kind of suburb. It's got a ⁵_____ interesting history, in fact.
A: In what way?
B: Well, it was specially designed as a model village for workers at the chocolate factory to live in. You know, to keep them happy and productive. And it really is ⁶_____ a special place to live.

7 Pronunciation *quite*, *fairly* and *pretty*

🔊 18 Listen to the conversations. For which items does speaker B mean '… but probably not enough'.

1. A: Are you warm?
   B: Mmm. I'm quite warm.
2. A: Are you feeling optimistic?
   B: Hmm … pretty hopeful.
3. A: How was the film?
   B: I quite liked it.
4. A: Is he interested in the job?
   B: Mmm. He's pretty keen, I think.
5. A: Are we late?
   B: We're in quite good time.
6. A: Is it safe?
   B: It's fairly safe.

8 Dictation talking about places

🔊 19 Listen to a conversation about a visit to Russia. Complete the answers.

A: How was your trip to Russia?
B: Great, thanks. We _____, but _____.
We started _____ Red Square. _____ the metro. Each _____. The _____.
A: And how did it compare to St Petersburg?
B: Very different. St Petersburg _____. Actually, it _____, Moscow _____. But _____. You _____ there.

21

3b Sky caves of Nepal

Reading mysterious dwellings

1 Look at the photo of some unusual caves. Then read the extract from an article about the caves and answer the questions.

1 What do you learn about the geography and climate of this area?
....
....

2 How many caves are there like the ones in the photo?
....
....

3 Why was this place important historically?
....

4 What was found in the caves?
....
....

5 What was the function of the earliest caves?
....

6 Why did people choose to live in them?
....

Sky caves of Nepal

Mustang, a former kingdom in north-central Nepal, is home to one of the world's great archaeological finds. In this [1] incredibly inhospitable, wind-savaged place, hidden within the Himalayas, there are an extraordinary number of human-built caves.

Some sit [2] completely by themselves, a single open mouth on a vast face of weathered rock. Others are in groups, occasionally stacked eight or nine storeys high, making a sort of a vertical neighbourhood. Some were dug into the cliff side, others were tunnelled from above. Many are thousands of years old. The total number of caves in Mustang, conservatively estimated, is 10,000. Why anyone would choose to build rooms which are [3] extremely difficult and dangerous to access has remained a mystery and the evidence that might supply an answer has been almost [4] totally erased.

We know that 700 years ago, Mustang was a bustling place: a centre of scholarship and art, and a key place on the salt trade route from Tibet to India. Salt was then an [5] extremely valuable commodity. Later, when cheaper salt became available in India, an economic decline set in. Soon the region was all but forgotten, lost beyond the great mountains.

Pete Athans first noticed the caves of Mustang while trekking in 1981. Many appear impossible to reach unless you are a bird and Athans, a [6] very accomplished mountaineer, was stirred by the challenge they presented.

Over a twelve-year period, Athans made several visits. Most of the caves he looked into were

empty, though they showed signs of domestic habitation. But in others the treasures he and his team found were [7] quite stunning. In one cave they discovered a 26-foot-long mural, in another 8,000 calligraphed manuscripts. Many caves seemed to be elaborate tombs full of [8] absolutely amazing riches.

Evidence now shows that the caves divide into three general periods. 3,000 years ago, they were used as burial chambers. Around 1,000 years ago, they became primarily living quarters. Because the territory was frequently fought over, people took refuge in them, placing safety over convenience. After AD 1400, when most people had moved to traditional villages, the caves continued to be used – as meditation chambers, military lookouts or storage units. Some remained as homes, and even today a few families live in them.

Unit 3 Design for life

Grammar intensifying adverbs

2 Look at the intensifying adverbs in the article. Then cross out the adverb(s) that could NOT replace each adverb in the article.

1 absolutely / extremely
2 entirely / extremely
3 completely / incredibly
4 absolutely / completely
5 absolutely / very
6 extremely / utterly
7 absolutely / very
8 incredibly / quite

3 Complete the exchanges about the sky caves story with these intensifying adverbs. There is sometimes more than one possibility.

| absolutely | completely | incredibly |
| quite | really | totally | very |

A: You must have to be a(n) ¹ _____ skilled climber to get into these caves.

B: Yes, you have to be ² _____ fearless.

C: I find it ³ _____ incredible that people could have lived in these caves.

D: I know. It must have been ⁴ _____ difficult to get provisions like food and water up to them.

E: I would ⁵ _____ love to be involved in this kind of work.

F: Yes. It must be ⁶ _____ exciting to discover what's inside the caves.

G: The entrances to some of the burial caves were ⁷ _____ sealed with large boulders.

H: Yes, that's right. The climbers had to ⁸ _____ literally risk their lives to open them up.

4 Pronunciation stress in intensifying adverbs

a 🔊 20 Listen to these sentences with intensifiers and underline the stressed syllables.

1 I'm utterly exhausted.
2 I'd really appreciate that.
3 It's so hot today.
4 It's OK. I quite understand.
5 You're absolutely right.
6 It's very difficult to say.

b Practise saying the sentences with the same stress.

Vocabulary adverb and adjective collocations

5 Match the adverbs (1–10) with the adjectives (a–j) to make collocations.

1 deadly   a amused
2 ideally   b familiar
3 hopelessly   c obvious
4 mildly   d optimistic
5 painfully   e reasonable
6 patently   f serious
7 perfectly   g slow
8 closely   h in love
9 vaguely   i suited
10 wildly   j associated with

6 Complete the sentences with collocations from Exercise 5.

1 I think your estimate that ninety per cent of the people will say 'yes' is _____. It'll be more like forty per cent.
2 His name sounds _____ to me. I think perhaps I met him at a party about three years ago.
3 I don't know why you're even asking me that question. The answer is _____.
4 Even if you bought the suitcase three years ago, it's _____ to ask for a refund if it has a five-year guarantee.
5 I thought she was joking when she said she was going to run the London marathon, but she was _____.
6 I wish he would get to the point sooner. I find his explanations _____.

Vocabulary features in a home

7 Look at these features in a home. Which are for:

a storage?
b health and fitness?
c enjoying the sun?
d leisure?
e convenience?

a conservatory   en suite bathrooms
a games room   a garage/workshop   a gym
a home cinema   a state-of-the-art kitchen
a library   a roof garden   a sauna
a walk-in wardrobe

23

3c Biomimetic architecture

Listening the influence of nature

1 🔊 21 Look at the photos and captions. Then listen to an interview with an architectural historian about 'biomimetics'. Answer the questions.

   1 What does 'biomimetics' mean?

   2 How do the three structures in the photos relate to biomimetics?

2 🔊 21 Listen again and choose the correct option (a, b or c). Pause the CD each time before moving onto the next question.

   1 According to the historian, the term biomimetics:
      a is relatively recent.
      b is an old science.
      c can be applied to anything that copies nature.

   2 The examples of new materials she gives are materials that copy:
      a water-based animals.
      b animals in general.
      c animals and plants.

   3 When designing the Sagrada Familia, Gaudi took inspiration from:
      a models he had made.
      b nature's forms.
      c the human body.

   4 The design of the Sagrada Familia:
      a confused the public.
      b divided public opinion.
      c brought Gaudi great fame.

   5 There are a lot of biomimetic buildings now that are:
      a named after animals.
      b known by the name of something in the natural world.
      c given nicknames by their creators.

   6 The Eastgate Centre in Harare uses biomimetics to avoid:
      a becoming too cold.
      b looking like a conventional office and shopping complex.
      c having to be cooled artificially.

Sagrada Familia, Barcelona

Swiss Re Tower, London

A termite mou Africa

3 Match these words in bold from the interview with the correct definition (a or b).

   1 … the term biomimetics, which was **coined** in the 1950s …
      a first created   b made popular

   2 … hi-tech swimsuits that **replicate** shark skin.
      a use   b imitate

   3 … he created a very **organic**-looking building …
      a simple   b natural

   4 … one of the most **hideous** buildings in the world.
      a beautiful   b ugly

   5 … to imitate the heating and cooling system in a termite **mound**.
      a small hill   b body

Word focus *ground*

4 Complete these sentences to make idioms with *ground*.

   1 He's only sixteen and enjoying enormous success, but it's very important that he .... **his** .... **on the ground**.

   2 You shouldn't give in to pressure just because it comes from people who have more experience. .... **your ground**.

   3 She refused to comment on the situation **on the** .... **that** it was a private matter.

   4 Using the latest laser technology, they are **breaking** .... **ground** medical surgery.

   5 He has some great ideas, but that's all they are: ideas. Because none of them ever .... **the ground**.

   6 Thanks – that was really productive. I'm amazed that we .... **so much ground** in just an hour.

24

Unit 3 Design for life

3d A lot to recommend it

Real life expressing opinions

1 🎧 **22** Listen to part of a discussion about a proposal to put a new coffee lounge into a large open-plan office, which is on the 14th floor of an office block. Write down two of the arguments mentioned in favour of the proposal and one against it.

For

_____

_____

_____

Against

_____

_____

2 🎧 **22** Complete the phrases used by the speakers to express their opinions. Then listen again and check your answers.

1 First of _____ , I should say that I think it's _____ a good idea.
2 It's got a lot of things to _____ it.
3 But I _____ say there's a risk in that.
4 I kind of _____ that. The thing about an open-plan office is …
5 The informal chats are something we _____ the importance of.
6 What I _____ is, if we assume that people relaxing and having coffee at work …
7 So I'm very _____ in _____ of this proposal, particularly _____ that we are all working in …
8 Oh, and _____ the _____ , including a screen with industry news on it in the room is a clever _____ .

3 Pronunciation linking vowel sounds (intrusion)

a 🎧 **23** Listen to these phrases and write the sound or letter that links *and* to the word before it.

1 food and water _____
2 tea and biscuits _____
3 vanilla and chocolate _____
4 wait and see _____
5 go and ask _____
6 you and me _____

b 🎧 **24** Look at these phrases and mark the words which are linked. If an extra sound (/w/, /j/ or /r/) is needed, write this too. Then listen and check your answers.

0 every so_w_often
1 first of all
2 with a bit of luck
3 as a matter of fact
4 as far as I'm aware
5 between you and me
6 let's be honest
7 at the end of the day
8 I've no idea, I'm afraid

c Practise saying the phrases in the same way.

4 Listen and respond giving your opinion

🎧 **25** Someone is going to ask your opinions on where we choose to live and the importance of our surroundings and also give their opinions. Respond with your own words. Then compare what you say with the model answer that follows.

1 *Would you prefer to have a large living space or somewhere that's small and cosy?*

Personally, I'd like to have a lot of space, but maybe that seems a bit selfish.

25

3e High-rise living

Writing an opinion essay

1 Look at the elements of an opinion essay (1–4). Then read the two paragraphs (a and b) from an opinion essay about whether it is good for people to live in high-rise buildings. Which elements do the paragraphs represent?

   1 analyse the question and set out your starting point
   2 give your opinion and present the arguments supporting it
   3 deal with opposing arguments
   4 make your conclusion

   a So, as with so many things, in the end we must balance the advantages and disadvantages and then make a choice. For me, even though there are great benefits of high-rise buildings, these benefits are outweighed by the cost to human interaction. After all, what use is a pleasant environment if most of the time you are isolated from other people in a small flat seventy metres from the ground?

   b The pressure for space in our cities has demanded that we build upwards, with taller and taller buildings, rather than build outwards. It is true that it is not particularly desirable to keep expanding our cities outwards into green, undeveloped land outside the city limits, but there are other solutions to providing more homes, such as the creation of compact living spaces. Some high-rise buildings could still be retained for non-residential activity, for example, as offices.

2 Do you think the writer is for or against high-rise living? What arguments does he/she concede to the other side?

3 **Writing skill** discourse markers

   Match the two halves of each comment about city life.

   1 Living in an apartment building in the centre is a bit noisy.
   2 Even though we live twenty storeys up,
   3 It feels very nice to live in an old house.
   4 Our building is not the tallest in the neighbourhood.
   5 Most of the flats are rented by companies for their employees.
   6 We wanted to be somewhere with a sense of community,

   a After all, very few individuals could afford to rent privately.
   b Having said that, it is extremely convenient.
   c that is to say, a place where people enjoy interacting.
   d Admittedly, the maintenance costs are higher.
   e our view of the city is blocked by other tall buildings.
   f Indeed, there are some buildings over sixty storeys high.

4 Write your own answer to the question: *Is it good for people to live in high-rise buildings?* Follow the structure suggested in Exercise 1. You can use ideas from those two paragraphs if you wish.

Vocabulary renting a flat

1 Use these words to complete the conversation between a student looking for a flat and a letting agent.

> advance   bills   budget   charges
> commission   deposit   furnished   landlord
> lets   move   properties   references   rent
> share   studio   tenant

S: Hi, I'm looking to ¹_____ a small apartment, like a ²_____ apartment, for three months. Do you do short ³_____?

LA: Yes, but only for ⁴_____ flats. Is it just for you or are you planning to ⁵_____? And when is this from?

S: Just me and I'm hoping to ⁶_____ in as soon as possible.

LA: OK. And what's your ⁷_____?

S: Well, including the ⁸_____ and ⁹_____, no more than $900 a month.

LA: OK. I think we have a few ¹⁰_____ that will interest you. You just need to know that we don't take any ¹¹_____ from you, the ¹², _____ just from the ¹³_____, who has to pay us a small fee. But you will need to pay a ¹⁴_____ of one month's rent and one month's rent in ¹⁵_____. And you'll also need to provide some ¹⁶_____, including one from your employer.

Learning skills listening: bottom-up strategies

2 When you listen to fast native speech, you will often be faced with the difficulty of decoding the sounds you hear. Look at this list of key things to recognize in native speech.

1 being able to recognize a word from its stressed syllable
2 understanding the place of weak forms (auxiliary verbs, prepositions, articles) in a sentence
3 understanding linking so that you can separate the words that have been linked
4 picking out the key word in a sentence (the one that carries the main meaning)

3 🔊 26 Look at the stressed syllables in the words in this sentence. Then listen to the sentence.

The de<u>vel</u>opment of <u>en</u>ergy-ef<u>fi</u>cient <u>homes</u> has <u>changed</u> the way <u>hous</u>es are <u>built</u>.

4 🔊 27 Underline the stressed syllables in the words in these sentences. Then listen to the sentences.

1 There are only two interesting buildings in the area around Newport.
2 The green belt should definitely be protected from developers.

5 Underline the stressed syllables in sentences from the listening extracts in this unit. Use the audioscript at the back of your book. Then listen and check.

Check!

6 Do the crossword. All of the words are in Student's Book Unit 3.

Across
5 poor (8)
8 past, present or future (4)
9 opposite of 5 across (4)
10 small and neat (7)
11 attached to the bedroom (2, 5)

Down
1 new, current (6)
2 slightly (1, 3)
3 appear (4)
4 with a lot of room (8)
6 lively (7)
7 discussion (7)

Unit 4 Innovation

4a The Boring Company

Listening future transport

1 🔊 28 Why do you think someone would name their company 'The Boring Company'? What does this have to do with future transport? Listen to a radio feature and check your answers.

2 🔊 28 Listen again and answer the questions. According to the speaker:
1. what are the three possibilities for overcoming an obstacle?
2. what can building new roads be compared to and why?
3. what is the problem with building 'roads in the air'?
4. what is the problem with building roads underground?
5. how would cars travel in Elon Musk's proposed underground system?
6. how would he make the tunnelling process cheaper?
7. how would he avoid congestion in the tunnels?
8. what technology might the Hyperloop tunnel use in the future?
9. how fast can pods travel in this system?

3 🔊 28 Complete these sentences and phrases used by the speaker. You have been given the first letter and a definition of the missing words. Listen again and check your answers.
1. We've already tried going round it by building **r**_____ **roads** around our cities …
   = roads which take you around the edge of a city
2. … have an impact on those below when **d**_____ falls from a height.
   = pieces of broken material, e.g. rock
3. And given his amazing record … he could **p**_____ this **off**.
   = make something a success
4. His latest **v**_____, The Boring Company, proposes building a network of tunnels …
   = a business enterprise or project involving risk
5. … so that there would be nothing to block them or **h**_____ them **up**.
   = delay
6. … Hyperloop project, has already been **t**_____ **and tested** …
   = experimented with and shown to work

Glossary
sled (n) /sled/ a small vehicle that slides over the ground
vacuum (n) /ˈvækjuəm/ a space that has had all the air removed from it

Grammar future probability

4 🔊 28 Complete the statements made by the speaker with these words. Then listen again and check your answers.

could   good chance   likely   might   possibly   should

1 … such solutions are never _____ to work because …
2 … rather than removing the problem, you _____ just be moving it somewhere else.
3 … collisions or accidents in the air _____ also have an impact on those below …
4 And given his amazing record …, there's a _____ that he could pull this off.
5 Musk's idea is that … his techniques _____ reduce the cost enormously.
6 In his mind, also, is the idea that in future, the tunnels will _____ use vacuum technology …

5 Rewrite the sentences from Exercise 4 so that they have the same meaning. Use the words in bold.

probably
1 _____

chances
2 _____

possible
3 _____

may well
4 _____

likely
5 _____

could
6 _____

6 Complete the answers to these questions about future transport using the correct form of the words in brackets.

Do you think that there's any chance this idea of Elon Musk's will become a reality?

It ¹_____ (may well). I think he ²_____ (almost certainly / come up with) a working model. He always does. Then it will be a question of whether city authorities are willing to support it. I think that some more forward-looking ones ³_____ (probably / be) supportive of it.

And, just leaving aside that possibility, what do you think our city streets will look like thirty years from now?

I think most of us ⁴_____ (likely / drive) electric vehicles. We're already moving in that direction. So we ⁵_____ (should / have) cleaner air in our cities. But there ⁶_____ (probably / be) some petrol cars on the streets too.

Why do you say that?

Because the oil companies are incredibly powerful. And that ⁷_____ (be / unlikely / change). Also, replacing petrol will need a whole new infrastructure in place of petrol stations and I think ⁸_____ (likelihood / that / happen) within thirty years ⁹_____ (be) very small.

Wordbuilding -able

7 Form the correct (positive or negative) adjective from the verb in brackets to complete these sentences. The negative adjectives can begin *un-*, *in-*, *ir-* or *non-*.

1 I think it's _____ (do). The question is: is it _____ (desire)?
2 I'm afraid the price is _____ (negotiate).
3 They're an advertising agency and they have this terrible slogan: 'Imagine the _____ (imagine)'!
4 I felt so bad about breaking her china plate. She said it was very rare and virtually _____ (replace).
5 There are problems with the plan, but I don't think they are _____ (surmount).
6 I couldn't go through another dental procedure like that again. The pain was _____ (tolerate).

8 Complete these sentences with a suitable adjective ending in *-able*.

1 If you don't like the shirt, I'm sure you can take it back to the shop. Things are usually _____ within two weeks of buying them.
2 These new glasses are supposed to be _____, but I sat on them and they snapped in half!
3 The tap water is _____ in the sense that it's safe. But I'm afraid it doesn't taste very nice.
4 How far is the station from here? Is it _____ or should I get a bus or taxi?
5 The label on this tablecloth says '_____', but actually I put it in the washing machine and it's come out fine.
6 I'm afraid I won't be _____ for the next few days; the place I'm staying in has no phone signal.

29

4b DIY innovators

Reading future transport

1 Read the article about DIY innovators and match the headings (a–d) with the four paragraphs (1–4).

   a What drives innovation
   b An unidentified need
   c Making do with bits and pieces
   d There's an inventor in all of us

2 Read the article again and complete these sentences using one word in each space.

1. The mistake we make about technology is that we think it is something only _____ can be involved with.
2. Thomas Jefferson's clock was unusual for its time because it could tell you the _____ .
3. The invention of eyeglasses for chickens solved something most people didn't think was a _____ .
4. Most DIY inventors are not really motivated by _____ .
5. In the Great Depression, some people created homemade versions of gadgets that they couldn't _____ .
6. Robert Goddard is an example of a scientist who did _____ using old household objects.

Glossary
DIY (abbrev) /ˌdiː aɪ ˈwaɪ/ do it yourself
hose (n) /həʊz/ a flexible water pipe
peck (v) /pek/ (of a bird) strike quickly with the mouth
piston rings (n) /ˈpɪstən rɪŋz/ metal rings that go around the cylinder of an internal combustion engine
scaffold (n) /ˈskæfəʊld/ a supporting structure used when repairing a building

DIY innovators

1 In today's electronic convenience age, many of us imagine that technology is something that brainy scientists in state-of-the-art laboratories create for us. But that isn't really a true reflection of how technology comes about – now or in the past. The strict definition of technology is designing a device to perform a particular task. Seen like that, we are all innovators, because we have all, at one time or another, improvised our own solutions to specific problems. It's just that some of us take it further than others. America's third president, Thomas Jefferson, filled his home with DIY gadgets. In his living room, for example, he had a homemade clock which, using a pair of cannonballs on ropes, told him both the hour of the day and the day of the week. He made himself a swivelling seat – an early version of the type of office chair many of us sit on today – and built an automatic signing machine so that he **didn't need to hand-sign** his letters.

2 DIY inventions rarely catch on, because often the inventor is providing a solution to something that is not generally perceived to be a problem. What was the inventor of glasses for chickens thinking? Obviously he thought there needed to be some way to prevent chickens pecking at each other's eyes. But he **should have realized** that they were never going to become a best-seller. Similarly, the self-tipping hat, which used parts of a clock to tip a man's hat when a lady passed him in the street, **must have seemed** to fill a need that was obvious to the inventor.

3 While a few DIY innovators in the past **might have been motivated** by money and the dream of making their fortune, others have been motivated by necessity. World War II servicemen in North Africa who **needed to wash** took empty oil drums and hoses, mounted them on scaffolds built from scrap wood and created improvised showers. Others have been motivated by economic hardship. During the Great Depression of the 1930s, some people **had to build** their own devices and equipment, because they couldn't afford new items in the shops. Cecil Burrell, when he wanted tables for his patio, made them from old piston rings from industrial engines.

4 But DIY can extend to professional scientists too. Dr Robert Goddard, who pioneered modern rocketry in the 1920s and 1930s, built much of his test equipment and rockets from bits and pieces he found lying around: clock parts, tobacco tins, etc.

30

3 Look at the words in bold from the article. Choose the correct definition (a or b).

1. a **swivelling** seat
   a turning   b with arms
2. rarely **catch on**
   a work   b become popular
3. to **tip** a man's hat
   a take off   b raise
4. **mounted** them **on** scaffolds
   a hang … from   b put … on top of
5. **scrap** wood
   a old but re-usable   b old and useless
6. who **pioneered** modern rocketry
   a was ignorant of   b led the way in

Grammar past modals

4 Match the past modal verbs (1–6) from the article with the functions (a–f).

1. didn't need to hand-sign
2. should have realized
3. must have seemed
4. might have been motivated
5. needed to wash
6. had to build

a. expresses what was expected
b. describes an obligation
c. talks about a necessity
d. talks about a lack of necessity
e. speculates about what was possibly the case
f. speculates about what was probably the case

5 Read the story in the next column about someone who got a bicycle puncture. Rewrite the underlined phrases with past modal verbs.

1. ___
2. ___
3. ___
4. ___
5. ___
6. ___
7. ___
8. ___

So there I was on a country road in the middle of nowhere with a flat bicycle tyre. ¹ Almost certainly I had ridden over a nail or something. ² The advisable thing would have been to take a puncture repair kit with me, but because the roads are very new around there I had imagined ³ it wasn't necessary. ⁴ One possibility was to wheel my bike back to the nearest town six kilometres away, but that would have taken ages. Besides, ⁵ I had an obligation to be home for supper, as a friend was coming to dinner. So I decided ⁶ it was my duty to find a way to fix the puncture. (In fact, ⁷ there was no need to worry because the friend had cancelled, but I didn't know that at the time.) All I had with me was a bicycle pump. What I needed was a patch for the puncture. I looked around on the road. ⁸ Perhaps someone had dropped something I could use. After some searching, I found some old chewing gum stuck to the road. It was very hard and I realized that there was only one thing to do …

---

6 Pronunciation weak forms in past modals

a 🔊 29 Listen to these sentences. Circle the weak forms.

1. I needn't have bothered.
2. She may have got lost.
3. It can't have been much fun.
4. You didn't need to wait for me.
5. It might not have been his fault.
6. She had to leave early.

b Practise saying the expressions in Exercise 6a in the same way.

Vocabulary phrasal verb *come*

7 Complete the text using prepositions to make phrasal verbs with *come*.

We've all eaten popcorn in the cinema, but few stop to think how the success of this all-American snack came ¹_____. I came ²_____ an article about its origins the other day when browsing the internet. It has an interesting history. The Guatemalans discovered popcorn thousands of years ago, presumably when someone had the bright idea of putting a corn kernel in a hot pan. But popcorn didn't really take off in the United States until the invention of the popcorn machine in the 1890s. Manufacturers spotted the growing trend, and came ³_____ with the idea of adding caramel and marketing it as a sweet snack. In the Depression of the 1930s, popcorn filled an important need because it was cheap. Since then, even though popcorn has come ⁴_____ against some opponents who say that it is unhealthy, it remains very popular and is even marketed today as a health food. Its success probably comes ⁵_____ to the fact that it is so cheap and easy to make.

4c The new philanthropists

Listening supporting good causes

1 🔊 **30** You are going to listen to a conversation about philanthropists. Read the definition. Then listen and make notes.

> **philanthropist** (n) /fɪˈlænθrəpɪst/ a person who cares about their fellow human beings; especially one who donates money to people less fortunate than themselves

1 two ways these new philanthropists made their money

2 two ways their approach to giving differs from philanthropists in the past

2 🔊 **30** Listen again. Are the sentences true (T) or false (F)?

1 The speaker implies that philanthropists in the past didn't have to work for their money.
2 The new philanthropists' attitude to their money is that they want to use it now.
3 The new philanthropists don't want the projects they invest in to be run by business people.
4 The Daniela Papi story shows how a social enterprise project can evolve and spread.
5 John Caudwell believes that success in life is just a question of hard work.
6 The speaker suggests that the new philanthropists ultimately care only about their business reputation.

3 🔊 **30** Complete these phrases from the conversation. Then listen again and check your answers.

| bring about | counterparts | ethos | return |
| seed money | self-confessed | self-made |
| no strings |

1 … so many more of these do-gooders are _____ businessmen and women …
2 … these philanthropists and their 19th–century _____ ?
3 … business terms like 'getting a good _____ on capital' …
4 The money they put into philanthropic projects is like _____ …
5 … helping to _____ positive change in areas where social problems exist.
6 … none of the old-fashioned '_____ attached' kind of giving …
7 He's a _____ capitalist who believes in people helping themselves …
8 I'd say that was very typical of the _____ of the new philanthropists.

4 Write the words from Exercise 3 next to the correct definition.

1 set of beliefs and values _____
2 early investment in a new company _____
3 profit _____
4 make happen _____
5 succeeding without help _____
6 someone who does the same job in a different time or place _____
7 admitting to being _____
8 without special conditions _____

Word focus *give*

5 Complete the expressions with *give*.
1 I **gave it my** _____ , but I didn't win – he was a much better player.
2 It's not a decision you can take lightly. You need to **give it some serious** _____ .
3 **Give her a** _____ . She's only 12. I didn't know what I wanted to do until I was 20!
4 I've never tried to steer a boat before, but I'll **give it a** _____ .
5 The council have finally **given them the go-** _____ to build a new factory on the site.
6 Don't rush it. You broke your leg. You need to **give it some** _____ to heal properly.

Unit 4 Innovation

4d An elevator pitch

Real life making a short pitch

1 🔊 **31** Listen to a short pitch for a product called the 'Solidarity Bag'. Listen and answer the questions.

1 Who is the product aimed at?

2 What is unique about this idea?

3 What problem does it solve?

4 What features does the bag have?

2 Speaking skill using rhetorical questions

🔊 **31** Listen again and complete these rhetorical questions.

1 What's _____ about that, you _____ ?
2 Why _____ children _____ to do _____ , when they have a desk at school and a table at home?
3 But _____ will _____ in poorer countries _____ to afford the bag?

3 Write the answers to the questions in Exercise 2.

1 _____
2 _____
3 _____

4 Complete these other rhetorical questions you might ask when pitching a new product or service.

1 Operation
  So how _____ ?
2 Cost
  Isn't _____ , you ask?
3 Need
  So why _____ ?
4 Ambition/Goal
  So, what _____ ?

5 Pronunciation word stress

🔊 **32** Look at the words in bold in these sentences and underline where you think the stress falls in each word. Then listen and check.

1 **Clearly**, we want to help others.
2 **Financially**, we are in a good position.
3 **Essentially**, it's a school rucksack.
4 **Practically**, it has many advantages.
5 **Of course**, this is not the finished design.
6 **Honestly**, I don't know the answer to that.
7 **Obviously**, not all kids need a bag that functions as a desk.
8 **To be honest**, I think people will pay extra.
9 **Basically**, we'd like to help kids learn.

6 Listen and respond defending your idea

🔊 **33** Imagine you have just presented this Solidarity Bag to a potential investor. Listen to their questions. Respond with your own words. Then compare what you say with the model answer that follows.

1
Can you just explain to me what your ambition is for this product?

Yes. We would like it to have successful sales in Europe and on the basis of that to be able to provide many of these bags to children in developing countries.

4e Problem or solution?

Writing a proposal

1 Read the proposal and answer the questions.
1. Does the company currently recognize the importance of innovation and if so, how?
2. What specific, concrete suggestions does the proposal make?
3. What recommendations does it make without giving specific examples?

2 Answer these questions about the structure of the proposal.
1. What is the purpose of the introduction?
2. In what two ways does the author make a list of points?
3. What phrase does she use to signal the conclusion?

3 Writing skill making recommendations

Choose the correct options to complete the recommendations.
1. We suggest employees *are / to be* given a structure in which to innovate.
2. We recommend the company *could / should* reward employees for their ideas.
3. We strongly recommend *to give / giving* innovation a more formal position.
4. We recommend that employees *have / having* scheduled discussion opportunities.
5. We also suggest that they *are to visit / should visit* other organizations to get ideas.

Introduction
This proposal suggests a new way to encourage innovation and creativity among staff.

Current situation
Our company needs innovation to be successful. At the moment, although we say that 'we encourage creativity and innovation', in fact we receive very few ideas from employees about how to improve our products and processes. Innovation is important because it can:

- help to make the company more efficient
- create new products and services for our customers
- motivate staff
- help to secure the company's future

So how can we achieve more creativity and innovation in practice, not just in words?

Possible solutions
First of all, we suggest that employees should be given a structure in which to innovate. This could take the form of a scheduled discussion between groups of colleagues every two to four weeks. Or it could involve giving employees the opportunity to visit other organizations to see how they work. Secondly, we recommend rewarding employees for good ideas. This does not have to be a financial reward, but it must involve recognition of their effort. Lastly, we believe that creating a more relaxed relationship between employees and management would also help the flow of ideas.

Recommendations
In summary, we strongly recommend that innovation and creativity are given a more formal position in the company's working practices. Until that happens, we are unlikely to see much innovation from staff.

4 Use these notes to write a proposal for a way to make students more aware of ways we waste energy.

Problem: Students are conscious of dangers of pollution, but not of their own waste of energy (leaving on lights, phone chargers, etc.)
Possible solutions: awareness-raising campaign, fines for wasting energy, offer free 'green' charging devices

Vocabulary partitives

1 Complete the partitive expressions using these words.

bit   bit   bite   drop   gust   hint   plot   shred   stroke   word

1. I'm really thirsty. I haven't had a _____ of **water** all day.
2. It was a _____ of **luck** getting those tickets. They were the last two.
3. I'm sorry. I didn't mean to offend you. It was just a _____ of **fun**.
4. We had a _____ of **trouble** finding the bus stop, but otherwise everything went smoothly.
5. A sudden _____ of **wind** blew my hat off and it landed in a puddle.
6. He tried to be positive but I think there was a _____ of **disappointment** in his voice.
7. They bought a _____ of **land** near the sea and they intend to build a house there.
8. Can I give you a _____ of **advice** before you start out on this venture?
9. There's not a _____ of **evidence** to suggest that there is life on other planets.
10. We'll get a _____ **to eat*** when we get there.

* used with a verb (*to eat*) rather than a noun (*of food*)

2 Which three expressions in Exercise 1 emphasize a small amount?

a _____
b _____
c _____

Learning skills vocabulary extension (1)

3 You can use your dictionary to extend your vocabulary. If you see a word that you think you know but the meaning does not seem to fit, check the other meanings of this word in the dictionary. Look at this example.

1. You see this sentence but don't know this meaning of *capital*.

   'Running a railway network is a very capital-intensive activity.'

2. You find these entries for *capital* in the dictionary (see the next column). Which meaning does it have in this sentence?

capital /ˈkæpɪt(ə)l/ noun
  1 the administrative centre of a country or region
  2 money or assets that are or can be invested

capital /ˈkæpɪt(ə)l/ adjective
  3 (of a letter of the alphabet) large
  4 (of punishment or crime) punishable by death

3. Note any new meanings in your notebook and write an example sentence for each one.

4 Look at these words with more than one meaning. What meanings do you know for each?

crane   fair   fine   sole

5 Read the sentences. Do you know the meanings of the words in bold in these sentences? Check other meanings in the dictionary. Write example sentences for the meanings that are new to you.

1. In Japan, the most popular origami shape is a paper **crane**.
2. I went to the Frankfurt book **fair** last week.
3. There's a **fine** line between confidence and arrogance.
4. It's not a company: he is a **sole** trader.

Check!

6 Answer these questions. All the answers are in Student's Book Unit 4.

1. What is the 'mother of invention'?
   _____
2. What adjective describes gadgets you can fold? '_____ technology'
3. What type of eye did you see on the opening page of this unit? _____
4. What is the name for a short presentation where we have a limited time to convince someone of our idea? _____
5. What do we call someone who wants to make money but help people at the same time? _____

7 Complete the sentences. The first letters of each word spell the name of Blake Mykoskie's company.

1. I'll certainly give your idea some _____.
2. It's a very risky venture. I'll be surprised if it comes _____.
3. It's unlike John to be late. He _____ have had a problem.
4. To make something smaller you can _____ it, bend it or fold it.

Name of company: _____

Unit 5 The magic of travel

5a In defence of the guided tour

Listening a traveller's view

1 🔊 **34** Look at these features of organized tour holidays. Think about which features appeal to you and which don't. Then listen to someone talking about the benefits of such tours and tick the items he mentions.

1 Being with knowledgeable guides ☐
2 Comfort and safety ☐
3 Meeting fellow travellers ☐
4 Having a fixed itinerary/schedule ☐
5 No planning – everything is arranged for you ☐
6 Known costs – no financial surprises ☐
7 Optional free time ☐

2 🔊 **34** Read the statements. Then listen again and choose the best answer (a, b or c) to complete each statement.

1 The speaker says that in the past he didn't consider organized tour holidays an option because:
   a he couldn't relate to the type of people who went on them.
   b he thought they were too controlled and restricting.
   c the destinations were not places he wanted to visit.

2 The speaker says that he joined the guided tour at the Metropolitan Museum of Art because:
   a he thought it would at least be a new experience.
   b it was still raining outside.
   c it was highly recommended by the museum staff.

3 The difference between the museum tour and one of his normal visits to a museum was that:
   a he learned a lot about a lot of things.
   b he learned a little about a lot of things.
   c he learned a lot about a few things.

4 Most of the guides on the Italy trip:
   a had also been guests on the trips before.
   b had done months of research before the trip.
   c had academic qualifications.

5 The speaker says the fact that everything is organized beforehand saves a lot of:
   a money.   b stress.   c time.

6 The speaker says many organized tour operators these days give their guests:
   a the option of more free time.
   b a choice of excursions to go on.
   c mini guided tours with local people.

3 Try to complete these expression used by the speaker. Use one word per space.

1 to be herded around like a ....
2 Never in a .... years!
3 Don't get me .... – I like museums.
4 It'll be an experience, if .... else.
5 Not holding .... much hope, I joined it.
6 Transport, hotels, food: it's all taken care ....

Vocabulary repeated word pairs

4 Complete these repeated word pairs with the correct word.

1 She only had her operation a week ago, but she's getting better day .... day.
2 The film went on .... on. I thought it was never going to end.
3 Yes, we met face .... face for the first time last week.
4 People ask me if I prefer writing the music or the lyrics, but actually the two things go hand .... hand.
5 Their new business is going .... strength .... strength.
6 We don't see eye .... eye on a lot of issues, but we're still good friends.

36

Grammar emphatic structures

5 🔊 34 Use the words in brackets to rewrite the sentences with emphatic structures you heard in Exercise 1. Then listen again and check your answers.

1 I want a bit of independence and freedom from travel. (what)

2 A guided tour I took changed my mind. (thing)

3 I like visiting museums. (do)

4 It made me reassess my whole attitude to organized tours. (did)

5 How knowledgeable and interesting some of the other travellers were surprised me. (what)

6 ... particularly if you're visiting a more remote or not-so-safe place. (it)

6 Read this account of family holidays. Rewrite the underlined sentences below as emphatic structures, using the words in brackets.

¹ I remember best about my childhood how amazing family holidays were. Every few years we took a camper van and set off somewhere new. We didn't have a strict itinerary. ² A rough idea of where we were going was enough. We just took things day by day, without any planned stops or timetable. ³ We stopped when we saw things that interested us. We went wild swimming. We cooked on our camp stove usually. ⁴ Money wasn't the issue. If we saw a restaurant or cafe menu that looked good, we'd stop and eat there. We packed as little as possible and stopped at laundrettes when we needed to wash clothes. ⁵ I loved the lack of any kind of routine. Sometimes we'd wake up early, sometimes late. We'd often take a nap in the afternoon at some scenic spot. ⁶ I like sleeping in the afternoon. The whole thing was magical. ⁷ When I have children, I'm going to recreate a similar experience for them.

1 _____ (thing)
2 _____ (it)
3 _____ (did)
4 _____ (it)
5 _____ (what)
6 _____ (do)
7 _____ (what)

7 Pronunciation *do, does* and *did*

🔊 35 Listen to these sentences and write in the missing emphatic auxiliaries. Note how the auxiliary verbs are stressed.

1 I _____ wish I had been able to spend more time there.
2 He _____ say that he'd help us.
3 We _____ prefer to take holidays close to home.
4 She _____ get very sunburnt.

Vocabulary describing people and places

8 Complete the crossword using the clues below.

Across
1 warm and comfortable (4)
4 not fast (4)
7 evoking feelings of love (8)

Down
2 using authority in a self-important way (9)
3 stylish and graceful (7)
5 cautious or suspicious (4)
6 large and impressive (5)

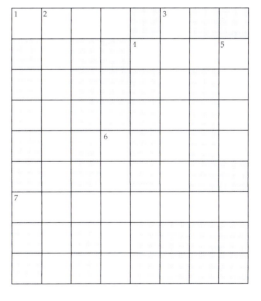

5b Pilgrimages

Reading their Africa

1 Read the article about the Pilgrimages project and answer the questions.

1 What is the aim of the Pilgrimages project?

2 What inspired the project?

3 How are the books different from the usual travel books we read?

4 What are the writers trying to avoid?

2 Read the article again and find words with these meanings.

a randomly (para 1)
b take hold of firmly (para 1)
c easily noticed (para 2)
d troubled (para 3)
e a picture (para 3)
f unoriginal (para 4)
g announce an order (para 4)

Pilgrimages

'For one month, nearly a billion eyes will follow the wayward movement of one small ball, bouncing about haphazardly on a lawn – controlled by the feet of 22 men speaking a language billions understand very well.' These are the opening words on the Pilgrimages website, a project set up by the Chinua Achebe Centre for African Writers and Artists, to seize the opportunity presented by the football World Cup in South Africa in 2010 to educate the rest of the world about Africa. The way the **association** did this was to ask thirteen African writers to write about their experiences of thirteen cities spread across Africa. Each **author** had two years, and help from a local guide, to produce a book of approximately 30,000 words on each city.

The result is travel writing of a very different kind. Rather than experiencing a place through the eyes of an outsider, Pilgrimages aims to reveal **it** as seen by Africans themselves. The advantage for each writer is that although they are visiting cities previously not well-known to them, many things are already familiar to them. **This** means that they can concentrate on observing the details and while **doing so**, not be as conspicuous as a non-African visitor **would**. Ugandan author Doreen Baingana, whose subject is the Somalian city of Hargeisa, says: 'Goats in a city, for example, do not surprise me in the way they would if I were from the UK.'

Among the **other thirteen** is Yvonne Owuor of Kenya, who has written about Kinshasa, the capital of Congo. The city is a great mix of different African cultures and languages with a turbulent history of colonization and struggle for independence. Like other Pilgrimages writers, Owuor is cautious about painting her portrait of Kinshasa with too broad a brush, fearful that what will emerge is a one-dimensional, stereotyped view of Africa.

This promises to be a refreshing series of travel books: not **ones** that throw out clichéd images and stereotyped views of other worlds. As Owuor says, when writers decree that a given place is like this or like that, then the reality disappears from view.

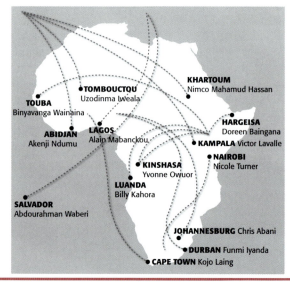

Grammar avoiding repetition

3 Look at the words in bold in the article and answer the questions.
1 What words have these words replaced to avoid repetition?
  a association (para 1)
  b author (para 1)
2 What clauses do these words refer to?
  a This (para 2)
  b doing so (para 2)
3 What nouns do these words refer to?
  a it (para 2, line 3)
  b This (para 4, line 1)
  c ones (para 4)
4 What words have been omitted after these words?
  a would (para 2)
  b other thirteen (para 3)

4 Replace the underlined words with other words or omit the underlined words to avoid repetition.
1 I was going to buy a new umbrella, but then I found my old <u>umbrella</u>.
2 I didn't want to go, but he persuaded me <u>to go</u>.
3 I want to phone her to find out what's going on, but if I <u>phone her</u>, she might think I'm being pushy.
4 I downloaded all the Bob Marley songs, but I didn't bother with the <u>other songs</u>.
5 The temperature is expected to drop to zero degrees tonight. <u>The temperature dropping to zero degrees</u> means there will be a frost.
6 It's a brilliant company. You couldn't find a better <u>company</u> to work for.
7 I'd love you to give me a hand moving this table, if you can bear <u>to give me a hand</u>.
8 It's not a cheap solution, but I understand why you might think <u>it is a cheap solution</u>.

5 Pronunciaton stress in short responses

a 🔊 36 Look at these exchanges. Mark the two (or three) words that you think are most stressed in each response.
1 A: Would you like to come to dinner one evening?
  B: Yes, I'd love to.
2 A: Do you need to borrow a pen?
  B: No, I've got one, thanks.
3 A: Are you coming?
  B: No, I'm afraid not.
4 A: I didn't get the assistant manager job.
  B: Oh, I'm sorry to hear that.
5 A: Are you going away this summer?
  B: I hope so.
6 A: Do you like detective stories?
  B: Oh, yes. I love a good thriller.
7 A: What are you doing here so early?
  B: Catching up on emails.

b 🔊 37 Listen to Student A's part of the exchanges. Respond using the correct stress.

6 Dictation a mystery tour

🔊 38 Listen to someone describing a mystery tour. Complete the paragraph.

I've been .... ,
but .... in Prague ....
And ....
....
If you .... ,
....
I'm ....
because ....
....
What ....
....
If ....
....

5c Heart of Darkness

Listening a voyage into the unknown

1 ♪ 39 You are going to listen to an extract from the book *Heart of Darkness* by Joseph Conrad. The setting is the Congo around 1880. The extract describes the beginning of the journey that Marlow, a ship's captain, makes to this area. Listen and answer the questions.
   1 What did Marlow dream about as a boy?
   2 What had happened to the place he had been most fascinated by?
   3 How did his dream become a reality?

2 ♪ 39 Listen again and complete these details of the description.
   1 What did you find on maps of the world at that time?
   2 In contrast, what had the map of this place (Congo) become filled with?
   3 What does he compare the river on the map to?
   4 What was the strategic importance of the river?
   5 What had happened to the captain that Marlow was replacing?
   6 What was his impression of the African coast as the boat sailed along it?

3 Look at these sentences from the extract and answer the questions about the descriptive words in bold.
   1 I would look for hours at South America, or Africa, or Australia, and **lose myself in** all the glories of exploration.
      Do you think *lose myself in something* has a positive or a negative connotation?
   2 But there was one [place] yet – the biggest, the most blank – that **I had a hankering after**.
      Have people who hanker after something experienced it yet or not?
   3 … a mighty big river, that you could see on the map, resembling an immense snake **uncoiled**.
      What is a snake usually doing when it is coiled?
   4 I went on along Fleet Street, but could not **shake off** the idea.
      Which of these things would you not try to shake off?
      a a cold   b a new skill   c a bad reputation
   5 Watching a coast as it slips by the ship is like thinking about **an enigma**.
      Do you think *an enigma* is:
      a a mystery?   b a new idea?
   6 … and always **mute** with an air of whispering …
      If *blind* means 'cannot see' and *deaf* means 'cannot hear', what does *mute* mean?

Word focus *matter*

4 Choose the correct options to complete these phrases with *matter*.
   1 Getting stuck in a lift underground might seem amusing, but believe me, at the time, **it was no *joking* / *funny* / *laughing* matter**.
   2 They say that you can control pain; it's just a question of *brain* / *mind* / *will* **over matter**.
   3 You should always use a safety belt, **as a matter of** *course* / *process* / *mode*.
   4 I'm sorry – I'm vegetarian. I don't eat meat **as a matter of** *belief* / *principle* / *morals*.
   5 **No matter which** *angle* / *point* / *way* **you look at it**, being a teenager isn't easy.
   6 Thankfully, it's not my concern; or yours **for** *that* / *any* / *what* **matter**.

40

Unit 5 The magic of travel

5d To my amazement

Real life telling an anecdote

1 🔊 **40** Listen to an anecdote about hitchhiking and answer the questions.

1 Where were the two men hitchhiking to and why?
2 What piece of good luck did they have?
3 What happened to change their mood for the worse and how did the story end?

2 🔊 **40** Listen again and complete these phrases that link or introduce the events in the story. Use one or two words per space.

1 Very few people still hitchhike, _____ .
2 _____ it can be dangerous.
3 _____, a group of us from university had a competition …
4 _____, within about ten minutes … we got a lift …
5 We couldn't _____ our luck.
6 … a resting point, which, _____, to have an area for pitching tents.
7 _____, we woke up early …
8 … but, to _____, it had gone.
9 _____, we started to pack up our tent.
10 But _____, we heard a loud horn sounding.

3 Speaking skill linking events

Substitute these phrases for a similar phrase from Exercise 2.

a As luck would have it, …
b Just then, …
c Despondently, …
d Nowadays, …
e To our great surprise, …
f Last summer …
g The next day, …
h To our horror, …

4 Pronunciation long vowel sounds

a Look at the underlined vowel sounds in these words and put them in the correct place in the table below.

am<u>a</u>zement   ann<u>o</u>yance   ast<u>o</u>nishment   del<u>i</u>ght
dism<u>a</u>y   emb<u>a</u>rrassment   frustr<u>a</u>tion   h<u>o</u>rror
regr<u>e</u>t   rel<u>ie</u>f   sh<u>o</u>ck   surpr<u>i</u>se

Long vowel sound	Short vowel sound

b 🔊 **41** Listen and check your answers. Say each word after you hear it.

5 Listen and respond telling an anecdote

🔊 **42** You are going to tell a story about falling asleep on a train and ending up in the wrong place. A friend will ask you some questions. Respond with your own words. Then compare what you say with the model answer that follows.

1 *So, tell me what happened?*

Well, a couple of weeks ago, I got the train to go and visit my aunt. She lives in Newville.

5e Book of the month

Writing a review

1 Read this book review of *The Siege of Krishnapur* by J.G. Farrell and mark the parts of the review that do the following.

1 describe the theme of the book
2 give the reader's opinion of the book
3 describe the setting and the plot
4 describe the style of writing

Early morning at Victoria Memorial, West Bengal

It is 1857 and the British Empire in India is facing severe unrest from the indigenous population. For the ruling British class in the northern town of Krishnapur, life is calm and polite until the sepoys at a nearby military fort rise in mutiny and the British are forced to retreat into the British Residency. Food and other supplies become short, disease sets in and the inhabitants' resources are tested to the limit.

This is the first part of J.G. Farrell's empire trilogy, an examination of the British Empire in its decline. *The Siege of Krishnapur* serves as a metaphor for this decline as each character is forced to examine their own view of the world.

Although the situation is desperate, Farrell describes it with great elegance and humour, conveying the ridiculousness of the British position. Some would argue that in not describing the hardship and injustice suffered by the local Indian population, Farrell has done them a great injustice. But I do not think that was his aim. What he has done is to write both a gripping story and a thought-provoking study of colonial life.

2 Which of these techniques (a–e) has the writer used to begin this review?

a giving an opinion about the book directly
b talking about the writer's background
c describing the opening of the story
d giving a short summary of the whole story
e discussing the topic or theme of the book

3 Writing skill descriptive words

Complete the definitions of words describing books and writing with these words.

| convincing | fetched | going | poorly |
| provoking | uneventful | uninspiring |
| wrenching |

1 A book that makes you think is a thought-_____ book.
2 A book that is difficult to read is said to be heavy-_____ .
3 A story in which nothing much happens is _____ .
4 A plot which is very difficult to believe is far-_____ .
5 A fictional character who you believe could really exist is _____ .
6 An ending which is extremely sad is heart-_____ .
7 A book which is a bit dull and flat is _____ .
8 The opposite of *well-written* is _____ written.

4 Think of a novel you have read and write two short alternative opening paragraphs. For the first, give a short summary of the whole story. For the second, discuss the topic or theme of the book.

1
2

Wordbuilding synonyms

1 Complete these sentences using a synonym for the underlined word. You have been given the first two letters of the missing words.

1. It's a very picturesque <u>place</u> and a great sp_____ for a picnic.
2. I didn't <u>succeed</u> in finding cooking chocolate, but I ma_____ to get some ordinary chocolate.
3. It didn't <u>spoil</u> my enjoyment of the book generally, but it ru_____ the ending.
4. It's the most <u>durable</u> suitcase I've ever had. It's made of a very to_____ kind of plastic.
5. He <u>dealt with</u> the audience very skilfully and co_____ with every tricky question.
6. She showed enormous <u>bravery</u>, I thought. It takes co_____ to stand up to such criticism.
7. We had <u>hopes</u> that the film would do well, but it has surpassed all our ex_____ .
8. Can you <u>recognize</u> that figure on the left of the picture? I can't ma_____ it ou_____ .
9. We <u>started out</u> at 9 a.m. and the others se_____ of _____ an hour later.
10. The climb was <u>exhilarating</u> and reaching the top was even more th_____ .

Learning skills vocabulary extension (2)

2 You can use pictures to extend your vocabulary. Follow these steps.

1. Find a picture that interests you and look at the objects in it. The picture could also include people's expressions, feelings or actions that are happening.
2. See how many items you can name in English and then write the other words in your own language.
3. Look up the English equivalents of these words in a bilingual dictionary. Check the example sentences to see that the meaning is the same and check the pronunciation.
4. Now label five new items in the picture with words you have just learned.
5. Look at the picture thirty minutes later and test yourself. Can you remember the new words?

3 Look at the photo and follow the steps in Exercise 2. You will find a larger version of the photo on the Unit 5 Opener of your Student's Book (page 57).

Check!

4 Complete these sentences about characters and events with the correct form of the words given. All the answers are in Student's Book Unit 5.

1. The travel writer in the Opener referred to a bad experience with an _____ museum curator in Paris. (official)
2. In 5a, the writer says his trip to Chile, where he stayed at a _____ lodge on a nature reserve, fulfilled his _____ . (sustain, expect)
3. In 5b, the speaker describes going on a _____ mystery tour to an _____ destination. (magic, know)
4. In 5c, the writer describes Hergé's *Tintin* books as _____ novels. (graph)
5. In 5c, we learn that Hergé was not just a great _____ but also a great storyteller. (cartoon)
6. In 5d, we looked at adverbial linking phrases like 'to my _____ ,' and '_____ '. (relieve, worry)
7. In 5e, the writer describes the *Bridge of San Luis Rey* as a _____-_____ book. (think, provoke)
8. In 5f, the writer describes a _____ experience that he had while walking in Spain. (transform)

Unit 6 Body matters

6a Here comes the sun

Listening a healing regime

1 🔊 **43** Listen to a man describing his search for an exercise regime to help him recover from an injury. Answer the questions.

1 Where did he travel to?

2 What was he hoping to heal?

3 Was the exercise regime successful?

2 🔊 **43** Listen again. What is significant about each of these numbers in the story?

1 1968: the date when

2 40: the number of

3 hundreds of thousands: the number of

4 200: the number of

5 6.50: the time when

6 20 centimetres: the height of

7 two weeks: the length of

8 30 minutes: the length of time that

3 Choose the correct synonym (a or b) for the words in bold from the extract.

1 … at least **put off** the day when I would have to face back surgery.
  a postpone   b cancel

2 … it supports around 200 disadvantaged boys – some **orphaned** …
  a without homes   b without parents

3 There were no other distractions – no New Age tunes playing, no yoga **outfits** …
  a equipment   b special clothing

4 The yoga carried on in a **serene** way for two weeks, never causing me even to break sweat.
  a calm   b intense

5 The **persistent** pain hasn't entirely gone away, but it has subsided.
  a constant   b irritating

6 I can now **put up with** it because I've given up worrying about it.
  a tolerate   b forget

Grammar phrasal verbs

4 🔊 **43** Look at these phrasal verbs that the speaker uses. Then listen again and write the object of the transitive verbs. If there is no object, write *intransitive*.

1 turn up
2 end up
3 get over
4 put off
5 look for
6 pull in
7 put up
8 work on
9 carry on
10 put up with
11 give up

5 Answer these questions about the transitive phrasal verbs in Exercise 4.

1 Which of the verbs is clearly a separable verb?

2 Which of the verbs is clearly inseparable?

3 Of the rest, which do you think are separable and which inseparable?

6 Add the pronouns to these sentences.

1. The pain is quite bad, but I've learned to put up with. (it)
2. I got the injury playing football and it took me a long time to get over. (it)
3. If you think going to yoga classes will help, then there's no point putting off. (it)
4. I used to ski a lot, but I gave up. (it)
5. Reducing the cost of the course for students really pulled in. (them)
6. Can you put up for the night on Tuesday when I'm in town? (me)
7. I'm not as supple as I used to be, but I put down to my age. (that)
8. I can't touch my toes yet, but I'm working on. (it)

Vocabulary phrasal verbs

7 Choose the correct phrasal verb to complete the definitions.

1. To *come across / come out of* something means 'to find it unexpectedly'.
2. To *set apart / set aside* money or time means 'to reserve it'.
3. To *pick up / take up* a new hobby or sport means 'to begin practising it'.
4. To *put someone off / turn someone off* something means 'to discourage them from doing it'.
5. To *go up for / go in for* an activity means 'to like doing it'.
6. If something *takes off / lifts off*, it becomes successful.
7. To *get away from / get out of* a difficult task means 'to avoid having to do it'.
8. To *carry out / carry off* a task means 'to perform it'.
9. If something *comes about / comes up*, it happens or comes into existence.
10. To *fall back on / go back on* something means 'to use it as a reserve or back-up'.

Vocabulary exercise and health

8 Complete this conversation using one word in each space.

A: How do you ¹_____ so fit, Bella? Do you ²_____ loads of exercise or something?

B: Not so much these days. I used to work ³_____ at the gym twice a week, doing weights and working on the running machine.

A: So what's the secret? How do you keep in such good ⁴_____ ?

B: I think I'm just lucky really. I've never been ⁵_____ any kind of diet and I find that if I ⁶_____ reasonably active, I don't really have to ⁷_____ my weight.

A: I think that's my problem. I just never seem to find time to exercise.

B: What about going ⁸_____ a run with me one evening after work?

A: Yes, that would be good – as long as it's not too far.

9 Dictation fitness crazes

🎧 **44** Listen to this conversation between two people about fitness classes. Complete the conversation.

A: The other day _____ .

B: Did you _____ ?

A: Not really. I didn't _____ .

B: You mean like Zumba?

A: Yes. I knew Zumba _____ , _____ .

B: And do you? _____

A: Yes, I do. _____ .

6b Cross-training

Reading advice for athletes

1 Read the article and underline the three sentences that tell you the following.

1 the definition of cross-training
2 its most significant benefit
3 what cross-training teaches us

2 Read the article again and choose the correct option (a, b or c).

1 The main benefit of swimming to a cyclist is to help them:
   a relax.   b build muscle.   c have more stamina.
2 Marathon running is given as an example of a sport which is:
   a anti-social.   b boring.   c lonely.
3 Cross-training helps athletes to avoid injuries by adding:
   a variety.   b gentler exercise.
   c breaks from exercise.
4 The writer implies that an athlete's career is relatively:
   a dangerous.   b short.   c easy.
5 The word *diet* in paragraph 3 could be replaced by:
   a routine.   b menu.   c day.
6 The result of taking up a new form of exercise is that your body:
   a becomes stressed.   b feels happy.
   c gets stronger.

Cross-training

In recent years, there has been an increased focus among practitioners of all types of sports on cross-training. It has become in fact a critical part of most top athletes' regular routines. Simply put, cross-training **means practising** other sports or forms of exercise to improve, indirectly, your abilities in your main or target sport. An example of this would be a cyclist going swimming a couple of times a week. Swimming **requires you to control** your breathing and so it can also **help more generally to increase** a cyclist's endurance. It also **lets you build** strength in a more relaxed way because the support of the water puts less strain on joints and muscles.

There are several benefits to cross-training. First, it **tends to be** more interesting for the athlete to be engaged in different activities. If their sport is a solitary one, like marathon running, playing a team sport like football could provide a social aspect to their training. Secondly, it can strengthen and improve joints and muscles that are vital if they are to **succeed in performing** their sport at the highest level. Finally, and most importantly, it **prevents athletes from getting** the kind of repetitive strain injuries that they often suffer if they only practise the same activities day in, day out. It can not only improve performance, but also extend an athlete's life. In recent years, several footballers have used yoga to **enable them to continue playing** into their late thirties and even in some cases, their early forties.

Cross-training is not just useful for the elite sportsperson either. It has benefits for all of us. To stay injury free, I **recommend everyone incorporate** the following elements into their exercise diet:

- two parts cardio-vascular exercise (e.g. running, swimming, cycling, skipping, tennis)
- one part strength building (weight training)
- one part stretching (e.g. yoga, dance, aerobics)
- one part balance training (e.g. yoga, surfing, gymnastics)

The lesson of cross-training is that the body reacts well to new experiences. Each time you embark on a new form of exercise, whether it be weight-lifting or cycling, the body must **learn to deal with** new stresses and new demands. And in doing that, it will naturally strengthen.

Grammar verb patterns

3 Look at these verb patterns (1–6). Complete the table with examples of the verb patterns from the article.

1 Verb + *to* + infinitive	
2 Verb + object + *to* + infinitive	
3 Verb + object + infinitive	
4 Verb + *-ing*	
5 Verb + preposition + *-ing*	
6 Verb + object + preposition + *-ing*	

4 Complete the sentences using the correct form of the verbs. You sometimes also need to use a preposition.

1 Many people forget .... properly before taking exercise. (warm up)
2 Sports therapists encourage athletes .... cross-training as a way to extend their careers. (do)
3 I don't recommend .... more than one hour of intensive exercise a day. (do)
4 You can't make people .... , but you can help them .... the benefits. (exercise, see)
5 I miss .... football, but at my age it's just not worth the risk of injury. (play)
6 If I worried .... injured all the time, I would never try anything new. (get)
7 I thank my teacher .... me interested in rowing. (get)
8 The best exercise routines seem .... the ones which incorporate different elements of exercise. (be)
9 I started .... tennis when I was ten, but then I switched to basketball. (play)
10 I love .... sports, but I dislike .... (play, train)

Vocabulary injuries

5 Complete the sentences with the correct form of these verbs to make collocations.

bruise   bump   chip   graze
lose   pull   sprain   stub

1 He fell over in the playground and .... **his knee**.
2 I got up in the night and .... **my toe** on the bed leg.
3 I didn't notice how low the doorway was and I .... **my head**.
4 I bit on a nutshell in my cereal and .... **my tooth**.
5 The doctor said nothing was broken – I've just .... **my ribs**, apparently.
6 Sorry, I've .... **my voice**. I was talking all day yesterday to a group of schoolchildren.
7 I trod in a hole in the pavement and .... **my ankle**.
8 I can't play tennis this weekend. I .... a **muscle** in my shoulder the last time I played.

6 Complete these idioms with prepositions. Then replace the underlined expressions in the sentences with the idioms.

to be .... a bad way	to pass ....
to be .... colour	to be .... the mend
to be shaken	to be run ....

1 It was so hot in the room, I practically <u>fainted</u>.
2 I'm glad Pete's <u>getting better</u> now; he seems to have been ill for ages.
3 I've been working solidly for months and I'm very <u>lacking in energy</u>.
4 I think she felt very <u>distressed</u> by the incident, even though no one got hurt.
5 You look a bit <u>pale</u>. Are you feeling OK?
6 So sorry to hear about Jim falling off the stepladder. Is he <u>seriously hurt</u>?

7 Pronunciation stress in two-syllable verbs

a 45 Circle the verbs that have stress on the second syllable. Which two do not? Then listen and check your answers.

admire   avoid   convince   delay   expect
insist   involve   postpone   practise
prevent   rely   require   succeed   welcome

b What is the difference between the two verbs that have stress on the first syllable and the others?

6c The beauty industry

Listening globalizing beauty

1 🔊 46 Listen to an interview with an expert on the fashion and beauty industry. Which of these statements (a, b or c) best summarizes her views?

a Globalization has made us all aspire to the same ideal of beauty.
b Companies have come to realize that local traditions are important.
c Companies try to convince us to want the same things because it's cheaper for them.

2 🔊 46 Listen again and complete the examples that the speaker gives to illustrate the following points. Pause the CD each time before moving onto the next question.

1 General economic growth has affected our view of beauty.
   a The global cosmetics industry _____ .
   b Americans _____ .

2 New markets keep being found.
   _____ brings in over $30 billion.

3 In the early 20th century, cosmetics companies were peddling a western and 'white' ideal of beauty.
   Some promised that _____ .

4 The more recent era of globalization is one in which companies definitely have to be more conscious of local traditions and values.
   A company like _____ .

5 Multinational companies adapt their products to include local and traditional ingredients.
   a _____ for skin cleansing
   b the Huito fruit _____

3 Replace the words in bold from the interview with one-word synonyms.

1 Has a globalized world made our ideal of beauty more **homogenized**?
2 If you go back to the early 20th century … cosmetics companies were **peddling** a Western ideal of beauty.
3 … if people everywhere could aspire to the same **notion** of beauty …
4 … McDonald's **alters** its menu to suit the tastes of each local market …
5 … a clear skin, healthy-looking hair, a youthful **glow** …

Word focus face

4 Complete this conversation using one word in each space.

A: Why the ¹_____ face? Are you depressed about something?
B: Yes, I'm going to a school reunion and all my clothes make me look too old. The last time I saw all those people I was 26!
A: Well, be careful. If you wear something that makes you look like you're obviously trying to look younger, no one will be able to **keep a** ²_____ face.
B: I know. I think I should just go as I am and **put a** ³_____ face on it.
A: Well, **let's face** ⁴_____ , none of them are going to be looking any younger either.
B: I wouldn't bet on it. Sue Williamson always used to spend loads on her appearance. She looked fantastic the last time I saw her.
A: Well, I don't see what the big deal is. If she thinks she's going to ⁵_____ face by looking old, that's her problem, not yours …
B: No, you're right. It's all very superficial. I'll just choose something smart and go and **face the** ⁶_____ . If they want to make judgements, let them.

48

Unit 6 Body matters

6d It'll do them good

Real life discussing proposals

1 🔊 **47** Listen to four speakers each discussing a different proposal for the workplace. Write the number of the speaker (1–4) next to the proposal they discuss (a–f). Note that there are two extra proposals.

_____ a a way to help people feel less stressed
_____ b a way to help people get more exercise
_____ c a way to reduce car use
_____ d a way to have a healthier atmosphere
_____ e a way to help people eat more healthily
_____ f a way to build team spirit

2 What was the specific proposal in each case?

1 do without a _____
2 do without _____
3 provide a _____
4 provide opportunities for _____

3 🔊 **47** Listen again and note down the possible problem with each proposal.

1 _____
2 _____
3 _____
4 _____

4 Speaking skill proposing and conceding a point

🔊 **47** Complete the phrases the speakers used to propose and concede points. Then listen again and check your answers.

1 A better _____ would _____ to have just one which can be a service lift.
2 I _____ that sometimes people who have heavy things to move … will sometimes want to use the lift, but we can _____ work _____ that.
3 It _____ be _____ better just to have straightforward fresh air sucked in from outside.
4 _____, it wouldn't always be cool air, _____ it would be a lot healthier – and cheaper.
5 I haven't really thought _____ who should be responsible for making the list, but I do think it's important to make one.
6 I _____ not _____ will want to join in in that way, but for a lot of people the social element will really be a big attraction.

5 Pronunciation toning down negative statements

a 🔊 **48** Listen and underline the words which have most stress in these sentences.

1 I'm not very much in favour of the proposal.
2 It's not exactly what I had in mind.
3 It's not a particularly cheap option.
4 It hasn't proved to be so successful.
5 I'm not entirely convinced.

b Practise saying each sentence in Exercise 5a in the same way.

6 Listen and respond giving your opinion

🔊 **49** Imagine you are at a meeting to discuss a proposal to install a gym in your workplace to help staff keep fit. Your colleagues ask you questions. Respond with your own words. Then compare what you say with the model answer that follows.

1 *What do you think of the proposal?*

I think it's a great idea. It would really help staff to keep in shape and get exercise during their lunch hour or after work.

6e A balanced diet

Writing a formal report

1 Read the report and answer the questions.

1 What prompted the report to be written?

2 What was the main finding?

3 What action is proposed?

Background and aims

There is concern that children at the school are not eating healthily enough, and this is affecting both their general health  and their academic performance. In view of this, a short study was commissioned to look into children's diets and make recommendations. The aim of this report is to present those findings and make recommendations.

Findings

Most children are not getting a balanced diet. In the 14–16 age group, only 55 per cent of children have school meals. Overall, the lunches provided are a good balance of meat or fish, vegetables and carbohydrates (bread, potatoes, etc.). However, it is a self-service system and there is no obligation for pupils to choose a good variety of foods. Accordingly, children tend to choose mainly the carbohydrates, especially items like chips and sweet puddings rather than healthier items.

The remaining 45 per cent of pupils bring in a packed lunch. The content of these lunches varies greatly – from crisps and sweets to sandwiches and fruit, and apparently, the school makes no specific recommendations on what packed lunches should include.

Recommendations

Although pupils at the school are given options as to what they can have for lunch, most are making choices that are not balanced; specifically, this means they are eating too many sweets and not enough protein. We recommend that school meals should be compulsory for all pupils. We also suggest that they are given the choice of different meals, but not a choice of different elements within each meal, i.e. they must have a balance of vegetables, protein and carbohydrates.

2 Find words and phrases in the report with the following meanings, but expressed more formally.

1 Because of this
2 In general
3 But
4 So
5 people say
6 in particular

3 Writing skill avoiding repetition

a Find these words (1–6) in the report. Then find different ways of expressing the same idea later in the report.

1 children in the school
2 meals
3 balanced diet
4 The content of these lunches
5 options
6 We recommend

b Express these ideas in other words.

1 The canteen staff …
   Those
2 Most children …
   The
3 Hot meals would be good for children
   Hot meals would

4 Write a report encouraging school children to do more sport using the notes below. Write three paragraphs.

Background and aims
Local school wants to encourage everyone to do sport, not just in school teams.

Main findings
Pupils sit around at break times; no equipment; not enough PE lessons.

Recommendations
Organized group early morning exercise; semi-organized sports at break times.

Glossary
PE (n) /ˌpiː ˈiː/ physical education: a school subject where students do exercise and play sport

Wordbuilding compound words

1 Choose the correct options to complete these sentences.
1. The film is about Jim when he's an old man, but it contains a lot of *cutbacks / flashbacks* to his earlier life.
2. The *turnout / turn-up* for the election was over 70% this time, because many more young people registered to vote.
3. This is probably the most important *break-in / breakthrough* in medical science for thirty years.
4. I sent her a *follow-on / follow-up* letter stressing how interested we are, but I still haven't heard.
5. Sorry, I can't really stop now, but I'd love to meet soon for a proper *catch-up / round-up*.
6. There's been a complete *breakdown / clampdown* in relations between the two sides – they're not even talking anymore.
7. You should try and get a gig at the Beat Café. They're always on the *lookalike / lookout* for new musical talent.
8. She had a kind of *faraway / getaway* look in her eyes.
9. We reported the *break-in / break-up* to the police, even though nothing valuable was stolen.
10. The final will be a *showdown / show-off* between the two best teams in the division.

2 Underline the compound word to complete each definition.
1. A *break-up / getaway* is a quick escape.
2. A *cutback / clampdown* is a reduction in spending.
3. A *turn-up / clampdown* is a severe restriction on activity.
4. A *lookalike / show-off* is a person who is always drawing attention to their achievements.
5. A *turn-up / follow-on* is an unexpected (positive) event or result.
6. A *break-in / break-up* is a separation or disintegration.

Learning skills using phrasal verbs correctly

3 Read the notes below about using phrasal verbs.
1. Often in dictionaries you will find one-word synonyms given for phrasal verbs. These can be misleading. For example: *make up = invent*.
2. Most phrasal verbs are limited in the contexts in which they can be used. You can *make up a story* or *make up an excuse*, for example, but you can't *make up a new product*.
3. So a full definition would be: *make up = invent an account of something*.
4. When you learn a new phrasal verb, you must also learn its limitations before you start to use it.

4 Look at these phrasal verbs and their full definitions, and tick (✓) the words that collocate with the phrasal verbs.
1. *call off* = cancel (a scheduled event)
   I called off:
   a the meeting.
   b the hotel booking.
   c the football match.
   d the wedding.
2. *put across* = communicate (one's ideas or feelings)
   She put across:
   a her proposal.
   b her views.
   c her decision.
   d the news by email.
3. *set up* = establish (a new organization or connection)
   We set up:
   a a good relationship.
   b our own company.
   c a video link.
   d a daily routine.
4. *find out* = discover (an answer by consulting or by experience)
   I found out:
   a an old map in his attic.
   b a new car.
   c why she left.
   d the meaning of the word.

Check!

5 Complete these sentences about exercise and beauty. All the answers are in Student's Book Unit 6.
1. Swogging is a mixture of _____ and _____.
2. Radio Taiso is a callisthenic exercise routine in _____.
3. Yoga originated in _____.
4. Ultrarunning means running _____ distances.
5. Women of the Paaung tribe in Myanmar put copper coils around their _____ to make them longer.
6. People say that beauty is _____ deep (but 'ugly' goes clean to the bone)!
7. In Washington State, USA, restaurants have to say how many _____ are in each dish.
8. In 6e, the writer reported on a proposal to make smokers pay more for their _____.

Unit 7 Digital media

7a The Star Cave

Listening digital exploration

1 Look at the photo and the heading *digital exploration*. How do you think this woman is able to see this image?

2 🔊 50 Listen to a podcast about Albert Yu-Min Lin and the Star Cave. Answer the questions.
   1 What is Lin's job, and how does he do it differently from others in his profession?
   ....
   ....
   2 What is the Star Cave?
   ....

3 🔊 50 Listen again and choose the correct option (a, b or c).
   1 What are the podcaster's feelings about technology?
      a mixed
      b that it is beneficial on the whole
      c that it creates more problems than it solves
   2 What do Lin's digital immersive technologies mean that he can do?
      a He can stay in California to work.
      b He doesn't necessarily have to go into the field to excavate.
      c He can use more sensitive and accurate equipment.
   3 What is the tomb of Genghis Khan given as an example of?
      a a place which is deep under the earth
      b a very sensitive subject for local people
      c a place which historians found but never mapped
   4 Which of these things ISN'T mentioned as something you can do in the Star Cave?
      a survey the landscape as if you were in a plane
      b navigate through underwater cities
      c compare a landscape to past accounts of it
   5 What is the future for this type of technology?
      a to be used in biological research
      b to create a complete 3D map of the world
      c to be used in many different disciplines

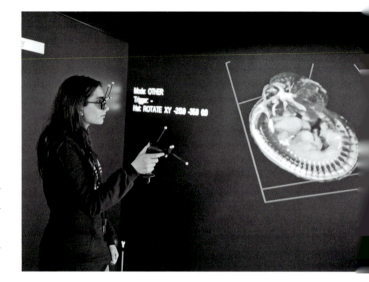

4 Answer the questions about the words in bold in these phrases from the podcast.
   1 ... plastic debris in our oceans is believed to be changing marine ecosystems **irreparably** ...
      Irreparably means it can't be fixed. What root word has *irreparably* been built from?
   2 Lin has **swapped** his spade and trowel for an array of digital 3D immersive technologies.
      What do footballers swap after a match?
   3 What this allows him to do is visualize data using **cutting-edge** tools ...
      Cutting-edge here means 'very advanced'. What object normally has a cutting edge?
   4 ... the tomb is considered to be an extremely **sacred** place ...
      Sacred means it has religious significance to people. Can you think of another word for *sacred*?
   5 ... disturbing it could **trigger** a **curse** that would end the world.
      a What triggers a house alarm to go off?
      b Do you think a curse brings good luck or only bad luck?
   6 ... the labs where all this data is **crunched** ...
      Crunch literally means 'to break up into small pieces, particularly when biting hard on food before swallowing'. What does it mean here?

52

Grammar passive reporting verbs

5 Write these sentences from the podcast using passive reporting verbs.

1. Technology (generally / think / be) a positive thing.
   ....
2. Plastic debris in our oceans (believe / change) marine ecosystems irreparably as we speak.
   ....
3. The quest (know / frustrate) scientists and historians for centuries.
   ....
4. The tomb (consider / be) an extremely sacred place.
   ....
5. Lin learns from an ancient text where a particular mountain (suppose / be) in the past.
   ....
6. These new approaches (expect / benefit) all kinds of projects in the future.
   ....

6 Rewrite these sentences using passive reporting verbs.

1. People think that Lin is unusual because of his varied interests.
   Lin ....
2. People say that Lin was inspired by an art historian who uses digital imaging.
   Lin ....
3. We know that Genghis Khan died far from his homeland.
   Genghis Khan ....
4. People also know that he wanted to be buried in some mountains in the north.
   It ....
5. Records reported at the time that he asked to be buried in an unmarked tomb.
   He ....
6. We don't expect to find his tomb any time soon.
   His tomb ....

Vocabulary digital media

7 Cross out the incorrect option in each sentence.

1. You can *download / upload / listen to* **music** for free on this website.
2. Feel free to *blog / post / write* **a comment** and tell us what you think.
3. I can use this software to *chat / network / talk* **online** to my parents 8,000 miles away in Australia.
4. I don't really *go on / tweet / use* **social networking sites**.
5. I always look online to see if others have *posted / recommended / reviewed* **a hotel** before I book it.
6. I've *posted / blogged / uploaded* the photos onto the website so you can see them.

8 Dictation photographing Paris

🔊 51 Listen to this blog post by a photographer in Paris. Complete the blog post.

I was ....
....
....
I didn't .... ,
like the Eiffel Tower, ...
....
But ....
.... ,
instead, I ....
....
So ....
They ....
....
.... :
more like ....
I'll ....
....

53

7b Follow us!

Reading exploiting social media

1 Look at these statements about businesses using social media. Do you think the statements are true (T) or false (F)? Then read the article and underline the sentences that provide the evidence for your answers.

1 There are many different social media sites, but they are all essentially the same.
2 Bad use of social media by a company can actually be worse than not using it at all.
3 Social media has become an integral part of the way companies communicate with customers.
4 Measuring the success of social media marketing is something anyone can do quite cheaply.
5 Ideally your social media marketing will offer something to the customer that they have not seen elsewhere.
6 The numbers of people who see your campaign is the most important thing.

2 Find these words and phrases in the article. Choose the correct meaning (a or b) for each.

1 a minefield
  a something full of unseen risks
  b something certain to end in disaster
2 go about
  a achieve   b approach
3 coherent
  a consistent and logical
  b simple and effective
4 in a roundabout way
  a secretly   b indirectly

Follow us!

For those businesses which are unfamiliar with it, social media marketing can be a minefield. Because there are so many different channels to choose from – Youtube, Instagram, Linkedin and Twitter to name just a few – each with a different user profile, it is difficult to know where to begin. And although every business has the same ultimate goal of selling more, each one will want to go about this in a different way through its social media campaigns, for example, by trying to attract more visitors to its website or by encouraging customers' interest in a specific product. If you use social media incorrectly, it can actually put customers off; yet not using it is not really an option any longer, since it has become a key area in which companies compete with each other for customers' attention. There are, however, some simple principles you can follow to make sure that you are successful.

The first thing is to plan a list of measures that are both achievable and measurable (there are various analytic software tools available at a relatively low cost that monitor both customer traffic and the reaction of those who see your campaign). The second point is to create content that has an equal mix of promotional material, new ideas and engaging or relatable content. Thirdly, it is important to keep your brand identity strong and your message coherent in your social media marketing; just as it is in any other type of advertising that you run. And lastly, as mentioned above, it is vital to choose the right social media channels to reach your target customers. Remember that it is not how many people you reach but whether you reach people with a message that appeals to them.

A good example of a company which has successfully followed these principles is TOMS shoes. TOMS is a social enterprise which, for each pair of shoes it sells, gives a pair of shoes to a child in need. The company asked followers to go without wearing shoes for one day and then post a photo of this on Instagram. They wanted to make people more aware of the millions of children in the world who walk barefoot. The campaign served in a roundabout way to promote TOMS' own 'Buy a pair, Give a pair' model. With the help of Instagram they were able to tell a visual story that their customers could engage with and also gave them immediate feedback on how successful their campaign was.

Unit 7 Digital media

Grammar nominalization

3 Rewrite the sentences from the article with nominalized forms. Use the prompts in brackets.

1 Because there are so many different channels to choose from, it is difficult to know where to begin. (wide choice / makes)

2 If you use social media incorrectly, it can actually put customers off (incorrect use)

3 There are, however, some simple principles you can follow to make sure that you are successful. (ensure / success)

4 Thirdly, it's important to keep your brand identity strong and your message coherent. (strength / coherence)

5 Remember that it is not how many people you reach but whether you reach people with a message that appeals to them. (number / matters / appeal)

6 They wanted to make people more aware of the millions of children in the world who walk barefoot. (aim / raise / awareness)

4 Complete the sentences using nominalized forms so that they mean the same as the sentence above.

1 We are not concerned about how much the work costs. It's more important to us that it is done quickly.
Our _____ is not the _____; the _____ is more important.

2 Their advertising campaign did not affect people immediately. It took about three months after they had launched it to become really popular.
The _____ advertising campaign was not immediate. Its _____ came three months after its _____.

3 Very few people were interested in the jumpers at first, but when David Beckham was spotted wearing one, suddenly they started to sell thousands of them.
There was _____ in the jumpers initially, but when David Beckham was spotted wearing one, _____ took off.

4 Fewer people booked camping holidays, because summer was very late in arriving.
_____ camping holidays were down owing to the _____ of summer.

Idioms business buzz words

5 Complete the sentences with these business buzz words.

| ballpark | box | loop | page |
| practice | reality | rocket | win |

1 I'd say 10,000 is just a _____ figure – who knows what the real potential is?
2 The CEO wants to be kept in the _____ on this project. He's keen that all goes smoothly.
3 I don't see how we can go wrong here. It's a _____-win situation.
4 I think our salespeople will understand the product. It's not _____ science.
5 Distribution is the key. We need to look at examples of best _____ in the industry and follow that model.
6 Are we on the same _____ here? I have the impression that you have different expectations for this initiative.
7 Innovation only happens when people think outside the _____.
8 We need a _____ check. Very few people use fax machines any more.

6 What more everyday words and phrases do you think the business buzzwords in bold in these sentences are alternatives for?

1 We've had a few **issues** with our supplier, so we can't send you the goods as promised.

2 Can you **reach out to** the sales team and see who is interested in doing the presentation?

3 We have a lot of talented people working for us, but we're failing to **leverage** that talent.

4 Why would you buy a product for $40 from a shop when you can get the same thing online for $25? It's **a no brainer**.

55

7c The Cleanweb hackathon

Listening hacking to a brighter future

1 Look at the photo and the heading *hacking to a brighter future*. What do you think a *hackathon* is?

2 🔊 52 Listen to an interview with a journalist and compare your idea with what the journalist says. What was the focus of the hackathon she attended?

3 🔊 53 Listen to the first part of the interview and make notes on the following.
   1 two alternative expressions for a *hackathon*
   2 the typical length of a hackathon
   3 three kinds of technology Cleanweb uses to solve environmental problems
   4 four areas of environmental improvement that they address
   5 what 'the resource cloud' was being used to encourage
   6 one thing that a neighbour might want to borrow from another

4 🔊 54 Listen to the second part of the interview and answer the questions.
   1 What did one of the organizers of Cleanweb say we all needed to do?
   2 What was the atmosphere at the hackathon like?
   3 What does the app Econofy allow you to do?
   4 What additional reward did the inventors of this app get?
   5 In what category would Amrita put Cleanweb?

Word focus *break*

5 Complete the sentences to make expressions with *break*. You have been given the first letter of the missing words.
   1 We've already spent $2,500 on new equipment. Another $50 isn't going to **break the b**_____ .
   2 So, he's going to have to share an office with four other people. Shall I **break the n**_____ to him or will you?
   3 I've bitten my nails since I was five years old and it's very difficult to **break the h**_____ .
   4 Thieves **broke i**_____ and stole $10,000 worth of electronic equipment.
   5 I always tell a few jokes before I begin a training session to help **break the i**_____ .
   6 It's a very difficult piece of translation, but I think I've **broken the b**_____ of it now.
   7 We **broke e**_____ in our first year and this year we'll make a small profit.

Unit 7 Digital media

7d Sauroniops

Real life making a podcast

1 🔊 **55** Listen to this podcast about a dinosaur find and complete the table.

What is it?	
Where was it found?	
Who found it?	
What does the discovery tell us about this part of Africa?	

2 Speaking skill hedging language

🔊 **55** Complete these statements from the podcast using hedging language. Use one or two words per space. Then listen again and check your answers.

1 … which _____ to have terrorized North Africa some 95 million years ago.
2 Cau has been able to conclude that this was _____ a large two-legged meat-eater …
3 … and _____ measuring as much as twelve metres in length.
4 The long shape of the skull _____ Sauroniops had a large jaw …
5 The fossil also revealed a large bump on Sauroniops's already thick forehead, from which it _____ this dinosaur used its head in fights …
6 … this area of North Africa _____ have been particularly popular with predatory dinosaurs.
7 Such dinosaurs _____ gather where there was an abundance of food …
8 _____, says Cau, they targeted different prey and had no need to compete for food.

3 Pronunciation new words

a Look at these words from the podcast. Using what you know about prefixes and suffixes, (stress patterns, rules for short or long vowels, etc.) say them as you think they will be pronounced.

abundance
blade
comprise
fossil
geological
jaw
predatory
ripping
skull
two-legged

b 🔊 **56** Listen, check and repeat.

4 Listen and respond historical objects

🔊 **57** Imagine you have found an old object of historical interest. Think about what it is, the period it is from and its significance. Then listen to the questions a friend asks you about it. Answer each question using hedging language. Then compare what you say with the model answer that follows.

1 So what did you find?   It seems to be some kind of old oil lamp.

7e World's smallest

Writing a news report

1 Look at the photo and then read the news report. Underline the parts of the report that answer these questions.

1. Who features in the story?
2. What did the zoologists do?
3. Where did this happen?
4. How did they do it?
5. When did this happen?
6. Why is this important?

Brookesia micra

David Attenborough is one of the world's best-known nature documentary makers, and there are few places on the planet that he has not been and few marvels of nature that he has not seen. So finding the pygmy chameleon on the island of Madagascar half a century after he first began looking for it was very likely a moment of huge personal satisfaction for him.

In 2012, German zoologists found an even smaller species, *Brookesia micra*, on one of the smaller islands off the coast of Madagascar. Attenborough found his pygmy chameleon by looking on the forest floor among the leaf litter, where they generally live during the day. The German team used a different method to find *Brookesia*: searching with torches at night when the tiny chameleons climb into the trees and are said to be easier to spot.

The discovery is significant because it seems to suggest that in certain circumstances, such as being confined to an island, some animals grow smaller in order to adapt to a restricted habitat. *Brookesia* is almost certainly not the only chameleon to be part of this phenomenon.

2 Writing skill cautious language

a Read the report again and find examples of the following types of cautious language.

a the verb *seem* (para 3)
b a passive reporting verb (para 2)
c an adverb of degree (para 3)
d an adverb of frequency (para 2)
e adverbs that speculate about a fact (paras 1 and 3)

b Make these sentences from the report more cautious using the words in brackets.

1. David Attenborough is one of the world's best-known nature documentary makers.
   .... (probably)
2. Attenborough found his pygmy chameleon by looking on the forest floor.
   .... (seem)
3. In 2012, German zoologists found an even smaller species.
   .... (apparently)
4. The German team used a different method to find *Brookesia*.
   .... (appear)
5. Some animals grow smaller in order to adapt to a restricted habitat.
   .... (believe)

3 Write your own news report using these notes. Write approximately 150 words.

> We already know some species of snake can fly.
> Some can glide up to 100 metres.
> But how?
> New study from Virginia Tech has a possible answer.
> Snakes flatten their bodies to make a wing.
> Heads up, tails down and glide.
> Probably no significance for aeroplane or military technology.

Wordbuilding verb prefixes

1 Look at the meanings of the verb* prefixes below. Then add the correct prefix (*out*, *over* or *under*) to each verb. (*out* = more than / better than; *over* = too much; *under* = too little)
   1 Don't _____ **estimate** her. She's a lot more capable than most people think.
   2 Statistics show that on average women _____ **live** men by approximately three to five years.
   3 I think you _____ **charged** me for these drinks. It should have come to $12, but you charged $18.
   4 There are disadvantages to making children stay at school until they are 18, but these are _____ **weighed** by the advantages.
   5 I'm amazed he still plays computer games at the age of 45. You would imagine he would have _____ **grown** them by now.
   6 This chicken is _____ **cooked**. It's still pink in the middle.
   7 I don't know why you are so angry with him. He was only doing his job. I think you are _____ **reacting**.
   8 'At the end of the day' is an expression that is _____ **used** in British English. It has become a bit meaningless.
   9 The people in favour of going on were _____ **numbered** by those who wanted to turn back.
   10 The girls' performance is good, but boys at the school are _____ **achieving**. They are capable of much better results.
   11 Internet security firms face a constant battle to _____ **smart** the hackers.
   12 This washing machine _____ **performs** its competitors in every aspect: it's quieter, uses less water, cleans better – and it's not that expensive.

   * Note that item 11 is an adjective, not a verb.

Learning skills intensive reading

2 To build your reading speed and ability to comprehend more complex texts, you need to practise intensive reading. Read the notes. Then answer the question.

> Intensive reading is when you read for an accurate and close understanding of the ideas and details in a text. This will often be necessary in work or study.
>
> Which of the following would you do if you were reading intensively?
> a check new words in a dictionary
> b skim the text first for a general understanding
> c try to break down complex sentences into manageable chunks

3 Breaking down text is a key skill with more complex writing. Read this complex sentence and then follow the steps (1–3).

Setting aside for a moment the question of whether you agree with his methods of collecting data or not, the evidence that Jenkins has supplied implies that there is an increase rather than a decrease in the number of people under the age of fifty suffering from memory loss.

1 Identify the main verb, the basic subject of the main verb and the basic object of that verb.
2 Now define more precisely what the subject and object of the verb are.
3 Finally, look at any subordinate clauses and say what the extra information they give relates to.

4 Follow these steps with other complex sentences in something you have to read in English.

Check!

5 Complete the sentences. Use the first letter of each word to spell a key word from Unit 7a. All the answers are in Student's Book Unit 7.

> 1 Unit 7b explains how companies use _____ media to market their products and services.
> 2 If you don't make a profit or a loss, you break _____ .
> 3 The video in 7f was about saving disappearing _____ .
> 4 At the Defcon convention, participants took part in a competition called 'Capture the _____ '.
> 5 Artist Liu Bolin is known as 'The _____ man'.
> 6 An _____ is a symbol used in messaging, like a smiley face or a sad face.
>
> Word: _____

Unit 8 The music in us

8a Ukulele master

Listening Jake Shimabukuro

1 🔊 58 Listen to an interview with ukulele player Jake Shimabukuro and answer the questions.

1 When did Shimabukuro start playing?

2 Where are he and his ukulele from?

3 What kind of music did he play at first?

4 What kind of music does he play now?

5 Why does he think everyone should play the ukulele?

2 🔊 58 Look at these statements. Then listen again and write the word or phrase Shimabukuro uses that has a similar meaning to the phrases in bold. (You can pause the CD each time to give yourself time to write.)

1 When he played the ukulele, Shimabukuro was instantly **addicted**.

2 The ukelele is **Hawaii's traditional instrument**.

3 At high school, there were **small groups of people** with specific interests in music styles.

4 Shimabukuro's **approach to the instrument was quite individual**.

5 People were **shocked** by his version of 'More Than Words'.

6 For him, music communicates **powerful feelings**.

7 His grandmother and her friends **enjoy** playing the ukulele.

8 Modern life and modern technology doesn't give us **time to stop and think**.

3 🔊 58 Read what Shimabukuro said about the importance of music. Complete the text. Then listen again and check your answers.

In this day and ¹_____ we live in, where technology always expects us to multi-task and give ² _____ our contemplative time, we're always expected to respond so quickly; it can be ³ _____ . So coming home after a long day, ⁴ _____ up the ukulele and playing it feels like a ⁵ _____ session to me! It gives you the chance to let loose and act ⁶ _____ !

4 Match these words (1–5) from the interview with their definitions (a–e).

1 recorder   a a melody
2 chord   b a version of someone
3 tune   else's composition
4 note   c a single musical tone
5 cover song   d a wind instrument
                       e a group of single musical tones played together

Grammar the adverb *just*

5 Replace the words in bold in these sentences with *just* and write it in the correct position in the sentence.

1. We got back from holiday **very recently**.
2. The new museum is **simply** stunning.
3. That's what I think **exactly**.
4. We **only** use bicycles; we don't own a car.
5. There are **a little** under three million people living in the city.
6. Hang on. I'm trying to call the bank before it closes, **right at this moment**.

6 Write *just* in the correct place in the numbered lines.

> One of the song titles on Shimabukuro's album *Peace, Love and Ukulele* consists
> 1 of three numbers: 143. Shimabukuro says that the song was written for his fiancée at the time and that the significance is that
> 2 in those days they had pagers, not mobile phones. 143 means 'I love you' in numeric code. So he used to page her with that code,
> 3 in the same way that some people now text the letters *ILY*. Even after pagers were replaced with mobile phones, they still used
> 4 the code, because it was something they
> 5 both understood. So the song is a piece of nostalgia, really.

7 Look at the pairs of sentences. Then choose the correct meaning of *just* (a, b or c) for each sentence.

1. My mom taught me my first three chords, and I was just hooked. ....
2. My mom has just taught me my first three chords, and I am hooked. ....
   a very recently   b only
   c quite simply
3. I remember playing 'More Than Words' by Extreme and everyone just freaked out! ....
4. I just remember playing 'More Than Words' by Extreme and everyone freaked out! ....
   a simply   b exactly   c only
5. It's a more intimate connection than just having a conversation with someone. ....
6. It's taken just over two years to build up that more intimate connection. ....
   a very recently   b a little   c only
7. My grandmother has just started playing it. ....
8. Just my grandmother started playing it. ....
   a exactly   b recently   c only
9. I believe just taking that step to give any kind of instrument a try will bring people immense joy. ....
10. I believe taking that step to give any kind of instrument a try is just the right thing to do. ....
    a simply   b exactly   c a little

8 Pronunciation expressions with *just*

a 🔊 59 Match the questions (1–6) with the correct responses (a–f). Then listen and check.

1. Will that work?
2. Shall we go?
3. How are you doing?
4. Can I help you?
5. Why do you ask?
6. Is Jaz there?

a No, thanks, I'm just looking.
b I'm just curious.
c No, he's just left.
d Yes, that's just the job!
e Yes, I'm just coming.
f Just fine, thanks.

b 🔊 59 Now listen again to the questions and pause the CD so that you can respond yourself.

Vocabulary extra music

9 Complete the table with these words.

busker   eclectic   folk   hum   naturally-gifted   upbeat

Genres of music	
Moods of music	
Types of musician	
Ways of singing	
Tastes in music	
Attributes of a musician	

10 Read the conversation. Then put the words in bold in the correct category in the table in Exercise 9.

A: I saw John Williams in concert last night. You know, the **composer** and guitarist?
B: Yes, he's very **accomplished**. I've heard some of the stuff he did with Segovia: it's very **expressive** – and **romantic**, too.
A: Yes, it is. Last night he surprised us with some West African pieces. I'm not sure the audience, which was quite **conservative**, enjoyed it that much. I think they were expecting him to play his better-known **classical** compositions.

8b Music therapy

Reading active and passive

1 What do you know about music therapy? What kind of conditions do you think that music therapy would be helpful in treating? Read the article and make a list of the conditions it mentions.

2 Read the article again. Are these sentences true (T) or false (F)?

1 The stereotypical view of music therapy is completely wrong.
2 Active music therapy stimulates parts of the brain that are not functioning properly.
3 Passive music therapy is used to help learning as well as for relaxation.
4 The 'Mozart Effect' helps patients to sleep.
5 Most people know that music can have an uplifting effect.
6 The Cochrane research means that fewer drugs may be used in future to treat depression.

Music therapy

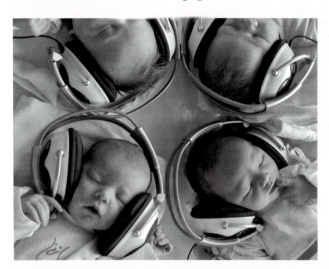

A stereotypical image of music therapy is a sing-a-long at an old people's home organized to alleviate the boredom or to stimulate nostalgic memories of days gone by. But like all stereotypes, while founded on some element of truth, it is such a simplified view that it does not give anything like a complete picture of music therapy's potential to heal.

There are essentially two types of music therapy: active and passive. Active music therapy includes composing lyrics or music, playing instruments, chanting or choral singing, exercising to music and dance. The principle is to get participants actively involved so that they will use parts of their brains and bodies that would otherwise be disengaged. Active therapy is proven to be highly effective in the treatment of neurological disorders, such as Alzheimer's, dementia, multiple sclerosis and Parkinson's.

Passive music therapy, as the name suggests, involves a more relaxing type of participation, usually simple listening exercises. The idea here is to use music in order to make the subject feel less stressed. So passive therapy can be effective in reducing anxiety and blood pressure, lessening post-operative pain, but also it can also be used for improvement of concentration and memory.

There is now so much research into this field that new applications for music therapy are being found all the time. In a Slovak hospital, newborn babies are played classical music through headphones for twenty minutes at a time. Doctors believe that this helps them to feel less stressed after birth and to remain healthy at a critical time, as most of them either fall asleep or lie quietly while the music is being played. This seems to agree with the 'Mozart Effect' reported some years ago in *Nature* magazine, which showed that listening to a Mozart piano sonata for ten minutes prior to taking an intelligence test improved students' scores.

In another study by the Cochrane Collaboration, music therapy was found to offer real benefit to people suffering from depression. A lot of us use music to lift our spirits or at least are aware of its potential to do that, but up to now this has not been clinically proven. Doctors have for a long time been looking for alternative therapies to avoid being so dependent on drugs to treat depression and the Cochrane research offers real hope in this area.

Unit 8 The music in us

Grammar purpose and result

3 Read these extracts from the article. Then rewrite the phrases in bold using the words in brackets.

1. It is **such a simplified** view that it does not give anything like a complete picture. (so)
   This view _____ that it does not give anything like a complete picture.
2. The principle is to get participants actively involved **so that they will use** parts of their brains and bodies that would otherwise be disengaged. (so as to)
   The principle is to get participants actively involved _____ parts of their brains and bodies that would otherwise be disengaged.
3. The idea here is to use music **in order to make the subject feel less** stressed. (to prevent)
   The idea here is to use music _____ stressed.
4. There is now **so much research into this field that** new applications for music therapy are being found all the time. (such)
   There is now _____ new applications for music therapy are being found all the time.
5. It can also be used **for improvement of** concentration and memory. (to)
   It can also be used _____ concentration and memory.
6. A lot of us use music **to lift our spirits**. (because)
   A lot of us use music _____ our spirits.
7. Doctors have been looking for alternative therapies **to avoid being** so dependent on drugs. (so as not to)
   Doctors have been looking for alternative therapies _____ so dependent on drugs.

4 Match the actions (1–5) with the reasons for doing them (a–e). Then write the correct expression of purpose to connect the two parts.

1. He left his job at the bank
2. We perform live sometimes, but just
3. Please turn any phones or music devices off
4. You have to practise
5. Singers drink a lot of water

a. fun.
b. getting throat problems.
c. get better.
d. concentrate on playing music.
e. disturb other passengers.

Idioms music

5 Complete these idioms. You have been given the first letter of the missing words.

1. Let's not go in with a particular strategy. Let's just **p**_____ **it by ear**.
2. I don't know why she **made** such **a big song and d**_____ **about** having to stay late.
3. **You've changed your t**_____. Yesterday you said you really wanted to go.
4. The news was **music to my e**_____.
5. I don't mean to **blow my own t**_____, but I think that went pretty well.
6. What he said about the importance of hard work really **struck a c**_____ with me.
7. Don't worry about briefing me. I think **I know the s**_____.
8. OK. It's time to **f**_____ **the music**. I hope she's not too angry.

6 Dictation learn fast

🎧 **60** Listen to this advice about learning a musical instrument. Complete the paragraph.

Is there _____?
What _____?
The answer _____
_____.
To _____
You can _____,
_____.
You may _____,
_____.
I always _____:
_____;
practice – _____
_____; and _____.
Progress _____
_____
_____.

8c Delta blues

Listening Sonny Boy Williamson II

1 🔊 **61** You are going to listen to an account of the life of blues musician Sonny Boy Williamson II. Look at the photo and then listen and answer the questions.

1 What instrument did he play?

2 What kind of character was he?

3 How is he remembered by those who like the blues?

Glossary
acclaim (n) /əˈkleɪm/ applause, approval
aficionado (n) /əˌfɪʃəˈnɑːdəʊ/ an enthusiastic follower, a fan
jamming (v) /ˈdʒæmɪŋ/ playing with other musicians

2 🔊 **61** Listen again and choose the best answer (a, b or c) for each question.

1 Why is it surprising that so few people have heard of Sonny Boy Williamson II?
   a He was very famous in his own lifetime.
   b His music has been played extensively on the radio.
   c He was a very original musician.

2 What do we know about what things were like for him growing up?
   a nothing
   b that he worked on a plantation
   c that he probably had a tough life

3 Which of these describes Sonny Boy's life in the 1930s to the 1950s?
   a a family man
   b a wanderer
   c a man with a mission

4 What is it that sets Sonny Boy Williamson apart from other musicians?
   a his individuality and charisma
   b the consistency of his playing
   c the truthfulness of his lyrics

5 How did Jimmy Page feel after his encounter with Sonny Boy?
   a upset with him
   b grateful to him
   c admiring of him

6 Which of these statements about Sonny Boy's death is true?
   a It came at a point in his career when he was playing his best.
   b He was seventy when he died.
   c He was in good shape for his age.

3 🔊 **61** Complete this account of Sonny Boy Williamson's life. Then listen again and check.

Sonny Boy Williamson II was perhaps the first black media ¹ _____ of the American South. His ² _____ show in the early 1940s was very popular in and around Helena, Arkansas. Sonny Boy grew up in ³ _____ times and started playing the harp when he was ⁴ _____. He had a trick where he could play without using his ⁵ _____. He spent his early career ⁶ _____ around the south, ⁷ _____ with other musicians.

His music combines ⁸ _____ rhythms with powerful solos and although he sounds weary, there is no ⁹ _____ in his songs. Above all Sonny Boy had great ¹⁰ _____.

In the 1960s, he toured ¹¹ _____ and met young musicians who became ¹² _____ by his music. He loved the ¹³ _____ he was given. Sonny Boy died in 1965 when he was still at the peak of his powers. He has become a ¹⁴ _____ among those who listen to the blues.

Word focus *hit*

4 Complete the sentences using expressions with *hit*.

miss	nerve	note	record	nail

1 You've **hit the** _____ **on the head** there, Stephanie.
2 It's a bit of a **hit and** _____ approach, but it seems to work.
3 I'm sorry. Did I **hit a** _____ when I said that?
4 Great speech! You **hit just the right** _____.
5 'Born Blind' wasn't his first **hit** _____.

64

8d Desert Island Discs

Real life your favourite music

1 🔴 62 Listen to a 'castaway' talking about her life and music. Answer the questions.

1 What is Aleah's family background?

2 What do you think her profession is?

3 How did her parents influence her choice of career?

2 Speaking skill responding to questions

🔴 62 Complete the phrases that Aleah gave when she needed time to think before responding. Use between two and four words per space. Then listen again and check.

1 'Was it obvious to you that you'd go into music as a profession?'
'No, I never _____ that.'

2 'Why?'
'That's a _____ .'

3 'The settled life she never had, maybe?'
'I _____ know. But I don't think so.'

4 'Was it the pull of the music world that made you leave?'
'Mmm, _____ say. I don't think it was as simple …'

5 'And so you took off to India. Were your parents unhappy about that?'
'Do you know, I couldn't _____ .'

3 Pronunciation intonation to express uncertainty

a 🔴 63 Look at this list of phrases and tick (✔) which ones you expect to be pronounced with an uncertain or wavering intonation. Then listen and check.

1 I'm not sure. ☐
2 I've no idea. ☐
3 Perhaps. ☐
4 It could be. ☐
5 Of course. ☐
6 I doubt it. ☐

b Practise answering these questions. Use the uncertain answers from Exercise 3a with a wavering intonation.

1 Are these the final figures?
2 Is it cheaper to take the bus?
3 Are you coming to the party on Friday?
4 Is the bank open on Saturdays?

4 Listen and respond responding to difficult questions

🔴 64 Listen to someone asking you questions about your background and your music preferences. Respond with your own words. Then compare your response with the model answer that follows.

1 *Did music play a big part in your childhood?*

That's a good question. Certainly it was very important at high school. Your circle of friends tended to be influenced a lot by the kind of music that you listened to.

8e Filmi

Writing a description

1 Read the description of a style of music from India called *filmi* and answer the questions.

1. Who sings these songs and where can you hear them?

2. Does the writer recommend listening to this type of music?

2 Read the description again and find examples of the following.

1. two powerful adjectives (para 1)
2. a simile (para 1)
3. a description of the atmosphere (para 1)
4. a description of how the listener feels listening to this music (para 3)
5. the writer speaking directly to the reader (para 3)
6. two parallel structures (paras 2 and 3)

3 Writing skill parallel structures

Complete these parallel structures using your own words. Make sure that the elements of each half of the sentence balance.

1. Wherever you go in India, you are greeted with warm smiles and _____ .
2. The songs are not only rich in Hindi folk tradition, but also _____ .
3. *Filmi* songs vary in type. Some are gentle ballads, others _____ .
4. *Filmi* represents both India's traditional side _____ .
5. On a visit to the Bollywood studios I was captivated by the performance of the actors and actresses: singing along to the music, _____ and _____ .
6. While most film studios make a variety of film types, Bollywood _____ .

Produced in their thousands every year, *filmi* songs are a genre unlike any other. Go nearly anywhere in India, and you will be accompanied by the latest *filmi* hit blaring out from radios in taxicabs and roadside vendors' stalls. The songs fill the air like a throng of happy voices adding to the already hectic nature of Indian city life, an environment which threatens to overwhelm your senses with its vibrant colours, rich smells and deafening traffic.

Filmi are essentially movie soundtrack songs. In mass-market Indian films, the action is frequently interrupted by spectacular song-and-dance sequences, in which the actors lip-sync music sung by Indian pop stars. It's a simple commercial formula: match the prettiest faces on screen with the best voices around. The best-known *filmi* come from the Bollywood film industry. 'Bollywood', based in Mumbai, is the Los Angeles of India.

The music, a fusion of traditional Hindu folk music and a variety of other Western styles such as pop and hip hop, is joyous and infectious. You can't help tapping your foot along to the rhythm. It's not great music, it's feel-good music, made to be danced to, both on and off the screen. It's not really my kind of music and it may not be yours. But I'd be surprised if you weren't carried along in its happy wake.

Unit 8 The music in us

Wordbuilding onomatopoeic words

1 The word *hum* – as in to 'hum a tune' – is an onomatopoeic word; in other words it sounds like the action itself. Try to match these other onomatopoeic verbs with the correct noun or phrase.

1 beep   your head
2 bump   a guitar
3 clap   a balloon
4 gulp   the horn
5 mumble   your hands
6 pop   the air
7 sigh   with boredom
8 sniff   on the window
9 strum   with relief
10 tap   the words
11 tut-tut   down a drink
12 yawn   in disapproval

2 Complete the sentences using the correct form of six of the verbs from Exercise 1.

1 'I don't think I'll ever have an opportunity like that again,' she _____ .
2 He shook his head and _____ . 'That was naughty of you – to take advantage of their goodwill.'
3 She _____ the perfume and quickly put it down. It smelt awful.
4 Sorry, I can't understand what you're saying. You're _____ .
5 He _____ lightly on the door so as not to disturb the neighbours.
6 I think when I _____ he thought I was tired of his company, but actually I was just tired from lack of sleep.

Learning skills pronunciation

3 Use your dictionary to check the pronunciation of new words. You will need to do the following:

a recognize the phonetic symbols in this chart.
b note where the stress comes: after the stress mark ('), e.g. *interest* /'ɪntrest/.

iː	ɪ	ʊ	uː	ɪə	eɪ	
p<u>ea</u>ce	h<u>i</u>t	c<u>ou</u>ld	sch<u>oo</u>l	h<u>ere</u>	pl<u>ay</u>	
e	ə	ɜː	ɔː	ʊə	ɔɪ	əʊ
h<u>e</u>n	<u>A</u>frica	b<u>ir</u>d	b<u>a</u>ll	p<u>ure</u>	b<u>oy</u>	n<u>o</u>te
æ	ʌ	ɑː	ɒ	eə	aɪ	aʊ
m<u>a</u>n	b<u>u</u>t	st<u>ar</u>t	n<u>o</u>t	wh<u>ere</u>	l<u>i</u>ke	n<u>ow</u>

p	b	t	d	tʃ	dʒ	k	g
<u>p</u>en	<u>b</u>and	<u>t</u>en	<u>d</u>ance	<u>ch</u>ange	<u>j</u>ust	<u>c</u>an	<u>g</u>o
f	v	θ	ð	s	z	ʃ	ʒ
<u>f</u>un	<u>v</u>ery	<u>th</u>ing	<u>th</u>e	<u>s</u>ong	<u>z</u>oo	<u>sh</u>e	vi<u>s</u>ual
m	n	ŋ	h	l	r	w	j
<u>m</u>iss	<u>n</u>o	si<u>ng</u>	<u>h</u>is	<u>l</u>ike	<u>r</u>ed	<u>w</u>est	<u>y</u>ou

4 Look at these words related to different music styles written in phonetic script. Say what the word is and where the stress is.

Example:
/'klæsɪkəl/ = <u>clas</u>sical

1 /'reɡeɪ/ _____
2 /'kʌntrɪ/ _____
3 /kə'lɪpsəʊ/ _____
4 /ɪksperɪ'mentl/ _____
5 /'fjuːʒn/ _____
6 /'ɒprə/ _____

Check!

5 Can you remember the following from Student's Book Unit 8?

1 Two words for musicians:

a a _____ = an artist who plays by himself/herself
b a _____ = a group of musicians

2 Two musical words used in expressions:

a blow your own _____ = to talk proudly about your achievements
b strike a _____ = to say something that elicits a positive (emotional) response

3 Two words beginning with *f*:

a _____ = a melancholy style of song native to Portugal
b _____ the music = accept criticisms for something you have done

4 Two similar-sounding words:

a an _____ guitar = the opposite of an accoustic guitar
b _____ tastes = an interest in a variety of kinds of music

5 The word that sums up Bob Marley's message of unity to the world and completes the name of one of his songs:

'One _____ '

Unit 9 Window on the past

9a Letter to yourself

Listening a writing project

1 🔊 65 Listen to a news report and answer the questions.
1. Who wrote letters to themselves?
2. What did the letters contain?
3. In what way have they become 'historical documents'?

2 🔊 65 Listen again and answer the questions.
1. What did Farrer's students think his reasons were for giving them this assignment?
2. What did Farrer do with each letter?
3. What is Farrer's job now?
4. What does he mainly want his students to do with the letters?
5. What two things make returning the letters worthwhile?
6. What choice did he give to students writing the letters?
7. Why did the boy dream of marrying a Swedish girl?
8. What adjectives sum up Farrer's character?

3 Use these words to complete the phrases you heard in the report. Use the definitions in brackets to help.

| be / track   distinct   fulfil   profound |
| see / through   straightforward |

1. a .... purpose (clear and definite)
2. .... the job .... (to complete)
3. .... on the right .... (follow a good path)
4. a .... job (simple)
5. .... one's wish (achieve one's goal)
6. .... effect (deep impact)

Vocabulary extra prepositional phrases related to time

4 Look at this phrase from the report. What does *on* mean here?
'Twenty years on, he has fulfilled his wish.'

5 Complete the prepositional phrases in bold using these prepositions.

| at   back   from   in   in   to |

1. .... **time**, Farrer hopes that his students will come to appreciate what he did.
2. .... **the outset**, it was always Farrer's intention to send the letters back to his students.
3. He responded to them **one** .... **a time**.
4. .... **retrospect**, Farrer feels that he should have told them what he was going to do.
5. .... **in the days** when Farrer was a child, letter writing was a much more common thing.
6. .... **date**, he has sent over 1,000 letters back to former pupils.

6 Match the highlighted phrases from Exercise 5 (1–6) with each of these meanings (a–f).
a looking back
b up to now
c from the beginning
d individually
e eventually
f at a time in the past

Grammar linking words

7 Rewrite the sentences or pairs of sentences using the words in bold.

1 After they had handed them in, they forgot about them. **… and, subsequently…**

2 Although he retired fully from teaching in 2006, Farrer kept all the letters carefully filed. **In spite of …**

3 After he retired, he continued posting the letters back to his former pupils. **Following …**

4 The exercise is greatly valued by his past students, partly because letters are rarer and more precious nowadays.
… partly owing to …

5 He gets to find out how their lives have actually evolved and, in addition, receives their gratitude for going to the trouble of returning the letters. **As well as …**

6 Not all the pupils agreed for him to read their letters, but he has kept and is returning these letters too. **… Nevertheless …**

8 Rewrite these sentences or pairs of sentences using appropriate linkers of reason, contrast and addition as indicated. There is sometimes more than one option. Note that item 4 has three sentences and needs two linking words or phrases.

1 Some pupils were too embarrassed to make their letters public. Their letters were immature. (reason)

2 The exercise has had a profound effect on the students. Farrer remains modest about his part in its success. (contrast)

3 Farrer thought the idea would inspire his students to write more. He also hoped they would think more about the importance of education in their lives. (addition)

4 Another student wrote that he wanted to go to college and play football. He graduated from high school and went to work in a steel mill. (contrast / sequence)

Vocabulary examining evidence

9 Complete the conversation using these words.

clues   deduced   determined   evidence
indicated   uncovered

A: I hear that they've ¹_____ an old Viking ship on the banks of the river Thames.
B: Yes, that's right. They haven't actually ²_____ exactly what kind of ship it was, but some of the ³_____ they've found has ⁴_____ that it might have been a burial ship.
A: What does that mean?
B: It's when someone important was buried at sea. Their body was usually cremated and then placed on a boat with some of their possessions and put out to sea.
A: And were there any ⁵_____ as to who this person was?
B: Not really, but because of the size of ship they have ⁶_____ that it must have been someone very important.

10 Dictation gladiator school

🔊 66 Listen to this description of an archaeological find in Austria. It contains five of the most commonly misspelled words in English. Complete the paragraph.

Archaeologists _____

_____ Colosseum.

The facility _____

_____.

In addition _____

_____.

69

9b Three famous fraudsters

Reading notorious con artists

1 Read the description of three con artists. Write down their crimes and what punishment, if any, they received.

William Thompson
Crime(s): ....
Punishment: ....

Natwarlal
Crime(s): ....
Punishment: ....

Ferdinand Demara
Crime(s): ....
Punishment: ....

2 Read the article again and answer the questions.

1 In what way was William Thompson a fake?

2 What is the phrase meaning 'to trust someone' that William Thompson became known for?

3 What is meant by the phrase *a master of disguises* to describe Natwarlal?

4 What does the writer suggest happened to Natwarlal in the end?

5 What two things helped to make Demara a successful impersonator?

6 Why did his career in impersonating decline?

Three famous fraudsters

William Thompson was a small-time fraudster who was active in New York City in the 1840s. His main claim to fame is that he is said to be responsible for the coining of the term 'confidence trickster' or 'con artist'. Preying on upper-class citizens, he would engage them in polite conversation and at a certain point ask if they 'had confidence in him' to lend him their watch or some money until the following day. Believing him to be a gentleman (Thompson was always well-dressed and well-spoken), they would generally hand over the watch or money, never to see it again. He was arrested and put on trial in 1849 and subsequently sent to prison.

Mithilesh Kumar Srivastava, known as Natwarlal, was an Indian con man who was arrested nine times in his life and sentenced to a total of 113 years in prison for his crimes. Considering that he had been charged with over eighty crimes of fraud and forgery, the length of these sentences is not surprising. He was an expert forger and also a master of disguises, but the frauds for which he is best-known are those where he 'sold' various famous buildings, including the Taj Mahal, to tourists. On every occasion that he was caught, Natwarlal managed to escape again. He was last arrested in 1996 when he was 84 and, having given the police the slip at Delhi station on his way to prison, was never seen again, and presumably now never will be.

Ferdinand Waldo Demara, Jr. was known as 'The Great Impostor'. During his life, he impersonated a monk, an editor, a lawyer, a child-care expert and a psychologist, among other things. He claimed that the secret of his success was finding roles to fill that did not threaten other people's positions in an organization. Also, compared to other impersonators, Demara was unusual in that he seems not to have been interested in money. Having published the story of his exploits in the 1950s, Demara became quite a well-known figure in America, making it difficult for him to carry out further impersonations. Knowledge of his past also discouraged employers from giving him work, despite the fact that he was highly intelligent man. After a long spell in hospital, he died in 1982.

Unit 9 **Window on the past**

3 Look at these expressions from the article and choose the correct definition (a or b).
1 preying on (line 5)
  a circulating among b targeting as victims
2 put on trial (line 12)
  a convicted b prosecuted
3 give someone the slip (line 26)
  a escape capture b cheat someone out of money
4 exploits (line 39)
  a crimes b adventures
5 a long spell (line 45)
  a a long period b a long illness

Grammar present and perfect participles

4 Look at how the seven participles listed below are used in the article. Is the subject of each participle the same as the subject of the main verb? If so, who or what is that subject?

Participle
1 Preying (line 5) *Same   Thompson (he)*
2 Believing (line 9)
3 Considering (line 17)
4 having given (line 26)
5 compared to (line 36)
6 Having published (line 39)
7 Making (line 41)

5 Complete the sentences using the correct participle form of the verb in brackets.
1 _____ their trust, he then persuaded his victims to lend him money. (gain)
2 _____ the con artist displays a casual, good-humoured attitude, most people are usually fooled. (provide)
3 _____ bank drafts which he had forged, Natwarlal defrauded banks and jewellers of huge amounts of money. (use)
4 _____ that most bank transactions these days are done with pin numbers and passwords, Natwarlal's methods would not be so effective now. (give)
5 _____ that he must by now be dead, the authorities have given up looking for him. (assume)
6 _____ from his victims' point of view, Natwarlal's arrests were little comfort, as the money he stole was never found. (see)

7 While impersonating a ship's surgeon, Demara, _____ up about what he needed to do, performed successful surgery on a wounded soldier. (read)
8 _____ he was so intelligent and also that he had a photographic memory, Demara could easily have found a good job as himself. (consider)

6 Combine each pair of sentences using participles. You will need to change, add or delete some words.
1 She tried a few times. Then she gave up.

2 I stood in front of the White House. I was amazed at how much smaller it is compared to how it looks on TV.

3 He's so young. It's not fair to ask him to practise the piano for four hours a day.

4 She feared that she would be the first to arrive. So she walked around the block a couple of times.

5 Can I assume you're happy with the arrangements? If so, I'll send out the invitations.

Vocabulary crime and punishment

7 Complete this passage using ONE word in each space.

Jaime was caught on camera driving in a cycle lane in the town centre. Two weeks later he received a letter ordering him to appear in [1]_____. He was [2]_____ with [3]_____ driving. Jaime said that he was not [4]_____, claiming that he had moved into the cycle lane to let an ambulance past. The case was [5]_____ in front of three magistrates and Jaime was [6]_____ guilty and ordered to pay a [7]_____ of £500. He appealed [8]_____ the conviction.

9c Mutiny on the *Bounty*

Listening trouble in paradise

1 🔊 **67** You are going to listen to a story about a mutiny. Read the definition. Then listen to the story and answer the questions.

mutiny (n) /ˈmjuːtəni/ unlawful refusal to obey one's commander or the authorities, especially rebellion by sailors against their superior officers

1 When and where did this mutiny happen?

2 What was the motive for the mutiny?

3 Did the story end happily, or not?

2 🔊 **67** Listen again and answer these questions.

1 What was the reason for the ship's voyage?

2 What became of the captain and the crew that was loyal to him?

3 Who was in the band that landed at Pitcairn Island with Christian to start a new life?

4 What did Christian do to the *Bounty* after he arrived at Pitcairn?

5 What became of the mutineers who stayed on Tahiti?

6 What was the cause of the dispute between the Tahitians and the mutineers on Pitcairn?

7 What became of Fletcher Christian himself?

3 Answer the questions about the words in bold in these sentences from the story.

1 … one of the most **atrocious** acts of piracy …
   Did Captain Bligh see this as a 'daring' act or a 'terrible' act?

2 In a boat only twenty-three feet long, heavily **laden** with nineteen men …
   What word that is similar to *laden* could you put here?

3 Christian had **stripped** the *Bounty*, then run her ashore and burned her.
   What things do you think he took off the boat?

4 Christian knew the English Admiralty **had a long arm** …
   What does this phrase suggest that Christian feared?

4 Complete the summary of the story.

In 1787, the *Bounty* ¹_____ from Spithead in England on its way to Tahiti to collect ²_____ to take to the West Indies. After six months in Tahiti, the acting mate led a ³_____ against the ⁴_____ William Bligh. They put him and some of his crew in a ⁵_____ and cast him adrift in the ⁶_____. Miraculously, Bligh managed to survive and ⁷_____ to England. Some of Christian's crew stayed in Tahiti, but Christian himself, with eight crew and eighteen ⁸_____, journeyed on to ⁹_____, a small ¹⁰_____ island in the South Sea. Here he ¹¹_____ the ship. Following arguments between the ¹²_____ and the ¹³_____, fighting broke out, resulting in the deaths of all but ¹⁴_____ of the original crew.

Word focus board

5 Underline the correct words to complete these idioms.

1 I think we need to **go back to the** *drawing board / planning sheet* here. Our plan isn't really working.

2 There will be a 3% pay increase *across / throughout* **the board**. Managers will get the same rise as other employees.

3 I'll try to *bring / take* everyone's **views on board**, but I can't promise that everyone will be happy with the solution we come up with.

4 He's offering to sell you a brand new bike at half its normal price. Are you sure it's all *above / on* **board**?

5 It's just a fancy dress party. I think spending $100 on an outfit **is going** *outboard / overboard*.

9d I'll give you an example

Real life checking, confirming and clarifying

1 🔊 **68** Listen to a conversation about a lecture on table manners. Are the statements true (T) or false (F) about table manners in the Middle Ages?
1 People didn't wipe their hands or mouths after eating.
2 People helped themselves to whatever food was on the table.
3 It was normal for people to spit sometimes during a meal.
4 The use of forks came after spoons and knives.
5 The main speaker thinks that table manners have definitely improved since then.

2 🔊 **68** Complete the phrases for checking, confirming and clarifying information. Then listen again and check your answers.
1 What do you .... 'etiquette'? Like table manners?
2 .... you .... that they didn't really have food served up on individual plates?
3 So, in .... , it was a bit of a free-for-all.
4 By today's standards it *would* seem very rude, but .... is that politeness is a relative thing.
5 Am I .... thinking that forks came a bit later?
6 So, ... me .... this ....
7 Who's to say what's right and wrong? .... I .... was that that's when we can see the beginning of modern table manners.

3 Which phrases in Exercise 2:
a) check meaning?

b) clarify meaning?

4 Pronunciation silent letters

a 🔊 **69** Look at these words and underline the letters that are not pronounced. Then listen and check.
island
handkerchief
foreign
honour
salmon
castle
subtle
guesthouse
whoever
wrap
psychiatrist
Wednesday

b 🔊 **69** Listen again and practise saying the words in Exercise 4a.

5 Listen and respond checking facts

🔊 **70** Imagine you are talking to a friend who has seen a TV programme about the modern world of technology. Listen to each fact. Use the information to make a question or to ask for confirmation or clarification of what you have heard. Then compare what you say with the model answer that follows.
1

> *I saw a great programme last night about the making of the modern world.*

> *What do you mean by 'the making of' the modern world?*

9e The folly of war

Writing describing a past event

1 Read the essay about the Charge of the Light Brigade and answer the questions.

1 What was the result of this cavalry charge?

2 How does the writer express a view about this event?

The notorious Charge of the Light Brigade took place during the battle of Balaclava in 1854 between a joint British–French–Turkish force and the Russian army. The British and French were positioned to the west of a valley with the main Russian army and their guns facing them at the other end in the east. The Russians had some hours earlier captured British guns on hills on the south side of the valley in fortified positions called redoubts.

Viewing the scene from a hill behind the British lines, Lord Raglan ordered the British cavalry to attack the redoubts on the south side. He gave this order to Captain Nolan who rode down into the valley to pass it on to the commander of the cavalry, Lord Lucan. Lucan, who did not have the advantage of being able to see the situation from a high vantage point, asked what guns were to be attacked. Nolan mistakenly indicated the guns at the eastern end of the valley.

Accordingly, 600 cavalrymen set off down the valley straight for the main Russian force with guns firing at them from all sides. Approximately 200 returned. The following day, a French marshal, Bosquet, said of the action: 'It is magnificent, but it is not war; it is madness.'

2 Underline two time phrases in the article that do the following.

a indicate a time before the main event (para 1)

b tell you about an event that happened after the main event (para 3)

3 Writing skill sequencing events

Read the first sentence in each pair. Complete the reported version with a past time phrase.

1 He is working for a bank at the moment.
He was working for a bank _____.

2 Nowadays it is normal to do military service.
_____ it was normal to do military service.

3 She arrived a few days ago.
She had arrived _____.

4 Up to now no one has heard of aeroplanes.
_____ no one had heard of aeroplanes.

5 The election takes place tomorrow.
The election took place _____.

6 Last year there was an equally bad storm.
_____ there had been an equally bad storm.

4 In 1937, the Hindenburg airship exploded while docking at a naval station in New Jersey. Use these notes to write an account of an amazing escape from the Hindenburg disaster.

Hindenburg airship passes over Boston, morning 6th May.
Hindenburg left Germany for USA, 3rd May.
Bad weather delays landing at Lakehurst, New Jersey.
Cabin boy Werner Franz works in kitchen on board Hindenburg.
He plans to visit New York before Hindenburg returns to Germany on 7th May.
The captain is trying to steer the airship next to a docking tower.
There is a loud bang and Werner sees a big ball of flame.
The skin of the ship has broken and the hydrogen inside has ignited.
The ship crashes to the ground. Horrified onlookers run for their lives.
Franz opens the kitchen hatch where food is pulled up into the kitchen and jumps.
He runs to safety.
Ten minutes after the fire starts, there is nothing left of the airship.

Wordbuilding verb + preposition

1 Put these verbs in the correct group according to the prepositions that follow them.

account adjust base benefit count
long resign result specialize subscribe

1 _____ , insist } on

2 _____ , pay } for

3 _____ , refer } to

4 _____ , succeed } in

5 _____ , recover } from

2 Complete the sentences using the correct verb and preposition combinations from Exercise 1.

1 Don't worry. You can _____ me.
2 It took a while to _____ living in a new country, but I love it now.
3 How do you _____ the fact that married men live longer than single men?
4 She didn't _____ her job; she was forced out!
5 I _____ the day when people can live together in peace.
6 I suspect the cuts will _____ a lot of people losing their jobs.
7 No, I _____ paying for this. You paid last time.
8 It usually takes about six weeks to _____ the operation.

Learning skills revising in writing

3 In your Student's Book, various models are presented for different types of writing and it is always useful to follow a basic structure for each type of writing. Bear in mind, however, the following points about the act of writing.

1 Writing is not always a linear process of planning, drafting and revising. Everyone composes their writing in a different way.
2 Your ideas will develop as you write, so you don't have to stick to a pre-determined plan.
3 It doesn't really matter where you start. You could start with your introduction, your conclusion or in the middle, with examples or an analysis of the situation.
4 It's natural to rethink and revise your ideas while you are writing.
5 Wait until the end to check the grammar or sentence structure, or you will interrupt the flow of your thoughts.
6 Remember that the best writing is economical. So, when rereading at the end, pay attention to what seems unnecessary – and cut it!

4 Think about a piece of writing you have done on this course and how you approached it. How true are the points in Exercise 3 for you?

Check!

5 Look at the photos from Unit 9 in the Student's Book and complete the summaries of stories relating to each photo.

1 Archaeologists say: 'It's not what you _____ that matters it's what you find _____ .' The Stones of Stenness are _____ of a sophisticated society, while other objects that were uncovered give valuable _____ to this being a rich trading community.
2 W.E.B. Dubois was an American sociologist and civil _____ activist. He sent his daughter to school in England and, shortly _____ , sent her a letter telling her not to shrink _____ new experiences and to remember that her father believed _____ her.
3 Arnaud de Tilh was an _____ who pretended to be another man, Martin Guerre, in order to _____ his estate. He was accused _____ fraud, taken to court and _____ guilty.
4 The *Bom Jesus* was a Portuguese ship carrying _____ to India to trade in exchange for _____ . It was blown off course and _____ off the _____ of Namibia.

75

Unit 10 Social living

10a Social animals

Listening the thoughtful elephant

1 🔊 71 Look at the title and the photo below. Then listen to an interview with a naturalist and tick (✓) the adjectives that match her description of female elephant behaviour.

efficient	considerate	solitary
intelligent	aggressive	protective
cooperative	wild	

2 🔊 71 Listen again and choose the best option (a, b or c) to complete the sentences.

1 The interviewer wants to know which animals have the greatest:
  a collective intelligence.
  b social awareness.
  c organizational skills.

2 In elephant society, bull elephants:
  a are dominant.
  b frequently change family group.
  c live separately.

3 The story the naturalist tells concerns a young female elephant who:
  a was rejected by her own family.
  b couldn't find her own family.
  c left the herd when she was one year old.

4 What was strange was that the matriarch of the herd:
  a knew who was guilty without seeing the incident.
  b protected an elephant that wasn't her daughter.
  c knew that the young elephant was injured.

5 The purpose of the experiment in Thailand was to see if elephants:
  a were different to other species.
  b reacted to rewards.
  c were naturally cooperative.

6 The experiment:
  a supports other evidence.
  b does not prove they behave like this in the wild.
  c proved how intelligent elephants are.

Grammar adverbs and adverbial phrases

3 Look at the extracts (1–4) from the interview. First underline the adverb or adverbial phrase in each sentence. Then match them with the correct grammatical description (a–d).

1 I mean, which animals are the most socially aware? ....

2 Which species treats other members of its group in a considerate way? ....

3 They either leave voluntarily or are pushed out. ....

4 One way or another they don't remain long in the family group. ....

a verb + adverb
b adverb + adjective
c adverb with the same form as the adjective
d adverb formed with an adverbial phrase rather than the -ly suffix

4 Look at the elephant facts. The adverbs and adverbial phrases are in the wrong place. Rewrite the sentences, putting the adverbs or adverbial phrases in the correct position. Add commas if necessary.
1 Elephants eat normally around 200 kilos of food a day.
2 Although they walk faster than us (approx. seven km/h), elephants still move in a leisurely way around.
3 However, they can move if they need to fast at speeds of up to forty kilometres per hour.
4 Elephants do not 'run' because they do not lift technically all feet off the ground at the same time.
5 In spite of their thick skin, elephants are sensitive to touch extremely and can feel a fly if it lands on them.
6 Male elephants leave the herd when typically they become 'teenagers'.
7 Elephants have excellent memories, undoubtedly, which they use to remember the whereabouts of food and water.
8 Around fifty elephants are killed every day for their ivory illegally.

5 Look at these other sentences from the interview. Rewrite the adjective in brackets in the correct adverbial form. Then place it in the correct place in the sentence.
1 What makes them intelligent? (social)
2 This is documented. (good)
3 She was wandering around. (disoriented)
4 This group rejected her – they pushed her away. (literal)
5 She marched over to the other herd. (straight)
6 She seemed to know which of the elephants in the other herd had been responsible. (strange)
7 If they pulled on their rope, a table with corn on it appeared before them. (simultaneous)
8 The elephants learned to coordinate their pulling. (fast)

Vocabulary social actions

6 Complete the text with these verbs.

| do | have | lend | play | show | take |

I think it's very important that all sections of society – young and old, rich and poor – ¹_____ a part in the life of their community. Of course, some will be able to contribute more than others, but in fact everyone can ²_____ their bit. The first thing is to ³_____ your say in decisions that affect you. That means voting at elections or taking part in debates. If you don't do this, you cannot complain when things don't go as you want them to. The second thing is to ⁴_____ concern for those who are less fortunate than you: for example, to ⁵_____ a helping hand to an elderly neighbour if there is something they cannot manage to do. The last thing is to be aware that the local environment is there to be enjoyed by everyone so everyone must ⁶_____ responsibility for keeping it clean and pleasant.

7 Dictation animal facts

🔊 72 Listen to five facts about animals. Complete the facts.
1 Research suggests that crows _____.
2 If one dolphin _____.
3 Meerkats _____.
4 Young _____.
5 Killer _____.

77

10b How play made our world

Reading the influence of games

1 Read the article about Steven Johnson's book, *Wonderland: How Play Made the Modern World*. Find and underline two sentences that sum up his main argument in the book.

2 Write down one 'serious' innovation that each of these toys or games were part of the story of, according to Johnson?
 1 Banu Musa's robotic elephant
 2 Vaucanson's music box
 3 Pokémon Go

3 Look at the article again and explain what these phrases mean in this context.
 1 It usually works the other way around (para 1)
 2 a golden age (para 2)
 3 they led to huge transformations (para 2)
 4 a 'programmable' weaving machine (para 4)
 5 confined to the past (para 5)

How play made our world

We tend to think of play as one of the benefits of technological progress. But actually, according to Steven Johnson, author of *Wonderland: How Play Made the Modern World*, it usually works the other way around. Many of our most important innovations have their origins in human beings just having a bit of fun.

One of the key examples he gives is a place in Baghdad during the Islamic golden age called the House of Wisdom. Here two brothers, the Banu Musa, designed various toys like robotic elephants or automated flute players. Not only were these engineering feats ahead of their time (they appeared 400–500 years later in Western Europe), but they led to huge transformations, like industrialization and mechanization.

In the 18th century, another golden age of innovation, a Frenchman, Jacques de Vaucanson, took one of the ideas of the Banu Musa – the music box – and improved on it. He created a rotating cylinder with little pins in it that corresponded to the song you wanted to play (this is still the principle used in most music boxes today).

Little did anyone realize at the time the huge implications this invention would have, because Vacunson did not stop there. He then began to think about how this system could be used for other purposes such as weaving patterns in cloth. His idea, taken up by Joseph-Marie Jacquard, became a 'programmable' weaving machine, the Jacquard loom, which revolutionized textile design and production. In turn, this had great influence on the ideas of Charles Babbage who invented the first computers. And all this came from a music box, in other words, from our desire to play.

Johnson says that in no way is this phenomenon confined to the past. 'We find the future wherever people are having the most fun.' He points to the video game, Pokémon Go, where players run around capturing imaginary monsters in the real world. The game overlays a virtual experience on a real-world environment, a technology otherwise known as augmented reality. In practical applications, augmented reality will in future allow us to overlay useful (and serious) information onto real-world objects.

Grammar negative adverbials and inversion

4 Find three sentences that use negative adverbials and inversion in the article. Then say:
1. what the negative adverbial is in each case.
   a .... (in para 2)
   b .... (in para 4)
   c .... (in para 5)
2. why the writer has used inversion here.

3. how you would rewrite the sentences without inversion.
   a ....
   b ....
   c ....

5 Complete these sentences using ONE word in each space.
1. Only when you see it for yourself .... you believe it.
2. I can't ask her to do that! I .... know her.
3. No sooner had she accepted the job .... she realized she had made a mistake.
4. I want you to know that in no way .... this change my opinion of you.
5. Nowhere .... in Italy do you find such rich food as in Sicily.
6. We .... go to the cinema anymore. It's too expensive.
7. .... had I opened my mouth when he told me to stop talking.
8. Not only .... she very successful, she's .... very modest about it.

6 Rewrite the sentences using inversion and the adverbs or adverbial phrases in bold.
1. You shouldn't drink water from the tap under any circumstances.
   under no

2. The Queen very rarely attends public functions these days. She's very elderly now.
   only very

3. As soon as the news broke, hundreds of journalists gathered at the presidential palace to get more details.
   no sooner

4. You can only apply for a working visa when you have been in the country for five years.
   only when

5. I've never heard such nonsense.
   never

6. I'd barely had time to put on my waterproof jacket when the most torrential rain started.
   barely

7 Pronunciation sentence stress

a 🔊 73 Underline the two words that you think are most stressed in these sentences. Then listen and check.
1. Under no circumstances should you open it.
2. We barely speak anymore.
3. Not only did he win; he won convincingly.
4. It's hardly a success, is it?

Vocabulary having fun

8 Put the words in each expression into the right order to complete these sentences.
1. Don't keep looking up the answers on the internet. / takes / of / fun / it / out / the / it / .

2. Dana's great fun. We always / laugh / such / a / have / things / about / .

3. He loves chess and when he doesn't have a human partner. He likes to / against / wits / pit / the / his / computer.

4. A good example of / a / making / on / words / play / is this joke: Q. Why did the actor fall through the floor? A. It was just a stage he was going through.

5. I think you were very mean to / joke / on / a / play / Katja.

6. Try to / see / it / of / the / funny / side / . At least you didn't break a leg.

10c Rebuilding society

Listening Leymah Gbowee

1 🎧 74 Listen to the story of Nobel Prize winner Leymah Gbowee and answer the questions.

1 What did she win her Nobel Prize for?

2 Whose help did she enlist to achieve her aim?

3 What does she do now?

2 🎧 74 Listen again and complete these facts.

1 Ellen Johnson Sirleaf was the first _____.

2 Liberia had suffered for many years from a _____.

3 Gbowee became the head of a _____ movement.

4 When she returned to Liberia, she trained as a _____.

5 She believed that in order to move forward victims must _____ the person who wronged them.

6 She mobilized women and mothers to renew _____ in society.

7 She and her supporters spread this message in _____.

8 Ultimately their actions led to _____.

3 🎧 75 Read the extract about reconciliation from Gbowee's book. The words in italics are synonyms of the actual words used. Complete the extract with the actual words Gbowee used. Then listen and check.

> ❝ The person who *injured* [1] _____ you … If you are still angry at that person, if you haven't been able to forgive, you are *tied* [2] _____ to him. When someone *insults* [3] _____ you and you haven't let go, every time you see him, you grow breathless or your heart *misses* [4] _____ a beat. Perhaps even you *wish for* [5] _____ revenge. Above you is the Mountain of Peace and Prosperity where we all want to go. But when you try to climb that hill, the person you haven't forgiven weighs you down. It's a personal choice whether or not to let go. But you can't *progress* [6] _____ until you break that chain. ❞

4 Match the words from the story (1–6) with the correct synonym (a–f).

1 meaningful   a determined
2 tireless   b group
3 underpin   c leaflet
4 reconcile   d significant
5 faction   e be at the heart of
6 flyer   f bring together

Word focus *free*

5 Complete the idioms in these conversations using one word in each space.

1 A: Katie's just gone off to India for a month, leaving Jack to look after the kids.
   B: Yes, I heard that. She**'s a free** _____.

2 A: I thought they were giving their advice for free, but they've sent me a bill for $300!
   B: Well, **there's no such thing as a free** _____.

3 A: Did you have to pay a fine for parking on a yellow line?
   B: No, I told them I'd parked there in an emergency, so **I got off** _____ -**free**.

4 A: Can I just borrow your phone for a minute to check the cinema listings?
   B: Sure, _____ **free**.

5 A: Do I have to follow any particular guidelines?
   B: No, you've got **a** completely **free** _____. Do whatever you think best.

10d Showing interest

Real life making conversation

1 🔊 **76** TED talks are short educational talks given by experts in various fields, which are then posted on the internet. Have you ever watched one? Listen to a short conversation about a TED talk and answer the questions.

1 What was this TED talk about?

2 What idea did the speaker in the TED talk criticize?

3 What does he suggest we do instead?

2 Which of these points are characteristics of a good listener? Tick (✓) the three points that the person listening to the description in Exercise 1 did.

a showed appreciation ☐
b tried to predict what the other person is going to say ☐
c waited before giving their views ☐
d asked questions ☐
e related what they hear to their own experience ☐

3 Speaking skill showing interest

🔊 **77** Both speakers used short responses and phrases to show interest, to agree and to make the conversation flow more easily. Complete the phrases. Then listen and check your answers.

1 A: What are you doing?
   B: _____ a TED talk on my laptop.
2 A: He's a really good speaker actually.
   B: Yes, he is, _____ ?
3 B: Yeah, well, I'd go along with that.
   A: Mmm, me _____ .
4 A: … those who just are at the bottom of society also deserve to be there – and to stay there.
   B: Oh, yes, I _____ .
5 B: I hadn't thought about it like that before.
   A: No, me _____ .
6 A: And he's saying that that can be pretty crushing for people.
   B: Yes, I _____ .
7 A: Shall I send you the link?
   B: Yes, _____ .
8 B: Is it very long?
   A: I haven't got to the end yet, but I _____ .

4 Pronunciation elision

a 🔊 **78** Which words and sounds are elided (disappear) in these short responses? Underline the sounds which you think are not pronounced. Then listen and check your answers.

1 I doubt it.
2 I expect so.
3 I couldn't tell you, I'm afraid.
4 I'm afraid not.
5 I suppose so.
6 It's a good idea, isn't it?

b Practise saying the responses in Exercise 4a in the same way.

5 Listen and respond showing interest

🔊 **79** Imagine you are with some friends. Your friends ask you some questions or make statements. Respond with your own words. Then compare what you say with the model answer that follows.

1 *What are you doing this evening?*   *Staying in, I think.*

Unit 10 Social living

81

10e Social mobility

Writing a discursive essay

1 Despite dropping out of college early, Bill Gates (pictured above) managed to build a hugely successful company, Microsoft. How do you think he was able to achieve this? Can you think of anyone else who has done something similar?

2 Look at the essay title and think about whether you agree with it. Then read the essay and answer the questions.

'With hard work and dedication, anyone can achieve anything they want in life.' Discuss.
  1 What is the writer's main argument?
  2 What evidence do they provide to support it?

3 Writing skill referring to evidence

a Find and underline two verbs in the second paragraph that refer to what the evidence tells us.

b Rewrite the sentences below using the verbs in bold.
  1 This example shows that people with good social skills go further in life.
     illustrates
     This _____.
  2 This example implies that people with good social skills are likely to go further in life.
     infer
     We _____.
  3 This demonstrates without doubt that the workplace is changing.
     proves
     This _____.
  4 This example indicates that there is a big difference between those with good social skills and those without.
     points to
     This example _____.

4 Write your own discursive essay on the same subject:

'With hard work and dedication, anyone can achieve anything they want in life.' Discuss.

Organize your essay into three paragraphs and use as evidence a study from the University of California that showed that people who have a positive mental attitude were more successful in their careers.

In modern society, we are often told that we can achieve anything if we want it enough and are prepared to work hard enough. No goal is out of reach: successful business person, top medical surgeon, even president. Clearly, without hard work and dedication, you will achieve little. But is this really all there is to it? My belief is that your ability to manage relationships with others as you progress through your career is at least as important, if not a more important factor.

A recent survey conducted in Singapore suggests that it is social skills, not academic qualifications, which will have the greatest influence on success in the future. Researchers questioned various organizations, both commercial and non-commercial, to find out what skills they valued most highly in their employees. The ability to listen, to work with colleagues and to persuade others were all at the top of their lists. This implies that human interaction, rather than analytical skills, is becoming a more important aspect of the modern workplace compared to the workplace of the past.

This does not mean that we should ignore other types of job training. However, it does mean that we should put more emphasis on the development of social and communication skills at school and university. Simply telling students that they can achieve anything they want through hard work will only lead to disappointment when they find themselves socially unprepared for the wider world.

Wordbuilding animal verbs

1 Read the example with the animal verb in bold (see page 118 of the Student's Book.) Then answer the questions below.

Everyone was **beavering away** trying to get the stadium ready for the opening ceremony.

1 What kind of animal is a beaver? What is it known for doing?
2 What does the verb 'beaver away' mean?

2 Look at these other animals and think about what each is known for. Then complete the sentences with the correct animal verb.

duck	hound	monkey	parrot	ram
swan	wolf			

1 He's always trying to .... out of doing the housework.
2 Please don't .... around. This is a serious business.
3 How can she .... into work an hour late and pretend that's normal?
4 Why does he always .... down his food? It can't be good for his digestion.
5 It can't be easy being famous, especially when press photographers .... you all the time.
6 The car behind didn't .... into us hard, but it was still quite a shock.
7 I wish he wouldn't always just .... the views of other people. Why doesn't he try to think for himself a bit?

Learning skills speaking skills

3 Even at your level of English, you may sometimes feel frustrated at not having the right expressions for everyday situations. Try to build your range of these expressions. Look at the following situations. What would be a natural thing to say in each?

1 Someone tries to help you fix your computer, but can't. You say:

2 You give someone a lift to the station. The next day they bring you a box of chocolates. You say:

3 Someone says they will be seeing a former colleague of yours tomorrow. You say:

4 In a bus, someone says: 'You're standing on my toe.' You say:

5 You're at a conference sitting next to a stranger, waiting for a talk to begin. You say:

6 A colleague invites you to lunch, but you have too much work to do. You say:

4 Think of other everyday situations where you are not sure what would be the right thing to say. Ask your teacher what the correct phrase would be. Keep a note of these phrases.

Check!

5 Look at the words and phrases (a–h) which describe the stories about society and communities that you learned about in Student's Book Unit 10. Match two words or phrases with each photo.

a collective intelligence
b rich cultural heritage
c letting go
d colonies
e free spirits
f lose oneself in the present
g second-generation immigrants
h hunter-gatherers

Unit 11 Reason and emotion

11a Hikikomori

Listening a lost generation

1 **80** Listen to a radio report of people in Japan known as 'hikikomori'. Answer the questions.
   1 Where do hikikomori spend their time?
   2 Who does this condition affect mainly?
   3 What two things could be responsible for it?

2 **80** Listen again and choose the correct option (a, b or c) to complete each statement.
   1 What do people who pity the hikikomori say they are a sign of?
      a a society which is too selfish
      b a society which isn't working
      c a society which ignores its youth
   2 Which of these adjectives does NOT describe how hikikomori feel?
      a angry   b depressed   c insecure
   3 The Hikikomori condition is associated with:
      a western society.
      b Japanese society.
      c wealthy people.
   4 In the past, male university graduates in Japan could expect to get:
      a lifelong employment.
      b society's respect.
      c well-paid jobs.
   5 It is suggested that the parents of hikikomori cannot accept:
      a their children's failure.
      b their children's immaturity.
      c their own poor parenting.
   6 The speaker says that hikikomori need to be helped to:
      a understand their personal feelings.
      b discover their lost confidence.
      c become more sociable again.

3 Complete the expressions used by the speaker using these verbs.

   | Inclined locked lost pulled trod |

   1 … it's high time that these young people _____ **themselves together**.
   2 But their children are _____ **in a cycle of** depression …
   3 … middle-class Japanese males _____ **a** fairly **sure path** from high school to university …
   4 … companies **are less** _____ **to** offer long-term employment, anyway.
   5 … somehow these _____ **souls** need to be reintegrated into society …

4 Match the expressions in Exercise 3 (1–5) with their meanings (a–e).
   a don't really want to
   b followed a route
   c recovered control of their emotions
   d people with no direction in life
   e unable to escape from a repeating pattern

Grammar unreal past forms

5 Look at these examples of the unreal past (1–5) from the radio report. Match them with their uses (a–e).
   1 It's high time that they **pulled** themselves together.
   2 The hikikomori would rather their parents just **left** them alone.
   3 Many end up wishing they **had not worked** so hard for this empty dream.
   4 The young hikikomori wish they **could emulate** their parents' success.
   5 If only the parents **would act** more firmly, the critics say, the problem would not exist.

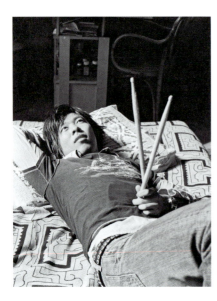

a describes a wish for action to do or stop doing something
b describes a preference for what someone should do
c describes something not yet done that needs to be done urgently
d describes a wish about a past situation
e describes a wish about a present situation

6 Complete these sentences by putting the verbs in the correct tense. Sometimes there is more than one possibility.

1 Supposing you _____ (be) in my position, what _____ (you / do)?
2 If only we _____ (leave) earlier, we _____ (not / get) stuck in all this rush hour traffic.
3 I would rather you _____ (tell) her than _____ (tell) her myself.
4 I wish you _____ (live) nearer. Then we _____ (be) able to meet up more often.
5 It's time that we _____ (stop) treating these people as problems and _____ (realize) that they actually need our help.
6 I wish that he _____ (just / talk) to someone about what he is feeling, rather than bottling it all up inside.

Grammar extra prepositional phrases + -ing

7 Rewrite the sentences using prepositional phrases with -ing. You will need to change or add words.

0 If only parents would act more firmly. Instead, they shield their children from the outside world.
   If only parents would act more firmly **instead of shielding** *their children from the outside world.*
1 He wrote the letter without any thought for the consequences it might have.
   He wrote the letter without _____ .
2 I'm not against a face-to-face meeting with them, but skyping would be easier.
   I'm not against _____ .
3 Before we decide, shall we ask Naomi what she thinks about it?
   Before _____ .
4 I was able to log onto the computer with your old password.
   I was able to log onto the computer by _____ .

5 I think I got the injury because I use a mouse all day.
   I think I got the injury from _____ .

Vocabulary feelings: adjectives and idioms

8 Match the strong feelings with the milder ones.

Strong		Mild
1 astonished	a	content
2 ecstatic	b	cross
3 livid	c	despondent
4 miserable	d	scared
5 petrified	e	taken aback

9 Match the idioms (1–8) describing feelings with the adjectives (a–h).

1 all over the place	a	exhausted
2 a bit down	b	optimistic
3 done in	c	nervous
4 hot under the collar	d	confused and disorganized
5 on edge	e	astonished
6 speechless	f	cross
7 thrilled to bits	g	ecstatic
8 upbeat	h	fed up

10 Complete the sentences using an appropriate adjective or idiom from Exercises 8 and 9. Sometimes there is more than one possibility.

1 Don't worry about Sue. She's just _____ because she has to work on a public holiday.
2 We've had a great season and are feeling very _____ about our chances of winning the league this year.
3 It was a great opportunity to get a free holiday so I was rather _____ when he refused.
4 I'm not going to come out tonight. I've been working all day and I'm completely _____ .
5 She's _____ that everyone else knew about the concert, but that no one told her. She really wanted to go.
6 I have a good job and a nice place to live. On the whole I'm pretty _____ .
7 I always feel _____ before I have to give a talk, but once I begin I'm fine.
8 Sorry, I can't help you. We've just moved house and I'm _____ at the moment.

85

11b Don't overthink it

Reading taking hard decisions

1 Look at the question and then read the statements by four different people. Which one best describes you?

What part do reason and emotion play when you have to make a difficult decision?

> In the case of difficult decisions, I always try to let fate decide – in other words, let the decision be taken out of my hands. So supposing there was a popular show I wanted to see but the tickets were really expensive. I'd wait a couple of days and then ring up to buy the tickets. If they had sold out, then I'd accept that and go "Oh, well, perhaps it wasn't for me, anyway." But if there were still some left, then I'd buy them. In either case, I would feel that fate had decided for me. AB

> When it comes to difficult decisions, I find often I just have to go with my gut feeling. If I try to use reason, sometimes I go round and round in circles, because there are just too many factors to consider. I think what's important is not to have regrets, once you've made a decision. So if you've made the choice to move to a new flat, don't start torturing yourself with thoughts like, "If I'd stayed where I was, I'd probably have been much happier. JT

> You're going to think this idea is a bit forced, but I find the easiest way to make a difficult decision is to use a points system. So, for example, if you're thinking about whether to take a new job or not, then make a list of advantages and disadvantages. Put a score of one or two points next to each advantage and a score of minus one or two next to each disadvantage. Then add them up and see if the total is positive or negative. PT

> People say that you shouldn't let your feelings interfere with your decisions. But anyone who says they can make decisions in a completely rational way is kidding themselves. You can't just shut off your feelings. At some point you'll have to deal with them. So I think you just need to accept that and accept that making the wrong decision now and then is just part of life. CL

2 Read the statements again and say which speaker(s):
1 stress(es) a logical approach to decision-making.
☐ AB ☐ JT ☐ PT ☐ CL
2 think(s) that you should listen to your emotions when making a decision.
☐ AB ☐ JT ☐ PT ☐ CL
3 don't/doesn't really have any particular method for decision-making.
☐ AB ☐ JT ☐ PT ☐ CL
4 stress(es) the importance of not looking back at decisions once they have been taken.
☐ AB ☐ JT ☐ PT ☐ CL
5 is/are resigned to the fact that they will not get every decision right.
☐ AB ☐ JT ☐ PT ☐ CL
6 try/tries to detach themselves from the decision-making process.
☐ AB ☐ JT ☐ PT ☐ CL

3 Find phrases in the statements that mean the following.
1 allow something to stop being in my control
2 instinct
3 not make any progress
4 making yourself suffer
5 unnatural
6 is deceiving themselves

Grammar conditionals and inversion

4 Rewrite these conditional sentences from the text as inverted conditional forms using the prompts.
1 But if there were still some left, then I'd buy them.
   But were _____.
2 If I'd stayed where I was, I'd probably have been much happier.
   Had _____.
3 If you're thinking about whether to take a new job or not, then make a list of advantages and disadvantages.
   Should _____.

5 Complete these conditional sentences by putting the verb in the correct form.
1 I think if I _____ (take) the job, it will probably lead to other opportunities.
2 If I _____ (not / leave) when I did, I think I _____ (still / be) there now.
3 Life _____ (be) easier if people _____ (spend) more time on simple decisions and less time on complicated ones.
4 If you _____ (doubt) what I say, read Jonah Lehrer's bestselling book, *How we decide*.
5 If my husband _____ (not / have) a well-paid job in London, we _____ (move) out to the countryside years ago.
6 Things would be very different if I _____ (know) then what I know now.

6 Rewrite sentences 1–6 from Exercise 5 as inverted conditionals using the words in brackets.
1 _____ (Were … to)
2 _____ (Had)
3 _____ (were .... to)
4 _____ (Should)
5 _____ (it not for)
6 _____ (had)

7 Pronunciation heteronyms

a 🔊 81 Look at the sentences and decide how *-ate* is pronounced (/ət/ or /eɪt/) in each word in bold. Then listen and check your answers.
1 They sent us four **duplicate** copies of the contract to sign.
2 Can you just **elaborate** on that?
3 I wish I was as **articulate** as Beth. She speaks so well.
4 They had to **deliberate** for a long time before coming to a decision.
5 Please **separate** the recyclable waste from the non-recyclable.

b 🔊 82 Listen to these heteronyms and underline the stress in each word in bold. What rule can you make about these words?
1 a What's that strange **object**?
  b I don't **object** to the idea.
2 a Did they **contest** the decision?
  b It wasn't a fair **contest**.
3 a How much did the price **increase**?
  b It's a big **increase**.
4 a It's a **refuse** collection truck.
  b I couldn't **refuse** the offer.
5 a What an interesting **project**.
  b We can't **project** far into the future.
6 a We **import** furniture from Japan.
  b Our main **import** is sugar.

8 Dictation a personal decision

🔊 83 Listen to someone describing a decision they had to make. Complete the paragraph. Then say what you think they should do.

OK, so here's _____

87

11c RoboBees

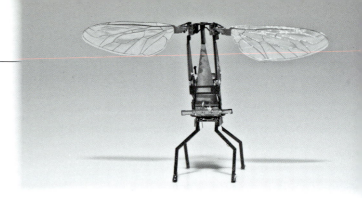

Listening insect robots

1 🔊 **84** Look at the photo and the title *Insect robots*. Answer the questions. Then listen to a report about RoboBees and check your answers.

1 What technical challenges do you think a designer of an insect robot faces?

2 What useful tasks could insect robots perform?

Glossary
hive (n) /haɪv/ a house for bees to live in
pollinate (v) /ˈpɒləneɪt/ to take pollen from one flower to another so that it can produce seeds

2 🔊 **85** Answer the questions. Then listen to the first part of the report again and check your answers.

1 What kind of animal robots have we seen up to now?

2 What inspired the scientists to make RoboBee?

3 What did they think they could use RoboBee to do?

4 Rather than an individual robot, what do they hope to create with RoboBee?

5 What will RoboBee use to respond to their environment?

3 🔊 **86** In the report, the speaker made a number of comparisons between RoboBee and real bees. Listen to the second part of the report again and complete the table.

	RoboBee	Actual bees
1	uses a computer chip brain	have a
2		are amazing flying machines
3	uses a hive as a	live in a real bee hive
4	has a variety of purposes	make and
5	uses cameras and sensors to navigate	use

4 🔊 **87** Listen to the last part of the report again and complete the summary. Use one or two words per space.

Bees are not the only animals to have ¹_____ roboticists. Scientists have also used flies, fish and ²_____ to get ideas for robots. It is hoped that such research will create a new generation of machines based on the designs of ³_____, using the ⁴_____ that animals apply in the task of daily survival. The National ⁵_____ Foundation in the USA is convinced of the potential benefits and is putting ⁶_____ per year into the research.

5 Complete these collocations from the report with the correct verb.

adapt to   determine   face
flap   perform   take

1 _____ an operation
2 _____ changing conditions
3 _____ a challenge
4 _____ one's wings
5 _____ the cause of something
6 _____ advantage of

Word focus *beyond*

6 Underline the correct word to complete these expressions with *beyond*.

1 I last saw her when she was fifteen so she had changed **beyond all** *appreciation / recognition*.
2 The noise from next door has got **beyond** *a joke / a laugh*. I'm going to go and speak to them.
3 It's **beyond** *me / my thinking* how anyone can be so talented and so lazy at the same time.
4 Her loyalty to the company is **beyond** *doubt / uncertainty*.
5 Risking his life to save others from the fire was **beyond the call of** *service / duty*.
6 My father was an extravagant man who always **lived beyond his** *income / means*.

88

Unit 11 Reason and emotion

11d You look concerned

Real life recognizing feelings

1 🎧 88 Listen to three conversations in the workplace. Write the number of the conversation which discusses each subject. There are two extra subjects.

.... a someone worried that others have the wrong impression of them
.... b someone upset that they were not asked to a meeting
.... c what one person thought about another's proposals
.... d someone saying something too directly
.... e a joke that was taken the wrong way

2 🎧 88 Listen again and answer the questions.

1 In conversation 1, why is the second speaker upset with the first speaker?

2 In conversation 2, what does the second speaker worry that Sarah might think about her now?

3 In conversation 3, is Gary likely to be offended by what the second speaker said?

3 🎧 88 The speakers used phrases to acknowledge the emotional effect of what they said. Complete the phrases. Use one word per space. Then listen and check your answers.

Conversation 1

1 You .... a .... taken aback. I didn't mean to .... you during the meeting.
2 Anyway, I'm sorry if that .... wrong at the meeting.

Conversation 2

3 You .... worried. Is something bothering you?
4 Did I .... something to .... you?

Conversation 3

5 Sorry, why are you laughing? I don't understand what's ....
6 Sorry, perhaps that .... a bit abrupt.

4 Pronunciation adjectives ending in *-ed*

a 🎧 89 Are the following *-ed* endings pronounced /d/, /t/ or /ɪd/? Listen and check your answers.

1 shocked ....   6 minded ....
2 thrilled ....   7 surprised ....
3 worried ....   8 impressed ....
4 bored ....   9 frustrated ....
5 frightened .... 10 laughed ....

b Practise saying the words in Exercise 4a in the same way.

c 🎧 90 Listen to these words. What sound does *-ied* produce here?

1 terrified
2 preoccupied
3 mystified
4 satisfied

5 Listen and respond being sensitive

🎧 91 Imagine you are having discussions with colleagues at work. You want to understand the feelings behind what they are saying. Listen to each statement. Respond with your own words. Then compare your response with the model answer that follows.

1 *Well, I'm a bit surprised that you volunteered me for the project.*

Oh, I'm sorry. I hope I didn't upset you. I didn't mean to put you in a difficult situation.

89

11e Don't get me wrong

Writing an email message

1 Writing skill avoiding misunderstandings

Read emails 1–4 and underline the phrases which help the reader to avoid a misunderstanding.

---

1 Hi John

I'm still waiting to hear back from you about buying some of my old furniture. Were you that horrified when you saw it? I'm joking of course! I don't want to pressure you in any way – it's just that I'm moving in two weeks' time and I need to sort something out.

Let me know.

Best wishes

Hakim

---

2 Dear Sian

Many thanks for getting back to me so quickly. In your haste, you attached the wrong document. It's the photo of the main university entrance that I need, not the one of your holiday in the south of France! Can you resend?

Thanks.

Jen

---

3 Dear Sarah

Just to let you know that we won't need you on Sunday after all. Frederica has volunteered to help us with the packing. Please don't take this the wrong way. We do really appreciate your offer.

See you soon, I hope.

Paul

---

4 Hi Barney

That wasn't the answer I expected! I thought you wanted to be involved in this project. Don't worry – I'm not offended in any way. It just took me rather by surprise.

Speak soon.

Graham

---

2 Read emails 5–8 and match them with the impression that they give (a–d).

a This person seems offended not to be asked.
b This person seems too busy to deal with correspondence.
c This person seems annoyed to be kept waiting.
d This person seems to be making a rude comment about the reader.

---

5 Hi Des

That was a very long answer you sent me. I will reply to you when I have time to read it properly.

Jeff

---

6 Dear Brigitte

Great to hear from you! Your spelling hasn't improved much since we were at school. I had to re-read your email three times before I could understand it. Your idea of meeting up on 8th December sounds perfect. Let me know where you'd like to meet.

All the best

Rosalie

---

7 Dear Mr Nasri

I sent you a quotation as promised a week ago, but you have not replied. Are we to suppose that you are not interested?

Kind regards

David Temperley

---

8 Dear Berni

I received your email saying that you don't want to take up my offer of advice about the design of your website. I hope the person you have found to help you with this does a good job.

Yours

Jasper

---

3 Rewrite emails 5–8 so that you avoid the possibility of the reader misunderstanding or being offended by them.

Wordbuilding heteronyms

1 Match the words (1–8) with their definitions (a–h).

1 delegate (n) /ˈdelɪgət/
2 alternate (v) /ˈɔːltəneɪt/
3 row (v) /rəʊ/
4 wound (n) /wuːnd/
5 tear (n) /tɪə(r)/
6 minute (n) /ˈmɪnɪt/
7 sewer (n) /ˈsəʊə(r)/
8 refuse (v) /rɪˈfjuːz/

a someone who works with a needle and thread
b change places periodically
c say no to something
d a drop of water from the eye
e a unit of time
f a representative
g a cut or injury
h propel a boat with oars

2 Look at the words in bold. What part of speech are they? What do they mean? How are they pronounced?

1 I **wound** a piece of bandage around the cut to protect it from infection.

2 Please try not to **tear** the material when you put the cover back on the chair. It's very tight.

3 They had a big **row** yesterday and now neither one is speaking to the other.

4 I put a **minute** amount of sugar in your coffee before I remembered you didn't take sugar. You won't taste it.

5 We have a job share. We work on **alternate** days of the week.

6 It is well known that rats live in the **sewers**.

7 Household **refuse** collection is on Thursdays.

8 Good managers learn how to **delegate** responsibility to their team.

Learning skills the internet

3 The internet has some great resources for learning English. Here are a few tips for using these.

News: Visit an English language news website and listen to a story that you are already familiar with. Write down new words that you learn.

Songs: Find a song sung in English that you like and try to write down the lyrics. Then do an internet search for the lyrics and compare.

Talks: Listen to TED talks. These are free and are categorized by subject. Listen without the transcript and see how much you can understand. Then listen again, this time following the transcript. Make a note of any new words. Also search for podcasts related to your interests.

Blogs: Try to find blogs about stories that have interested you in *Life*. Perhaps post a comment on their blog and start a conversation.

4 Do one of the things in Exercise 3 this week. Then tell a fellow student about your experience.

Check!

5 Do the crossword. All the answers are in Student's Book Unit 11.

Across

1 Unit 11a was about this kind of intelligence. (9)
5 *Thrilled to* _____ means 'very happy'. (4)
6 'You _____ worried. Is everything OK?' (4)
7 a bit down _____ (3)
9 the opposite of reasoned and logical (10)

Down

2 small facial gestures are called _____ - expressions (5)
3 and 8 a stronger way of saying 'I wish …' (2, 4)
4 the prize that Kahneman won (5)
6 very angry (5)
8 see 3 Down
10 artificial intelligence

Unit 12 Mother nature

12a Aerial view

Listening interview with Marie Arana

1　🔊 92　You are going to listen to an interview with Marie Arana, a journalist. Which kind of landscapes does she associate with North America and which with South America? Which photo(s) match her descriptions of North America and which South America?

....
....

2　🔊 92　Complete Marie Arana's descriptions of each of the places depicted in the photos. Listen again and check.
1　.................... - .... mountain
2　...................., green ....
3　great .... of grass
4　.................... towns

Glossary
hacienda (n) /ˌhæsiˈendə/ (of Spanish origin) a large estate used for farming
prairie (n) /ˈpreəri/ a large area of flat grassland
shanty town (n) /ˈʃænti ˌtaʊn/ a poor area of a town made up of shacks or insubstantial buildings

3　🔊 92　Listen again and choose the best option (a, b or c) to complete the questions.
1　Marie Arana has always had a strong awareness of landscapes because she grew up:
　a　near volcanoes.
　b　on a farm near the sea.
　c　on an island in the Pacific.
2　The American landscape felt foreign to her because:
　a　the land stretched so far in all directions.
　b　there were roads everywhere.
　c　people had settled everywhere.
3　What she loves about Peru is:
　a　how deserted it is.
　b　how varied the landscape is.
　c　how easy it is to get from one place to another.
4　Why had the cities she saw from the air grown so much?
　a　because of economic migrants
　b　because of people escaping various disasters
　c　because of industrialization
5　How did she feel when she saw the cities of South America from the air?
　a　moved and impressed
　b　confused
　c　surprised and saddened
6　What was the most difficult thing about taking photos from a small aeroplane?
　a　the wind and cold coming through the open door
　b　you don't have confidence in the plane
　c　your equipment doesn't always work properly

4 Look at these words and expressions from the interview and choose the correct definition (a or b).

1 **In all truth**, I was taken aback
   a to be honest   b in every sense
2 The urban centres have **burgeoned**
   a grown much larger   b become depressed
3 the shanty towns that had **sprouted up** around the cities
   a grown upwards   b that have appeared and grown rapidly
4 the **prevailing** beauty of the land
   a dominant   b hidden
5 the **visual feast** below us
   a delight for the eyes   b confusing image
6 **fierce gales** rushing through the open door
   a extreme cold   b very strong winds

Grammar approximation and vague language

5 🔊 92 Rewrite the sentences to make the statements you heard in the interview. Use these expressions of approximation and vague language to add to (or replace) the words and phrases in bold. Then listen again and check.

| around | hundreds of | -ish | kind of |
| or so | over | some | stuff |

1 My earliest memories are of earthquakes – there were **fifteen** by the time I reached the age of five.

2 … a place where you could drive for **miles** and human beings always be in evidence.

3 Having grown up in **a desert**, I had never seen great fields of grass.

4 Peru has five kinds of landforms … all of it in **close** proximity!

5 … the shanty towns that had sprouted up around the cities in the past **thirty years**.

6 The sights from **1,500 metres** in the air were astoundingly beautiful!

7 How Bobby was able to … manipulate **photographic equipment** under those conditions is still a mystery to me.

6 Make the information in this passage more approximate by adding to (or replacing) the expressions of approximation in the correct place on the line.

> We live on a big ranch in Montana. It's been in the family for 120 years. I guess my father is what you would call a cowboy. He has a herd of 300 cattle which is actually small for this region, but it keeps us busy! I still help out there, but next year I'm going back to college to continue my studies. I think we all have ambition to do something different from our parents – I'd like to be a car designer. I have ideas. If it doesn't work out, I can always come back and help out with work on the farm.
>
> ¹ ODD
> ² ROUGHLY
> ³ KIND OF
> ⁴ IN THE … OR TWO
> ⁵ SOME
> ⁶ DOZENS OF
> ⁷ STUFF

Vocabulary nature

7 Choose the best option to form collocations about descriptions of nature.

1 *dramatic / wooded / bleak* hillsides
2 *lush / sparse / cloudless* sky
3 *rugged / monotonous / rich* farmland
4 *bleak / lush / rugged* valleys
5 *snow-capped / lush / dramatic* scenery
6 *dramatic / sparse / monotonous* vegetation
7 *rugged / cloudless / sparse* terrain
8 *monotonous / rich / snow-capped* mountains
9 a *sparse / cloudless / monotonous* skyline
10 *a blot / a spot / a plot* on the landscape

8 Dictation approximate answers

🔊 93 Listen to a conversation where a speaker gives approximate answers to questions. Complete the answers.

1 Where do you live now?
   _____ Irbid,

2 Is that near where you work?

3 What's the countryside like around there?

4 Are you near the desert?

12b Nature's great events

Reading nature blog

1 Have you seen any of the following events in nature? What amazing natural events would you like to see?

- a double rainbow
- a solar eclipse
- a lunar eclipse

2 Read the blog about four amazing events seen by the writer. Which one(s):
1. are a bit frightening?
2. are to do with the sun?
3. are to do with water?
4. are unexplained phenomena?
5. take place in countries with cold climates?
6. produce an amazing effect?

3 Find words in the blog with the following meanings.
1. drops of water that appear on plants and the grass in cold weather (para 1)
2. the northernmost and southernmost points on the Earth (para 2)
3. poisonous (para 3)
4. burnt or made very dry by heat (para 4)
5. turning round and round (para 5)

Nature's great events

Nature can conjure up some pretty amazing spectacles. Some are on a modest scale and are quite easily found: a spider's web in the morning dew one autumn morning or frost formations on a window pane. Others are on a much grander scale and are not so easy to come by. I have been lucky enough to see four such spectacles on my travels and it's these I'd like to share with you.

The Aurora Borealis

This is an extraordinary light show in the far northern skies that I promised myself I would see one day – and I wasn't disappointed. The Aurora occurs when solar winds (a stream of plasma) interact with the Earth's magnetic fields, which are strongest at the two poles. As particles in the solar wind collide with gases in the atmosphere, they glow in wonderful greens, blues and reds.

Red tides

Also called the algal bloom, red tides are caused by an accumulation of algae in the ocean. It's an impressive, but also slightly alarming sight as the sea turns a blood-red colour. The algae is not dangerous to humans (although it is toxic for animals) but it can be irritating. We would always check for news of red tides before planning beach visits.

Sailing stones

One of the strangest things I've come across is the sailing stones of Death Valley in California. These single stones sit in the middle of vast expanses of scorched open desert and – extraordinarily – they move. Stones weighing over a hundred kilos drift across the sand. You would think this could be explained by the action of the wind or elements, until you learn that some stones that started in the same place have been known to move in completely different directions.

Ice circles

These are beautiful circular discs of ice, some measuring up to 150 metres across, that form in rivers. Most of us are quite used to seeing ice forming at the edge of rivers, but in the case of ice circles, it forms in the middle. They occur when a current turns slowly in a circular motion and the spinning water freezes. Ideally, I would have liked to have seen one of the larger ones, but even a twenty-metre diameter one is an amazing sight.

Grammar *would*

4 Look at the list of the uses of the modal verb *would* (1–7). Then match the sentences from the blog (a–d) with the correct use.

1 to make a polite request
2 to describe a hypothetical situation
3 to respond to a request or invitation
4 to describe a reported intention, expectation or decision
5 to describe a habitual action in the past
6 to indicate a person or thing's refusal to do something
7 to express an opinion or hope in a less forceful way

a This is an extraordinary light show that I promised myself I **would see** one day.
b We **would** always **check** for news of red tides before planning beach visits.
c You **would think** this could be explained by the action of the wind or elements.
d Ideally I **would have liked** to have seen one of the larger ones, but ....

5 Read the exchanges. Rewrite the underlined sections using phrases with *would*.

A: ¹Can I ask you to do me a favour?
B: Sure. What is it?
A: ²Take this cake out of the oven in ten minutes. I have to go to the shops.

C: Do you fancy coming for supper on Saturday? We're having a few friends round.
D: That ³sounds really nice. Can I bring anything?

E: What happened? I thought you were going to drive to work this morning.
F: I was, but ⁴I couldn't get the car to start.

G: Is this where you used to live?
H: Yes, that's my old house over there. And that's the café that we ⁵used to go to most evenings.

I: Did you stop at the shop for milk on the way home?
J: No, I ⁶meant to get some, but I didn't have enough time.

K: How was your holiday in Spain? Pretty hot, I ⁷expect.
L: We didn't go in the end. We decided ⁸to stay at home instead. But it worked out really well. We had a really relaxing time.

M: Are you loving your new job?
N: ⁹I'm not inclined to put it that strongly. But it's pretty good, thanks, yes.

6 Pronunciation *would*

a 🎵 94 Look at the sentences with *would*. Listen to how the underlined words are pronounced.

1 <u>Would you</u> like to go for a walk?
2 I <u>would love</u> to come with you but I can't.
3 I tried to talk to him, but he <u>wouldn't listen</u>.
4 When I was a student, I <u>would always walk</u> wherever I went.
5 <u>We would never have dared</u> to speak to our parents like that!
6 <u>You would imagine</u> that she knows what she's doing.

b 🎵 94 Listen again to the sentences. Try to say each one before you hear it. Pause the CD as necessary.

Idioms adjective collocations

7 Complete the adjective collocations with these words.

brand   fast   freezing   lightning   pitch
rock   sopping   stiff   sick   wide

1 I can't wear my coat – it's still _____ wet after I cycled home in the rain.
2 Is that a _____ new computer you've got there?
3 I fell _____ asleep in the lecture. It was so embarrassing when I woke up.
4 This bread is _____ hard. Can you get some more when you're out?
5 The room was _____ black. You couldn't see your hand in front of your face.
6 What a _____ cold wind. I should have brought my hat.
7 She's got _____ quick reactions. She'd make a fantastic tennis player.
8 Where have you been? I've been worried _____ about you.
9 The race is _____ open. Anyone could win.
10 I was scared _____ that he was going to fire me, but actually he was really nice about the mistake I'd made.

8 Look at these other adjective collocations (1–6) and answer the questions (a and b).

1 squeaky clean   4 bored stiff
2 dirt cheap   5 filthy rich
3 silky smooth   6 razor sharp

a In which collocation does the intensifying word come second? _____
b Which are pejorative, i.e. make a negative judgement about that quality?

Unit 12 Mother nature

95

12c Tigers as neighbours

Listening a lesson in conservation

1 🔊 95 Listen to someone discussing the future survival of tigers. How does he think the tiger population, and that of other wild animals, can best be conserved?

....
....

2 🔊 95 Listen again and choose the best option (a, b or c) to complete each statement.

1. The speaker says he will feel devastated if:
   a tigers become extinct.
   b there are no more tigers in the wild.
   c people are unable to live near tigers.
2. The speaker says that personally:
   a he would be happy to live near tigers.
   b he admires people who live near tigers.
   c he doesn't want to live near tigers.
3. Before 2016 the tiger population:
   a had been falling steadily.
   b had risen slightly.
   c had remained stable.
4. Because the tribes are vegetarian:
   a they don't eat tiger meat.
   b they look for different food from the tigers.
   c they don't look for food in dangerous places.
5. Tigers are good for farmers who:
   a grow crops.
   b keep small animals.
   c are worried about thieves.
6. For the Soliga tribe, the tiger is a:
   a vulnerable creature.
   b sacred creature.
   c evil creature.
7. The speaker says that local people killing tigers for their skins:
   a is a real problem.
   b is a concern of some.
   c is very unlikely to happen.
8. The speaker thinks that local tribes make good conservationists because they:
   a respect other living things around them.
   b understand environmental problems.
   c have sophisticated land management skills.

3 Complete the summary below. You have been given the first two letters of the missing words.

¹Mu .... as I love tigers, I don't really want to live next to one. Luckily for tiger conservation there are people who do. The local tribes of the Western Ghats of India ²co .... happily with tigers because, as vegetarians, the people don't ³co .... with them for food. The result of this ⁴he .... relationship is that tiger numbers are ⁵gr .... But conservationists think that it would be better if there were no people in these areas, so now the local tribes are being ⁶ev .... This is ⁷ir .... , because these are the very people who have made tiger conservation a success and the best chance that the tigers have of ⁸su ....

Word focus *move*

4 Underline the correct prepositions to complete the sentences.

1. I think we should **move** *on* / *off*, because this discussion is getting us nowhere.
2. Come on – **get a move** *in* / *on*. You may not want to get there in time, but I do.
3. She couldn't afford the rent on her flat anymore, so she's given it up and **moved back** *in* / *around* with her parents.
4. If we **move** the tables and chairs *around* / *off* a bit, we can create more space at the front of the room.
5. We stood on the dock and watched in dismay as the ship **moved** *off* / *out* with our passports and all our luggage on it.
6. Her speech **moved** everyone in the room *to* / *with* tears.
7. Jack is one of the last original residents of this street. The rest have all **moved** *over* / *out*.
8. **Move** *on* / *over*, will you? I need to sit down.

12d Environmental vandalism?

Real life a debate

1 Speaking skill interrupting

a Look at the phrases for interrupting and preventing interruptions. Complete phrases 2–8 using ONE word in each space.

1 Yes, but …
2 Sorry, can I .... interrupt you there?
3 Can I just .... what I was saying?
4 No, sorry. I have to stop you .... …
5 Can I just say something .... answer to that?
6 No, hang .... a minute.
7 Just a ...., please.
8 You can .... your point in a moment.

b Which phrases in Exercise 1a are used to interrupt (I) someone and which phrases are used to prevent (P) interruptions?

2 🔘 96 Listen to a debate between three friends about the building of a new golf course in a coastal area and answer the questions.

a What arguments are used in favour of the new golf course?

b What arguments are used against the golf course?

3 🔘 96 Listen again. Which phrases in Exercise 1 do the different speakers use to interrupt and to prevent interruptions?

4 Pronunciation intonation in interruptions

a 🔘 97 Look at these phrases for interrupting. Listen and say which ones are said with a polite and firm intonation. Which one is not?

1 I have to stop you there. ....
2 OK, you can make your point in a moment. ....
3 Can I just finish what I was saying? ....
4 Can I just say something in answer to that? ....
5 Just a moment, please. ....

b 🔘 98 Listen again to the exception, this time said with a polite intonation. Then practise saying all the sentences in Exercise 4a.

5 Listen and respond environmental vandalism?

🔘 99 You are going to hear a debate about the building of a new golf course on an area of natural beauty in your country. You believe it is a bad idea. Listen to each statement. Respond with your own words. Then compare your response with the model answer that follows.

1 *I was very pleased to hear about the new golf course. Weren't you?*

No, I wasn't actually. I don't see why they have to build it in a National Park.

12e To the editor

Writing a letter to a newspaper

1 Read the letter and answer the questions.

1 What was the subject of the article that prompted this letter?

2 What issue did the writer of the article ignore, according to the letter writer?

3 What recommendations does she make to remedy this situation?

2 **Writing skill** persuasive language

a Find examples of the following persuasive elements in the letter and underline them.

1 a personal connection with the topic (para 2)
2 a strong statement or statistic (para 2)
3 an emotive expression or phrase (para 2)
4 a short, clear sentence (para 3)
5 an appeal to shared experiences (para 4)
6 a view of what the future could be like (para 4)

b Look at these pairs of sentences and say which is more persuasive and why.

1
  a With a little more thought, drivers could reduce animal injuries on the roads.
  b Animal injuries are a direct result of drivers' thoughtlessness.

2
  a There are huge numbers of animal deaths on the roads each year.
  b A million animals are killed on the roads each day in the USA.

3
  a Our careless attitude is a poor reflection on us as a species.
  b By not caring about the lives of other animals we show that we are not a very good species to live with.

4
  a Such accidents are inexcusable.
  b Such accidents are a shame.

To the editor:
I enjoyed your article 'Something to cheer about at last' (Tuesday 7th June) and I agree that we should be proud (of ourselves and animals) that wildlife is thriving in our cities. But there is one area where we still have a lot of progress to make with animal welfare: our roads.

I am a vet and injury from road accidents is the most common reason animals are brought to our clinic. I am the first to accept that accidents can and do happen. What I cannot accept, however, is that we just shrug our shoulders and do nothing about it. Many accidents could be avoided if drivers were more attentive to animals on the roads. But more importantly, many animal injuries could be treated if drivers responded more sensitively to accidents.

So, be animal aware. And if you hit a wild animal while driving, stop the car safely and go and check on the animal. If it is injured, try to pick it up, protecting yourself with a thick item of clothing. Then take it to the nearest veterinary clinic. Even if the animal ultimately dies, it will have a far more humane death in the clinic than by the roadside.

We all know how upsetting it is to hit an animal in your car. But taking steps to lessen any negative consequences will make you – and the animal – feel a whole lot better.

3 Imagine you have read a newspaper article that urges drivers to be more attentive and careful when driving, especially at night, so as to avoid hitting and killing animals on the roads. Write a letter to the editor agreeing with the article. Use persuasive techniques from Exercise 2 and add the following ideas for improving the situation:
• lower speed limits on roads
• signs warning drivers that animals (deer, badgers, cats, etc.) are crossing
• laws making it illegal to drive away after hitting an animal

Wordbuilding adverb + adjective collocations

1 Look at these adverbs. Choose the most appropriate adverb to complete each sentence.

culturally   emotionally   environmentally
geographically   ethnically   industrially
internationally   physically   socially   visually

1 It wasn't a great story, but the effects in the film were .... stunning.
2 She's very natural with people and always puts them at their ease. I wish I was as .... gifted as she is.
3 The term 'third world' refers to poorer countries that are not .... developed – as if this was necessarily a bad thing!
4 It's important for young people to be .... active, because it keeps them healthy not only in body, but also in mind.
5 This map of the metro system isn't .... accurate. It just shows the arrangement of the different lines and stations.
6 It's important to be .... sensitive so that you don't offend other people when talking about their customs and habits.
7 He's an .... famous composer. In fact, I think he's better known abroad than in his own country.
8 It was an .... charged atmosphere at the meeting: a lot of people were very angry about what had happened.
9 All their products are sold in .... friendly packaging.
10 It's the most .... diverse university in the country with over 67 different nationalities and 42 different languages spoken.

Learning skills eliminating errors

2 You probably now understand most of what you hear and read and are easily understood by others. But you may feel there are some gaps in your knowledge and you are not always sure you are speaking accurately. Try to follow these 'social strategies' to overcome this.

1 Ask questions about the language, especially idioms or culturally specific items, when you are in the company of native speakers.
2 Check the precise meaning of words if you are not sure you are using them correctly.
3 Ask people to correct you if you make a mistake.
4 You may have some ingrained errors – mistakes that you have 'grown up' with. Make an effort to eliminate these. Ask friends or native speakers if they have noticed such mistakes.

3 Look at this list of the most common types of advanced learner error. Do you recognize any of them? Ask your teacher to give you a list of what he/she thinks are your ingrained errors.

1 mistakes with agreement (e.g. singular noun–plural verb)
2 mistakes with prepositions
3 mistakes with the present perfect tense
4 mistakes with tense choice in general
5 incorrect formation of a particular idiom or everyday expression
6 mistakes with verb patterns: gerund or infinitive

4 Look at these sentences. Identify and correct the mistake in each one.

1 We must ask if it is really worth to spend all this money on something that will bring only a small benefit.
2 At the end, it is a question of personal choice for each individual.
3 I had many strange experiences in my life, but nothing compares to that.
4 The resort, like the other resorts around it, are made up of a mixture of new and old hotels.
5 His employers had had enough. His attitude had become beyond the joke and so they fired him.

Check!

5 Answer the questions. Then rearrange the first letter of the answers to make the name of a vegetable. All the answers are in Student's Book Unit 12.

1 What is the adjective that describes a completely clear, blue sky? ....
2 What is the name for 'an understanding of how our world and the Earth's systems work' you read about in Unit 12a? ....
3 What was the name of the Japanese poet that you read about in Unit 12b? ....
4 How many syllables are there in a haiku? ....
5 In which city can you see mountain lions roaming in the hills? Los ....
6 What word describes a thing that spoils a landscape or view? a ....
7 What kind of pollution prompted the letter in Unit 12e? .... pollution
8 Who was the letter from question 7 sent to? the ....

Vegetable (plural): ....

IELTS practice test

LISTENING TEST

SECTION 1 Questions 1–10

Questions 1–3

*Choose the correct letter, **A**, **B** or **C**.*

Example

Where was the meeting?
A in a local public library
B in an educational institution
C in a company's headquarters

---

1 Who is paying for the project?
   A various business sponsors
   B a local government body
   C a charitable organization

2 What did Fiona need to take to the meeting?
   A a character reference
   B an identification document
   C a tutor's letter of recommendation

3 Applicants were chosen according to
   A their academic record.
   B their performance in a task.
   C their attitude towards certain issues.

Questions 4–10

Complete the notes below.

Write **NO MORE THAN TWO WORDS AND/OR A NUMBER** for each answer.

Hours of work:	4 .... per day maximum
Interviewers' appearance:	must wear 5 ....
Target interviewees:	minimum of 6 .... per cent in category A
Target number of interviews:	7 .... per week
Location of interviews:	informed by 8 .... daily
Delivery of data:	within 9 .... of interview
Name of website:	10 ....

SECTION 2

Questions 11–20

Questions 11–14

Choose the correct letter, **A**, **B** or **C**.

11 Which feature of the Phinda Reserve is unusual?
 A its extensive bush environment
 B its proximity to the ocean
 C its level of biodiversity

12 The speaker says that before recent initiatives in Phinda,
 A larger species had experienced falling numbers.
 B some key species had become locally extinct.
 C certain species had tended to predominate.

13 What does the release of the black rhino serve as an example of?
 A Phinda's international standing
 B the scale of the research programme in Phinda
 C the contribution of volunteers to Phinda's reputation

14 Volunteers at Phinda are most likely to do research connected with
 A big cats.
 B white rhinos.
 C small mammals.

Questions 15–17

Complete the notes below.

Write **NO MORE THAN TWO WORDS** for each answer.

Monitoring Projects in Phinda		
Animal	Volunteers' task	Method
White Rhino	developing a detailed 15	ear notching of individuals
Cheetah	tracking territories and movements	use markings around the 16 .... to identify individuals
17	recording sightings	tracking, darting and collaring

Questions 18–20

Which three facilities are provided for volunteers?

*Choose **THREE** letters, A–H.*

      A separate accommodation from the staff
      B money to spend locally
      C cooking facilities
      D land on which to grow food
      E access to international media
      F the equipment to watch movies
      G free transport to the beach
      H excursions to local places of interest

18 ....
19 ....
20 ....

SECTION 3

Questions 21–30

Questions 21–25

Choose the correct letter, A, B or C.

21 What's called 'ash dieback' disease first appears in
 A the shoots of young trees.
 B the leaves of healthy trees.
 C the bark of older trees.

22 When asked about the risk posed by the infection, Dennis explains that
 A other tree species can easily catch it.
 B it affects Asian ash trees less severely.
 C some species of ash tree are unaffected by it.

23 What do we learn the origin of the disease?
 A It remains a complete mystery.
 B It can be traced to one part of Europe.
 C It is likely to have existed in Japan for some time.

24 Dennis corrects Diana's suggestion that the European ash
 A may be divided into sub-species.
 B is particularly vulnerable to the disease.
 C has some natural resistance to the infection.

25 Dennis disagrees with the interviewer's ideas about
 A how quickly the problem might be solved.
 B how willing people will be to remove infected trees.
 C how many existing ash trees will survive the outbreak.

Questions 26–30

What facts would Dennis like to establish?

Choose FIVE letters, A–H.

> A the total number of ash trees in the UK
> B whether fungicides could control the disease
> C the geographical distribution of ash trees in the UK
> D the age of trees already infected
> E whether trees could be immunized
> F the regional spread of the disease
> G whether some groups of trees remain unaffected
> H whether ash trees in cities are equally affected

26 ....

27 ....

28 ....

29 ....

30 ....

SECTION 4

Questions 31–40

Questions 31–37

Complete the sentences below.

*Write **NO MORE THAN TWO WORDS** for each answer.*

The subject which the students are studying is called **31** ....

The speaker points out that interns will be **32** .... for the work they do.

The speaker recommends a document entitled the **33** ....

The internship report has three main features: a description of the company's business, a description of the intern's **34** .... , a **35** .... of a relevant topic.

Students will probably have to do mostly **36** .... during their internship.

In their reports, students need to show they are capable of **37** ....

Questions 38–40

What does the speaker recommend for internship reports?

*Choose **THREE** letters, A–H.*

- A using lots of technical terms
- B avoiding the use of acronyms
- C throwing away the first draft
- D using complex grammar
- E checking that spelling is accurate
- F getting feedback from a colleague
- G dividing the text into four sections
- H using a specific format

38 ....

39 ....

40 ....

SECTION 1

Questions 1–13

Read the text below and answer questions 1–13.

The North Dakota Fracking Boom

The Fort Berthold Reservation in western North Dakota is a vast area where advances in drilling and extraction technology have made it possible to remove oil from deep, widely dispersed deposits. Since early 2006, production from what's known as the Bakken formation has increased nearly 150-fold, to more than 660,000 barrels a day, moving North Dakota into second place among US states, ahead of Alaska.

No one but a handful of industry insiders saw that coming. Now some optimistic oilmen predict that the state's daily output could eventually close in on that of Texas – at two million barrels. The number of wells could increase from the roughly 8,000 operating today to between 40,000 and 50,000. By the time the frenzy ends, perhaps 20 years from now, as many as 14 billion barrels of high-quality crude may have been removed. Until more pipelines are built in this landlocked rural region, most of the oil and water will be transported by truck. So will everything else needed for swift, large-scale development: gravel, construction materials, tools, machinery. The prairie is being industrialized.

Change of such scope and intensity is bound to raise questions. Thousands of people are converging on the area, looking for work, looking for redemption, looking for trouble. And jobs are plentiful. In Williston, in the heart of the oil patch, the unemployment rate is less than one per cent. But how does a region of farms weather the human onslaught? Another risk is environmental damage. Most attention has focused on hydraulic fracturing, or fracking, by which large amounts of fresh water combined with sand and smaller amounts of other substances, some toxic, are driven under high pressure down wells drilled into deep layers of shale, creating cracks through which bubbles of trapped oil and natural gas can escape into the well. Where will all the clean water come from? How will the dirty water that's pumped out be prevented from contaminating groundwater, as has happened in other parts of the country? Stepping back for a broader view, can the inestimable values of the prairie – silence, solitude – be preserved in the face of full-throttle, regionwide development, of extracting as much oil as possible as fast as possible?

The implications are already reverberating far beyond North Dakota. Bakken-like shale formations occur across the US, indeed, across the world. The extraction technology refined in the Bakken is in effect a skeleton key that can be used to open other fossil fuel treasure chests.

North Dakota has boomed before, in the 1950s and 1980s. But besides being much larger and likely to last much longer, the current boom differs from earlier ones because it initially coincided with an economic recession. For refugees from its ravages, the Bakken is a chance – often the last chance – to escape ruin.

So it was for truck driver Susan Connell. While we head for the disposal site on a two-lane highway chewed up by truck traffic, she describes how she came to be behind the wheel of a Kenworth Anteater. The trouble started in 2009, when she and her husband could no longer find construction work in south-western Montana, where they still live. By the fall they were three months behind on their house payments. The bank sent threatening letters. Then Connell heard that truckers were needed in North Dakota. Earlier in her career, the Delaware native had driven a commercial bus between Philadelphia and Atlantic City, also an airport transit bus in Portland, Oregon. How much harder could an 18-wheeler be? But to qualify she would have to upgrade her licence, and for that she would need to attend a special training program. Cost: $4,000. At a time when Connell and her husband could scarcely buy groceries for their kids, they charged the fee to a credit card. 'It was a big gamble,' she says, referring less to the likely availability of work than to the reception she would almost certainly get in such a male-dominated environment.

IELTS practice test

> Trucking is one of the most lucrative enterprises in North Dakota. Driving an 18-wheeler tank truck can bring in $40,000 a month – if everything goes right. One night during the training program in early April 2011, waiting out the 'umpteenth blizzard' of the season with two dozen oil and water drivers at a gas station in Parshall, Connell insinuated herself into conversations, inquiring about jobs and collecting phone numbers of trucking firms. Someone asked her where she'd abandoned her vehicle. It turned out that Connell, the only female driver in the room, was also the only one who hadn't gone off the road during the storm. One of the guys, the owner of a small water-hauling company based in Killdeer, was so impressed he cold-called and offered her a job next day. Her pay jumped from $600 a week to $2,000. There would be no more worrisome letters from the bank. She'd saved the family house.

Questions 1–6

Complete the table below.

Choose **NO MORE THAN THREE WORDS** from the text for each answer.

Write your answers in boxes 1–6 on your answer sheet.

Fracking in North Dakota	
US state which currently produces more oil:	1 ....
Estimated daily amount of oil that Dakota might eventually produce:	2 ....
Key type of infrastructure currently lacking in the region:	3 ....
Traditional economic activity of the region:	4 ....
Main material introduced into wells during fracking:	water 5 ....
Name given to the waste material produced:	6 ....

Questions 7–13

Do the following statements agree with the information given in the text?

In boxes 7–13 on your answer sheet, write

    TRUE   *if the statement agrees with the information*
    FALSE   *if the statement contradicts the information*
    NOT GIVEN *if there is no information on this*

7 Extraction of oil from shale is likely to spread to other areas.

8 North Dakota is seeing rapid economic development for the first time.

9 Susan Cornell sold her home in order to move to North Dakota.

10 Susan has recently trained as a professional driver.

11 Susan found her special training course more challenging than she expected.

12 Susan was concerned about whether she would be accepted by other drivers in the industry.

13 Susan had to do a bad weather driving test as part of her job application.

READING TEST

SECTION 2
Questions 14–30

Read the text below and answer questions 14–24.

Why the Scottish wildcat is staring extinction in the face

A
Once found across Britain, this magnificent predator is now rarer than the tiger – with perhaps only 40 left at large. According to a report published last week, Felis silvestris grampia is now hovering at the edge of extinction and could be wiped out, in the wild, in the near future. A report just out, produced by the Scottish Wildcat Association, reviewed 2,000 records of camera trap recordings, eyewitness reports and road kills, and concluded there may be only about 40 wildcats left in Scotland in the wild today. 'However you juggle the figures, it's hard to find anything positive,' says Steve Piper, the association's chairman. 'The overwhelming evidence is that the wildcat is going to be extinct very soon.'

B
The prospect is alarming, to put it mildly. Not every wildcat expert agrees with the association's grim prognosis, however. A separate report, by Scottish National Heritage, last month concluded there may be up to 400 still living in the wild. That is certainly a more encouraging figure, but the future of this glorious, distinctive animal is worryingly uncertain, no matter how you stack up their numbers. But how has this happened and what can be done to save the wildcat?

C
Not surprisingly, the answer to the first question is a lot easier to provide than the latter and stems from recent studies into the origins of wildcats. These can be grouped into three main genetic clusters, say scientists: the European wildcat, *Felis silvestris silvestris*; the Middle Eastern wildcat, *Felis silvestris lybica*; and the southern African wildcat, *Felis silvestris cafra*. Crucially the Highland wildcat is a member of the first of these subspecies while the domestic variety is a member of the second.

D
So how did descendants of the Middle Eastern wildcat end up being domesticated and why is that important for the fate of our own native wildcats? The answer is straightforward: with the invention of agriculture in the Middle East ten thousand years ago, the first stores of grain were established. Mice and rats moved in and wildcats – of the Middle Eastern variety – turned up to hunt them. Soon the cats adapted to life with humans, who in turn came to rely on them as a means of pest control. As farming spread westwards, the cats came too. Today there are an estimated ten million ancestors of these early domestic cats across Britain.

E
And that is a real problem for the Highland wildcat. Its population had already been drastically reduced by loss of habitat in historic times, says David Hetherington, of the Cairngorms Wildcat Project. 'Wildcats disappeared in lowland England around 1800. Then they vanished from Wales and northern England around 1860. Finally, they went from southern Scotland. All we have left is a few hundred around the Cairngorms and places like the Black Isle.'

F
However, it is not the loss of habitat that is causing the imminent extinction of the species. It is the spread of the domestic cat. Occasionally household animals go wild and create breeding colonies of feral cats. These form at the edges of villages and in farms. Some of these feral animals meet up with wildcats and they mate. Female wildcats become pregnant and give birth to kittens that are not purebred wildcats. Slowly the species loses its unique status and vigour and animals become hybridized.

G
'Estimates suggest that there are now up to a hundred thousand domestic cats that have gone feral in the Scottish Highlands,' says Piper. 'The fact that domestic cats can survive there in such numbers shows that they are a very resourceful species. However, that success – measured by their ever-growing population – shows the kind of trouble that the Highland wildcat is in today. They are being outbred.'

IELTS practice test

Questions 14–20

The text on page 107 has seven sections, **A–G**.

*Choose the correct heading for sections **A–G** from the list of headings below.*

*Write the correct number (**i–x**) in boxes 14–20 on your answer sheet.*

i	disagreement over the root cause of the problem
ii	a steady contraction in range can be identified
iii	evidence that suggests concerted action can be effective
iv	findings that appear to provide conclusive evidence
v	how new research helps to establish the wider context
vi	how to prevent hybridization of the species
vii	the detailed explanation behind the current crisis
viii	the significance of reciprocal benefits over time
ix	the alarming scale of an ongoing trend
x	a slightly less pessimistic assessment

14 Section **A** ....

15 Section **B** ....

16 Section **C** ....

17 Section **D** ....

18 Section **E** ....

19 Section **F** ....

20 Section **G** ....

Questions 21–24

Look at the following list of statements 21–24 and the list of species below.

Match each statement with the correct species.

*Write the correct letter **A–C** in boxes 21–24 on your answer sheet.*

21 This subspecies of cat is now prevalent in Scotland.
22 This subspecies of cat no longer lives in the wild in England.
23 This subspecies of cat has long been domesticated.
24 This subspecies of cat is not found in Scotland.

List of species
A Felis silvestris silvestris
B Felis silvestris lybica
C Felis silvestris cafra

21 ....

22 ....

23 ....

24 ....

Read the continuation of the text below and answer questions 25–30.

The urgency of the problem led conservationists to meet in Scotland recently to develop a plan to save the wildcat. 'We cannot wait for another couple of years to do a new census,' says Piper. 'We need to act immediately.' The exact nature of that plan has yet to be finalized but almost certainly involves the widescale neutering rather than the culling of feral cats. 'That will bring numbers down and take the pressure off the Highland wildcat,' says Piper. The situation is, therefore, not hopeless, a point that is reinforced by the example of the Iberian lynx, a feline whose story shares many features with the Highland wildcat. Ten years ago, there were only around a hundred of these equally magnificent hunters left in the wild. However, its prospects have been transformed by a rescue project that boosted numbers to more than three hundred and which could reach a thousand by the end of the decade.

I recently joined conservationists working on the Iberian lynx project and was struck by the enthusiasm and commitment of its staff – and by the considerable resources they needed to do their work. Having persuaded local hunters and landowners to stop shooting and laying down snares in lynx territory, conservationists have since been capturing animals and relocating young adult lynxes in protected territory. Captive breeding centres have also been established and animals reintroduced into the wild thanks to those programmes. Warrens of rabbits – a lynx's prime source of food – have also been established.

As a result, lynx numbers have bounced back, though we note the price tag. A total of €33m – most of it provided by the regional government of Andalucía – has been spent so far on saving the lynx. And that, we should note, is the level of expenditure that is likely to be needed to save the Scottish Highland wildcat. Some would consider that disproportionate, whilst others would think it money well spent. We should, however, also consider the larger issue: it is relatively easy to drive a species towards extinction, but it is very expensive to bring it back from the brink.

Questions 25–30

Complete the summary below.

Choose **NO MORE THAN TWO WORDS** *from the passage for each answer.*

Write your answers in boxes 25–30 on your answer sheet.

Conservationists in Scotland are planning to act to save their local wildcat from extinction. The **25** .... of large numbers of feral cats is likely to be a feature. The **26** .... that has helped the Iberian lynx may act as a useful model for their efforts. Although conservationists in Spain also had to tackle the problem of hunting, and have been successful in reducing the use of **27** .... in areas where the lynx live, their work has focussed on **28** .... certain animals in protected areas. Centres have been set up and the **29** .... programmes organized there have proved successful. The writer acknowledges that critics may regard the cost of saving such animals to be **30** .... , however.

SECTION 3 Questions 31–40

Read the text below and answer questions 31–40.

NATURE OR NURTURE?

For years, academics have been divided over whether human personality, intelligence and health are determined primarily by genetic inheritance (nature) or by environment (nurture). Genetics is a relatively new scientific discipline. It took a major step forward in 1953 when Watson and Crick deciphered the code for human DNA, a discovery which has led to a great many medical breakthroughs. Today, a member of the public can have their DNA tested by a commercial company for only a few hundred dollars. Indeed, we are now able to access information about genes with such ease that the revolution in the field of genetics is sometimes taken for granted.

It seems that every week, the media announces the discovery of a new gene – the intelligence gene, the obesity gene – there appears to be a gene for everything. Many people now believe that human character traits and diseases are determined by a single gene, but, while this is an appealing idea, it's wrong, says Tim Spector, a professor of genetics at King's College London; in reality, many common illnesses are controlled by hundreds or even thousands of genes. It's one example of how scientists are re-evaluating the wealth of evidence now available. Similarly, for years it was accepted that an individual's genes were fixed and couldn't be changed. However, recently, researchers found that the diet of pregnant mothers could alter the behaviour of their children's genes. This raises the radical possibility that genes can, in fact, be changed by environment.

Both sides of the nature versus nurture debate are being forced to reconsider core beliefs. Epidemiologists – those who argue for the importance of environment – have for decades been the most influential of the scientists investigating causes of disease, receiving the majority of funding and publicity. But while environmental factors – such as tea, coffee, sunshine and exercise – get huge media coverage, Professor Spector estimates that these can explain or predict less than 5% of most diseases, the only exception being smoking, which has repeatedly been identified as a direct cause of disease.

However, supporters of the genetic argument are not necessarily getting the upper hand in the nature versus nurture debate. This may be partly because even some specialists are surprisingly misinformed. According to one study, the majority of family doctors believe there are millions of genes in the body, when in reality it is thousands, an overestimate by a factor of at least 1000.

This isn't the only example of misinformation. Historically, the importance of the role of genes was supported by the famous Jims study, which investigated two identical twins named Jim, who were separated at birth. The study appeared to show that the brothers shared an extraordinary number of similarities in later life, despite growing up in different environments. This was presented as evidence that genes are more influential than environment. However, closer analysis revealed that the study was misrepresented by the media: the brothers' environments were still quite similar and many pronounced differences in their lives were not revealed to the public.

The issue of how to interpret data is also raised by geneticist Professor Steve Jones. He gives the example of obesity, which is believed to be 70% inheritable. This has led some to suggest that obesity is predetermined by our genes and that little can be done about it. But Professor Jones takes a different view. He argues that while some people may have a genetic predisposition to obesity, the obesity epidemic is new and results from changes in environment, particularly the greater consumption of sugary drinks. Obesity can be addressed, according to Professor Jones, by changing that environment, perhaps by taxing drinks manufacturers.

A similar issue concerns human height, which is heavily determined by genetics. Yet since the 1870s, average male height has increased by 11 cm. This must be a result of the changing environment, though whether in the form of medical care, superior nutrition, more exercise or some other factor remains an open question. A final example is that of Kenyan runners, who have achieved remarkable success as Olympic athletes. Because the Kenyans all come from the same area, it has been widely assumed that they share some genetic characteristics which account for their success. But in fact the runners are not genetically linked and their success appears to result from a range of environmental factors. It's just one further illustration of how evidence can be misleading.

So where does all of this leave the debate about nature versus nurture? Professor Spector maintains that the most significant finding of recent years is that genes don't work alone and are usually dependent on their environments. To move the debate forward, he argues, the two terms should not be seen as separate or exclusive. Instead, they are parts of the same process.

Questions 31–32

Choose the correct letter, A, B, C or D.

Write your answers in boxes 31–32 on your answer sheet.

31 In the first paragraph the writer concludes that

    A there is still a great deal to be learned about human genes.
    B the advances made in gene science are easily overlooked.
    C businesses should not make a profit from gene technology.
    D the importance of some gene research has been exaggerated.

32 What is the writer doing in the second paragraph?

    A criticizing the way some research has been conducted
    B illustrating the range of treatments that are now available
    C contrasting the findings of two different research studies
    D summarizing some problems with certain established theories

Questions 33–40

Do the following statements agree with the information given in the text?

In boxes 33–40 on your answer sheet, write

    TRUE   if the statement agrees with the information
    FALSE   if the statement contradicts the information
    NOT GIVEN if there is no information on this

33 In the past epidemiologists had less financial support than geneticists.

34 Research suggests that smoking is the most important known environmental factor affecting health.

35 Most family doctors think nature is more significant than nurture in causing diseases.

36 The way the Jims Study was reported gave people an inaccurate impression of the research.

37 Professor Steve Jones argues that obesity can be reduced by targeting genes.

38 Research has proved that humans are growing taller because of eating a better diet.

39 Kenyan runners have participated in research investigating their athletic performance.

40 Professor Spector believes the old distinction between genes and environment is no longer helpful.

WRITING TEST

TASK 1

You should spend about 20 minutes on this task.

> *There have been some problems caused by very bad weather in your area recently.*
>
> *Write a letter to the local newspaper. In your letter*
> - *describe the problems that were caused by the bad weather*
> - *explain how these problems have affected people's lives*
> - *suggest how the local community could be better prepared for bad weather in the future*

Write about 150 words.

You do not need to write any addresses.

Begin your letter like this:

Dear Sir,

TASK 2

You should spend about 40 minutes on this task.

Write about this topic.

> *Some people say that workers over the age of fifty-five should be forced to retire so that it is easier for young people to find jobs.*
>
> *Do you agree?*

Give reasons for your answer and include any relevant examples from your own knowledge or experience.

Write at least 250 words.

SPEAKING TEST

PART 1 – INTRODUCTION AND INTERVIEW

Let's talk about advertising.
- How much notice do you take of advertising in the media?
- Do you think advertising affects you when you're choosing things to buy?
- Which type of advertising do you think is most effective?
- Is there a type of advertising that you particularly like or dislike?

PART 2 – INDIVIDUAL LONG TURN

Candidate Task Card

> Describe your journey to work or school/college each day.
>
> You should say:
>
> > how you travel
> >
> > why you choose to travel in that way
> >
> > how efficient you feel this type of transport is
>
> and explain what would make your daily journey easier.

You will have to talk about the topic for one to two minutes.

You will have one minute to think about what you are going to say.

You can make some notes to help you if you wish.

Rounding-off questions
- What changes would you make to public transport in this area?
- Do you think more people should try to work from home using the internet?

PART 3 – TWO-WAY DISCUSSION

Let's consider first of all public transport in general.
- How often do you use public transport?
- What are the advantages and disadvantages of using public transport?
- How can people be encouraged to use public transport more?
- Should people be actively discouraged from using private cars? Why (not)?

Finally, let's talk about public transport in the future.
- What type of public transport do you think we should invest in for the future? Why?

Audioscripts

Unit 1

1

Hello, everyone. My name's Herb Sokolowski and I'm a college graduate, just like you. You might have heard of me, because I used to present a TV programme called *Weird Science*. Currently, I'm writing a book about scientific inventions, and when I was asked to come and speak to you, I thought I'd talk about that. But then I thought: 'What's the use of that? It'll probably only interest a few of them.' So instead, I'm going to give you some rules of life that I read about fifteen years ago in a book by a guy called Charles Sykes. I believe the book was called *Dumbing down our kids*. Before that, I had believed myself to be – as you probably do now – one entitled individual. But it changed my attitude and, who knows, perhaps it'll change yours. I've reduced the number of rules a bit and put them in my own words. So, are you ready? Here we go.

RULE 1: Life's not fair; get used to it.

RULE 2: You will not make eighty thousand dollars next year. You won't be a vice president with a car phone, not until you've earned the right.

RULE 3: If you think your teacher is tough, wait till you get a boss.

RULE 4: Flipping burgers is not beneath your dignity. Many years ago, your grandparents had a different word for burger flipping; they called it opportunity.

RULE 5: If you mess up, it's probably your own fault. So don't whine about your mistakes: learn from them.

RULE 6: You probably thought growing up that your parents were pretty boring. But they were like that because at the time they were paying your bills, cleaning your clothes and listening to you talk about how cool you are. So before you go off and save the world, clean up your own room.

RULE 7: Over the last 20 years, schools have abolished the idea of winners and losers – but life hasn't. In school, they give you as much time as you want to get the right answer. That rarely happens in real life.

RULE 8: Be nice to nerds. Sooner or later, you'll end up working for one.

2

One of the problems with advice is that people tend to interpret it to suit their own purposes. An example of this is the wisdom of the 18th-century economist, Adam Smith. One of his main ideas was that if you allow people to seek wealth for themselves, they will naturally create jobs and wealth for others. He called this 'the invisible hand'. People trying to improve their own situation also help their neighbour to improve theirs, but without meaning to, as if with an invisible hand. Unfortunately, a lot of people took Smith to mean that it was all right to be greedy and selfish and not to help others directly, which is not at all what he meant.

4

Like many islands, Great Britain and its language, English, have been subject to many influences over the centuries. What developed as a result is a language with a very rich and large vocabulary. Later in British history, the influenced would become an influencer, an exporter of its language and culture, to a point where its language again became subject to changes made by others who use it to communicate with each other in the worlds of business or academia.

The first influence is that of the Romans and their language, Latin. The legacy of the Romans is evident in the Latin-based or Romance languages that still survive in many Western European countries. However, after the fall of the Roman Empire in the fifth century, Britain was invaded by various Germanic peoples and it was their languages, notably Anglo-Saxon, or what is now known as Old English, that became the dominant force.

When William I of Normandy conquered Britain in 1066, he established French as the official language, but instead of replacing English, French was assimilated into it and Middle English, a close relation to the language, is still spoken in Britain today. This is a language made up of German vocabulary and simplified German grammar mixed with French-derived – often Latin-based – words. The language continued to remain quite organic until the invention of the printing press and the wider publication of the written word, when it started to become standardized. You can see this very clearly if you compare the writing of the poet Chaucer in the 14th century, which is difficult to understand without reference to a glossary, with Shakespeare's writing two centuries later. Shakespeare is not easy, but in fact it is relatively similar to the English of today.

From this point in history – the 17th century through to the end of the 19th century – British colonialism thrived. This had two implications for the English language: the first was the importation into the language of yet more words – *pyjama* and *bungalow*, for example, from India; the second was the spread of English around the globe – to India, America, East Africa and so on. With its spread came adaptation. Each country stamped its own mark on the language used, making it something different from the English spoken in Britain. The writer George Bernard Shaw famously spoke of Britain and America as 'two nations divided by a common language'. The new English-speaking settlers in America were keen to set their language and their country apart from Britain, and so brought in new words and new spellings, as well as a new, more direct style of speaking.

People have argued that English was successful in its global reach because it was a versatile and flexible language. But in fact its spread had far more to do with economic factors. People needed a language to do business and English was in the right place at the right time.

Which brings us to the present day and to a situation where many versions of English now exist. The writer Robert McCrum has identified two types in particular: English as spoken by native speakers in different countries around the world and Globish, a simplified form of the language used by non-native speakers to communicate on matters of business or work. According to McCrum, this is a utilitarian kind of English where you learn a limited vocabulary – maybe 1,500 words at most – and grammar, enough to enable you to do your job at the call centre, for example.

Although this characterization is too simplistic – there are many shades and versions of English between Globish and the language of Shakespeare – it does make an important point: that English, like any language, is a tool that people adapt and exploit to suit their needs. No one version is right or wrong; the question, rather, is which version you aspire to speak.

Audioscripts

5
Conversation 1
T: What did you think of the talk?
A: Yeah, I thought it was really interesting: a lot of food for thought.
T: Sorry, I should have introduced myself. I'm Teresa. I'm one of the conference organizers.
A: Good to meet you, Teresa. I'm Ana Muñoz, from Deusto University in Spain.
T: Oh, yes, I've heard of that. Whereabouts in Spain is it?
A: In San Sebastián, in the north.
T: Oh yes, where the Guggenheim museum is. Fabulous building.
A: No, I think you're thinking of Bilbao. We're not a million miles from there, but it's a different branch of the university. Are you an academic too, Teresa?
T: Yes, I lecture in Social Sciences at Toronto University.
A: Really? That's my field as well. Look, I'm going to get a coffee before the next session. Do you fancy joining me?
T: Yeah, that'd be great. Um ... let me just get rid of all these papers and I'll come over to the coffee area.

Conversation 2
K: Is this the right place for the bus into the city centre?
J: Yes, it is. We've just missed one, I'm afraid. But they come every twenty minutes. Where are you heading?
K: I've just flown in from Amman in Jordan and now I'm going to my university accommodation.
J: OK. So, you have the address.
K: Yes.
J: Is it near the centre?
K: Yes, I think so. It's in Princes Street.
J: OK. That's very central – and near the bus station. But you've got a big bag, so I think your best bet would be to get a taxi when we get off. What are you going to be studying ... um, sorry, I didn't ask your name?
K: My name is Khalid. It's nice to meet you.
J: Hi, Khalid. Yeah, good to meet you too. I'm Jeff, by the way. So, what are going to be studying, Khalid?
K: I'm doing an M.Sc. in Quantum Physics.
J: Wow, that sounds impressive. Way above my head, I'm afraid .... I'm just a primary school teacher ... Hey, I think this is our bus now ...

6
1 What did you think of the exhibition?
2 Do you fancy going out for some fresh air?
3 What kind of company is it, exactly?
4 What's it like being the only boy in a family of girls?
5 Sorry, I should have mentioned that before.
6 How are you finding the course?
7 Shall we go and get a coffee or something?
8 So, have you been here before?

7
A= Antony, MA =Model answer
A: Hi there, I don't think we've met. I'm Antony.
MA: Hi, Antony. Good to meet you. I'm José.
A: So, how do you know Nicola?
MA: We're old friends. We were at school together, actually. And you?
A: Oh. I work with Nicola's husband ... at an electronics firm. So, are you from around here?
MA: No, I live in Spain. I'm just visiting.
A: Oh, I see. And what do you think of the city? Is it your first time here?
MA: Yes, it is. I'm really enjoying it, actually; though I have to say, I find it a bit expensive.
A: And what have you done while you've been here? Have you been to any of the museums or anything?
MA: Not yet. I only got here two days ago. I've walked around the centre a bit and I've done a bit of sightseeing.
A: I'm supposed to take my kids on a sightseeing boat at the weekend. They've never been on one. Have you?
MA: Yes, I've been on one in Paris. But it was raining the whole time so the views weren't fantastic. Still, the kids will love it, I'm sure.

8
So, everyone. There have been various rumours about what paid and unpaid time off staff are entitled to, and so the management would like to clarify the company's position so that everyone is clear on the situation. A short document will be sent to everyone's work email address to formalize these arrangements in a couple of weeks, but as I said, I just wanted to set the record straight now by talking to you. So, first off – sabbaticals, that's to say paid leave from work. The policy is that everyone on pay grade six or above is entitled to three months' sabbatical every six years worked. This applies only to full-time employees and not to part-time employees. Arrangements for part-time employees are being discussed, but these arrangements are to be confirmed.

Secondly, unpaid leave. This is purely at the discretion of your line manager. He or she will decide each case on the circumstances of the employee. For example, if they have a difficult situation at home, such as sick or elderly parents. Having said that, normally no unpaid leave will be allowed for any employee who's worked in the company for less than eighteen months.

9
Now I've called everyone here today because we're about to test out a radical new idea, which is to set no limits on how much or how little holiday each member of staff can take. That's right – no limits. Initially the company is going to try this new policy out for a limited period, that's to say six months. That's because we're not entirely sure if it's going to work or not, but we're pretty confident.

What are the reasons for this policy? Well, we think that it's much better to be adult and responsible about this. We all have busy working lives with meetings to go to and targets to reach. And we all also have busy lives outside work, with families to look after and interests to pursue. If we're given a little freedom, we can organize our own time better.

So what are your responsibilities in this new scheme? Note that this is not an excuse to take as much time off work as possible. Nor is it something you can organize completely independently: you'll still have to negotiate with colleagues in case the timing of your holiday disrupts business in some way. You'll also still have your work targets to reach.

And finally the details. The exact start date is to be confirmed, but it will begin in the second half of this year. The policy applies to every employee including part-time staff. It will be reviewed after approximately four months. And that's it. Any questions?

Unit 2

10
Take a walk on the mountain slopes of the Tibetan Plateau in May or June, and you are likely to come across groups of people on their hands and knees, intently searching the grass for something they cannot find. It's as if someone had dropped a valuable ring, and then asked their friends and relatives to come and help them search for it.

Actually, what they're looking for is a small fungus called *yartsa gunbu* which is so prized in China for its medicinal properties that half a kilo has been known to sell for up to $50,000. Not surprising, perhaps, when you realize

115

how difficult it is to find. One couple I talked to had been searching all day and found only thirty specimens.

Yartsa gunbu occurs in very specific conditions. Only found on the Tibetan plateau and the Himalayas, the mushroom is formed when the larva of a particular type of moth hatches underground and becomes infected with the fungus. As the larva grows into a caterpillar, the fungus eats it from the inside. In late spring, the fungus sends a brown stalk up through the dead caterpillar's head and out of the ground. It is this tiny stalk that the worm diggers are searching for.

For centuries, herbal doctors have prescribed *yartsa gunbu* for all sorts of medical problems: back pain, fatigue, asthma, poor eyesight. The Chinese are convinced it revitalizes a person's 'chi' or 'life energy'. Legend says that yaks that eat it grow ten times stronger. Now, with China's growing wealth, demand for *yartsa gunbu* has soared and so has the income of the locals who farm it. Thousands of poor Tibetan yak herders now own motorcycles and iPhones and flat-screen TVs. Some are even more successful. Zhaxicaiji, a former yak herder, started her own *yartsa* company in 1998 and, since then, the business has grown year on year. It now has twenty stores and a turnover of $60 million.

These communities are thriving on *yartsa gunbu*'s rarity. But that very rarity may also be their downfall. The harvest is currently roughly 400 million specimens, and ecologists say that if this overpicking does not stop and some stalks are not left in the ground, the cycle will stop, because the fungus that infects the larvae will have disappeared. Perhaps the next generation of golden worm diggers will be searching harder than ever.

🎧 11

/ɪ/	/iː/	/aɪ/
medicinal	previous	private
specimen	kilo	unscientific
specific	visa	survive
caterpillar		prescribe
artist		tiny
		revitalize
		financial

🎧 12

I = Interviewer, J = John
- I: So, John, how did you come across this story?
- J: I've been travelling in this region for many years and I'd seen this phenomenon before but never paid it much attention.
- I: And what was it that interested you this time?
- J: Well, often you'll visit a place with a particular story in mind. Then, while you're researching it, you find something else catches your interest.
- I: And what was that in this case?
- J: I was very struck by how well off people in the village seemed compared to when I'd last visited. So I decided to investigate and got this amazing story of the golden worm.

🎧 13

P = Presenter, RE = Daniel Raven-Ellison
- P: Could you cross a forest without touching the ground? What would you see if you walked through your entire city taking a photo every eight steps? How would it feel to locate a missing cat and return it to its owner? How far could you walk sucking on the same mint? This is geography Daniel Raven-Ellison style. A former geography teacher, Raven-Ellison uses films, books, websites and walks to take geography beyond memorizing dots on a map, challenging children and adults to experience every aspect of the world around them in a more meaningful, surprising way. Here is Daniel Raven-Ellison.
- RE: The internet makes us feel the world is becoming smaller and more available, but at the same time, many real, lived experiences are shrinking. For children, outdoor exploration improves mental and physical health, expands learning through risk taking, spurs innovative problem solving, and encourages empathy by meeting different people; yet too few children are allowed to play outdoors nowadays. As adults, although we share our cities with millions of other people, many of us are more disconnected than ever before, moving from the island of our home to the island of our car to the island of our office without meaningfully engaging with each other, nature or the places in between. But for our ancestors, adventure was normal. Adventure has now become something we only watch on TV though. In fact, there are amazing adventures to be had right outside our doorsteps.
- P: For Raven-Ellison, this road to adventure is 'guerrilla geography': asking people to challenge their preconceptions about places, engage in social and environmental justice, and form deeper community connections. His *Urban Earth* films demonstrate guerrilla geography in action. He created them by walking across Mumbai, Mexico City, London, and ten other UK and US cities from one extreme edge to the other, while photographing whatever lay directly in front of him every eight steps. All photos, edited together, become a film portrait of each city. Raven-Ellison again.
- RE: Travel shows and guidebooks select what they want you to see. They twist things. My films give you an unaltered look at the reality of a city as a whole. When you're not protected by the speed or armour of a car, you see what's actually happening neighbourhood by neighbourhood.
- P: With more than half of the world's people living in urban areas, Raven-Ellison hopes the films will break down boundaries that isolate communities. He says that we need to engage with each other to reduce conflict, instead of being afraid to explore certain neighbourhoods.
  Raven-Ellison's films have inspired innovative walks for groups. He starts by handing the map to someone else. In one walk, he launched ten teams of people from different points outside London, all headed towards the city centre, converging at a pub where they compared experiences and shared ideas about how to improve Britain's neighbourhoods.
- RE: The act of actually walking and experiencing that space gives you a different, more tangible perspective of our environmental impacts.
- P: The educational project *Mission: Explore* has guerrilla geography incorporated into its children's programmes. They've developed a website and series of books with hundreds of challenges that show geography's fun side, including mini field trips, neighbourhood explorations and creative science experiments. It's a hands-on format that's very accessible to children. Many of the tasks seem fun and simple but actually require quite high-level thinking. One challenge suggests children conduct a survey to see how friendly their community is, write to their local politicians with the findings, and offer ways the community could be improved for children. Another proposes you blindfold yourself and get a friend to help you explore by using your other senses. I'll leave you with a last word from Raven-Ellison.
- RE: Memorizing things for quizzes isn't enough. Children need to have skills for interpretation, analysis and understanding. Education can't be based just on how much you know, but must also be measured by how creative and innovative you can be. Giving children time and space to explore outdoors allows moments to happen that will be crucial for tackling issues like climate change, water shortages and other big problems.

Audioscripts

14
I = Interviewer, H = Hiroki Katagawa
I: So, can you tell me a little about yourself, Hiroki, and what attracted you to this graduate training programme?
H: So. Er … yes, thank you. My name is Hiroki Katagawa. I'm 24 years old and I'm master … I have a master's degree in Business Administration. So, my first degree was in Town Planning, um … Urban Planning. I spent one year in Japan working on a metro and transport hub in the city of Osaka – it's a major city on Honshu island. It was for work experience and I received a commendation when I left the project. So this is what attracted me to your company … because you are involved in such infrastructure projects.
I: And why do you think you are suited to this particular programme?
H: I have good planning and organization, and up-to-date IT skills. Perhaps you would like me to give you an example. In Osaka, I helped design the programme for planning work schedules for the staff working …
I: Sorry, you designed the programme or you were using bespoke software?
H: I'm sorry, what?
I: Was that software you adapted or created?
H: Oh no, it was a well-known programme used in Japan, but I had to adapt it, yes … So, as I was saying, it was for planning schedules for staff working on tramlines in the city. This work had to be arranged with the consent of the local authorities, the transport office of Osaka.
I: OK. Well, that is very relevant to what we do here …
H: And you also asked me about my suitability for this programme. I am very keen to join an international company. I am very open to different cultures, very interested in different cultures. I like travel very much and have made many friends and contacts in different countries. This is important for me – to work and live together with people from other cultures. I love to learn different approaches to life … in fact, in general I am very enthusiastic to learn.
I: OK. Thank you, Hiroki. A little earlier we gave you a form …

16
I = Interviewer, MA = Model answer
1
I: So can you tell me a little about yourself and what attracted you to this job?
MA: Yes, my name is Eduardo Torres and I'm a graduate in Hotel Management. I have been working for the last year at a country hotel and I would like to get a job with a bigger chain of hotels.
2
I: And what would you say your strongest qualities are?
MA: I'm well organized and I'm good at solving problems. In fact, I love the challenge of dealing with clients' problems and trying to find the best solution.
3
I: I see. And why do you think you would be suited to this particular hotel?
MA: I know this is a prestigious international hotel, so I imagine the challenge to maintain good standards is very high.

Unit 3

17
Speaker 1
You've probably heard of Glastonbury. It's in the west of England. It's fairly well-known around the world for its music festival, which is massive – over 170,000 people go each year. It takes place in the month of July on some agricultural land near the town, which is owned by a local farmer. Well, I live in the town of Glastonbury, which is not the same thing. I actually remember when it was just a small market town like others in the area: gentle countryside around it, pleasant period houses, a beautiful church, a few tea houses and quaint shops. All in all, it was quite a sleepy, traditional kind of English town. Well, that was before Glastonbury festival got big in the seventies and the hippies began to move in – I guess people had had such a transformative experience at the festival that they thought they'd stay to keep the magic alive somehow. Well, now the town is a rather odd mix of older, more conservative residents – I don't want to put myself in that category, mind you – and younger people who want an alternative lifestyle. So these days the High Street is full of vegetarian restaurants, second-hand music shops, bookshops that specialize in magic and ancient mysteries, shops selling healing crystals … it's all a bit wacky, really, but actually I quite like it!

Speaker 2
Ghent isn't my hometown but it was my adopted town for a while. Actually, it might be cheating slightly to call it a town. It's got around 250,000 inhabitants, which makes it more like a city, but it doesn't feel like a city, because it's quite compact. They say Ghent is Belgium's best-kept secret, because it's such an attractive place and yet remains relatively unknown. It doesn't get the number of visitors that Bruges or Brussels gets, which is also a bit odd because it's exactly halfway between the two. I guess part of its charm is that it's so many things rolled into one: it's a university town, a historic town, a port, an industrial town. So on one hand it feels a little like a working town, because of the industry around the old docks: there's a huge steel mill, a truck assembly plant, Europe's biggest fruit juice terminal … they say. But on the other hand, if you don't see that part, it seems like a well-preserved historic town. I was a student there and I had an amazing time. It was really lively and friendly. One of the benefits of having that kind of mix – I mean, old and new, academic and industrial – is that people tend to be quite open-minded and accepting. There's also masses to do – a good music scene, interesting museums and galleries, beautiful architecture, nice parks – but going out isn't particularly cheap. The other drawback is the weather, which is pretty terrible most of the time – grey and rainy. I'm from Italy and, I have to say, it got me down a bit at times.

19
A: How was your trip to Russia?
B: Great, thanks. We had quite a packed schedule, but it was very interesting. We started in Moscow and saw the sights around Red Square. Strangely, the thing I loved most was the metro. Each station is like a work of art in itself. The service is pretty efficient too.
A: And how did it compare to St Petersburg?
B: Very different. St Petersburg is a very grand and gracious city. Actually, it feels a bit closer in atmosphere to other cities in central Europe, whereas Moscow doesn't feel particularly European. But that's the thing about Russia. You don't realize what an enormous and diverse country it is until you travel there.

21
J = Jim, K = Kirsten Sommer
J: So I'm here with architectural historian Kirsten Sommer to talk about the subject of biomimetics and why it's relevant to architecture today. Kirsten, biomimetics – which I should explain to any listeners who are not familiar with the term – is the idea of

K: copying good design from nature and applying it to things that are man-made. It's something I associate more with material science and robotics, and things like that. But I think you've found strong evidence of it in the history of architecture too.

K: Yes, hello Jim, that's right. But first of all, I think we should be careful perhaps about how we label these things. We need to separate the term biomimetics, which was coined in the 1950s, from the practice of simply taking inspiration from nature's forms, which is obviously a much older phenomenon. The term Biomimetics is now used for the development of new technologies – like man-made fibres that can imitate the properties of duck feathers, or hi-tech swimsuits that replicate shark skin. A classic example of it is Velcro, which imitates barbs on the head of a thistle plant. But for a long time – and still very much today – architects have taken inspiration from the forms and shapes of nature.

J: Can you give us an example?

K: Yes, um … probably the best known building of this kind is Gaudi's Sagrada Familia in Barcelona …

J: That's not even finished yet, is it?

K: No. Its history is complicated, but before his death in 1926 Gaudi left very clear instructions – in the form of three-dimensional models – as to how he'd like it finished. The date for completion is now 2026. But anyway, Gaudi loved nature and understood that the natural world is full of curved forms, not straight lines. So with organic models in mind and the materials that nature uses to create its structures: wood, muscle, tendon, etc., he created a very organic-looking building in the Sagrada Familia, an architectural form that borrowed from nature in a way that no one had seen before.

J: It is, or certainly was, a controversial building, wasn't it?

K: Oh, absolutely. It's one of those buildings that people either love or hate. George Orwell called it 'one of the most hideous buildings in the world'. Others, like the surrealists, loved its originality and took Gaudi to their hearts. Gaudi's own explanation for its originality was that it had 'returned to the origin', in other words it was original in the sense that it had gone back to nature.

J: And who is using biomimetics these days in architecture?

K: Oh, my goodness, there are so many examples. You only have to look at the names of buildings to tell you that: The Swiss Re Tower in London is known as 'the Gherkin'; the Olympic stadium in Beijing, which people called the 'Bird's Nest'; Frank Gehry's 'Fish' in Barcelona. But it's about more than just the external shape and appearance of buildings. Architects are using biomimetics to create more environmentally friendly buildings.

J: Yes, I read about the Eastgate Centre in Harare being innovative in that way.

K: Yes, that's a very good example. It's not only unusual to look at – modern office and shopping complexes are typically all steel and glass these days. What's more interesting is the use of chimneys to imitate the heating and cooling system in a termite mound. It's called passive cooling, and it's very energy efficient and does away with the need for a modern air conditioning system. It works by storing heat that is generated inside the building in the walls and then letting this heat escape through the chimneys at night, so the building is nice and cool the following morning.

22

A: Well, first of all, I should say that I think it's basically a good idea – it's got a lot of things to recommend it: principally, that people won't have to waste time going down to the canteen to get their coffee. Also it'll encourage employee interaction, which of course is a good thing. But I have to say there's a risk in that, because if you make an area that's too comfortable or convivial, they might spend just as much time there as they did going down to the canteen – in other words, away from productive work.

B: I kind of disagree with that. The thing about an open-plan office is that it feels rather large and impersonal, and so the idea of putting in some area that feels more intimate and homely really appeals to me. I think you have to be careful about terms like 'productive work'. You said yourself that employee interaction was something to be encouraged and I think that can take different forms – from formal meetings to informal chats. The informal chats are something we shouldn't underestimate the importance of. What I mean is, if we assume that people relaxing and having coffee at work are wasting the company's time, then for me that is a sad state of affairs. So I'm very much in favour of this proposal, particularly given that we are all working in a rather impersonal environment, as I said before. Oh, and by the way, including a screen with industry news on it in the room is a clever touch.

25

C = Colleague, MA = Model answer

1
C: Would you prefer to have a large living space or somewhere that's small and cosy?
MA: Personally, I'd like to have a lot of space, but maybe that seems a bit selfish. After all, it's not a choice everyone can make.

2
C: Do you think that the architecture around you affects how you are feeling?
MA: Yes, I think it probably does. Not consciously maybe, but I don't think you should underestimate its impact.

3
C: I've heard it said that 80% of people end up living no more than 30 kilometres from where they were born. I think that's a rather surprising statistic.
MA: Do you? I disagree. I think most people like to stay near their family and friends. And also it's pretty clear that the bond that we form with our surroundings as we grow up is very strong.

4
C: I don't think there's enough new and radical design in architecture. There is for a few people who are prepared to pay for it, but most new buildings are just boring.
MA: I agree completely. A lot of new buildings either copy existing designs or go for the cheapest design. I'm in favour of people trying out new things and I don't think new always means more expensive.

Unit 4

28

There are three things you can do when you meet a physical obstacle – go round it, go over it or go under it. Now, imagine that physical obstacle is the traffic in our cities. We've already tried going round it by building ring roads around our cities, but, actually, such solutions are never likely to work because just as new channels around a sandcastle on the beach fill with water, so new roads fill with cars as soon as you build them.

That leaves two options: to build new traffic systems in the air or underground. But either way, rather than removing the problem, you might just be moving it somewhere else. The problem with the former is that collisions or accidents in the air could also have an impact on those below when debris falls from a height. The problem with the latter has always been the expense.

Until now that is. Because American entrepreneur Elon Musk thinks he has an answer. And given his amazing record of not only finding, but also implementing innovative solutions, there's a good chance that he could pull this off.

His latest venture, The Boring Company, proposes building a network of tunnels under cities that transports vehicles on high-speed electric sleds. The key to making this happen will be by speeding up the tunnelling process and making it a lot cheaper. Musk's idea is that by using smaller single-lane tunnels and more efficient boring or tunnelling machines, his techniques should reduce the cost enormously. Vehicles would then travel down each tunnel at high speeds and only in one direction, so that there would be nothing to block them or hold them up. In his mind, also, is the idea that in future, the tunnels will possibly use vacuum technology, in which pods carrying cars can travel at speeds of up to 900 kilometres per hour. This technology, part of Musk's so-called Hyperloop project, has already been tried and tested in an over-ground transport tube system in California.

30
P = Presenter, F = Freya Wint
P: Philanthropy is back in fashion – some say in America it never went out of fashion. Now a new generation of internet and mobile communications billionaires are supporting good causes like never before. The difference is that so many more of these do-gooders are self-made businessmen and women, whereas in the past they were individuals who relied on inherited wealth. Are there other differences between these philanthropists and their 19th-century counterparts? I put this question to social historian Freya Wint.
F: Very definitely. The philanthropists of the 19th-century tended to set up long-term foundations and scholarships so that their legacies would benefit future generations. What you have now is a number of people – Bill Gates being the most famous – who have made money relatively quickly in their lifetime and are now actively involved in doing good with it … and enjoying themselves. 'Giving while living' is the slogan.
P: And is there a difference in the way they give?
F: Oh, certainly. Because they are more hands-on, they are also more concerned to see the short-term benefits of what they are doing. In many cases, they treat their giving in much the same way as they treat their other business investments; they even describe their programmes in business terms like 'getting a good return on capital', 'making stakeholders accountable', and 'setting agreed and measurable targets'. The money they put into philanthropic projects is like seed money – they want to see the projects grow and prosper by themselves, become self-sustaining eventually.
P: Have you got any concrete examples of that?
F: Yes, a good example is Jeff Skoll, the Canadian founder of eBay, which is the world's largest online marketplace. He set up something called the Skoll Foundation which supports and promotes social entrepreneurship. The foundation aims to identify people and ideas that are already helping to bring about positive change in areas where social problems exist. I was particularly struck reading about one of the entrepreneurs he backed, a woman called Daniela Papi. She used to run voluntourism projects in Cambodia, where volunteers paid to come and help build schools there. But she soon realized that a more long-term and sustainable approach would be to promote teacher training and curriculum development in the schools. Then she realized that in these volunteers that came on her programme there was great potential … for them to go to other places and bring about positive change there. So now she focuses on that aspect too. I just thought that was a great example of how a little money behind the right person can develop into a much wider benefit and I think that's what today's philanthropists are all about.
P: So is there none of the old-fashioned 'no strings attached' kind of giving anymore?
F: Oh no … there are still a lot of donations – rather than investments – made to people who are in a bad situation and can't help themselves – medicines for HIV sufferers, water and food supplies for those who have been hit by drought or famine. John Caudwell, the man who made his fortune in the mobile phone business, gives most of his money to disabled children. He's a self-confessed capitalist who believes in people helping themselves, but he recognizes that there are some people that aren't born lucky like him. Essentially, by providing them with wheelchairs or walking aids, he's giving them greater independence and opportunity. I'd say that was very typical of the ethos of the new philanthropists. There's more emphasis on self-help than with former philanthropists.
P: It must make them feel good too.
F: Oh, absolutely. No one wants to be remembered only as the person who made a billion selling phones or laptops – they want to be remembered for the contribution they made to making the world a better place.

31
We have designed a school bag for children. What's so original about that, you ask? Well, this is a bag that also functions as a desk. So you can fold it out and work at it, anytime and anywhere you like. Why would children want to do that, when they have a desk at school and a table at home? Well, simply because not all children do have a desk at school or even a table at home. I'd like you to stop and just think about that for a minute. Our ambition for this school bag is that it will not only be used by children in Europe but also in developing countries. Because that is where it will really come into its own. It has numerous compartments for notebooks, pens and a water holder. Hydration, as you know, is very important for concentration. But how will people in poorer countries be able to afford the bag? Well, that's why we call it the Solidarity Bag. Because we're setting the price a little higher here in Europe to help lower the cost of a bag for a family in a developing country. So when you pay 35 euros for the bag here, you are helping to bring the price down to an affordable level elsewhere, showing solidarity with families less fortunate than you.

33
I = Investor, MA = Model answer
1
I: Can you just explain to me what your ambition is for this product?

MA: Yes. We would like it to have successful sales in Europe and on the basis of that to be able to provide many of these bags to children in developing countries.

2
I: And do you think that customers will support this ambition?
MA: Yes, I think that it's very important for people nowadays to feel they can do some good when they buy things. People want ethical products.

3
I: But the price of the bag is quite high for European customers.
MA: It is quite high, but it is a good-quality bag and I think people are prepared to pay a little extra for an ethical product.

4
I: And do you think the fact that it can function also as a desk is useful for children in Europe?
MA: It's not as useful as it is for children in some developing countries. But I think it is a feature that they will enjoy and it might encourage them to work in places where they didn't before.

5
I: And if we invest, what will you use the money for?
MA: The most important thing for us is to make people aware of the Solidarity Bag. So we will invest in an advertising and publicity campaign.

Unit 5

34

Maybe like me, you're one of those people who used to look at organized tours and think – never in a million years! Why would I want to be herded around like a sheep with a group of people I've never met before, tied to a strict schedule and taken to all the obvious tourist places rather than the more undiscovered ones? What I want from travel is a bit of independence and freedom.

Well, that's what I *used* to think. And the thing that changed my mind was a guided tour I took at the Metropolitan Museum of Art in New York. I was in New York on holiday and it was raining hard, so I dived into the museum to escape the rain. Don't get me wrong – I do like visiting museums; this just happened to be an unplanned visit. So I wandered over to the information desk and asked what was on and they said that, among other things, there was a tour of the museum's early Christian art collection and it was going to begin in a few minutes. OK, I thought to myself, it'll be an experience, if nothing else ... so, not holding out much hope, I joined it. Well, it *was* an experience – a really *good* one. Because rather than wander round the museum looking at 200 objects and not really taking in any of them properly, as I would normally have done, we were shown by this incredibly knowledgeable guide just a small number of ... maybe five or six really interesting artefacts. She explained the story and context behind each one in lots of detail – and it was fascinating. The experience didn't quite inspire me to want to become an expert on early Christian art, but it did make me reassess my whole attitude to organized tours.

A year later I went on a guided trip to Italy. Again, the guides were brilliant – mostly qualified archaeologists and historians. You know, to get that much information about somewhere, you'd have to do weeks, probably months, of reading beforehand. What surprised me too was how knowledgeable and interesting some of the other travellers were – not the sheep I'd ignorantly thought they'd be before ...

There are lots of other benefits too. Your transport, hotel, food: it's all taken care of; all the visits are pre-arranged, so you don't have to book anything. The convenience factor is *not* to be underestimated, like particularly if it's a more remote or not-so-safe place you're visiting. Imagine all the pressure and anxiety from planning and booking and missed connections that it cuts out. It's so liberating.

And, talking of liberating, what about free time? It's actually a myth that organized tours are too regimented – in fact, they've always factored in free time for people to go off and explore by themselves and these days they're even more sensitive to that than ever. A lot of operators offer you the option of not going on excursions if you'd prefer to make your own itinerary.

35
1 I do wish I had been able to spend more time there.
2 He did say that he'd help us.
3 We do prefer to take holidays close to home.
4 She does get very sunburnt.

37
1 Would you like to come to dinner one evening?
2 Do you need to borrow a pen?
3 Are you coming?
4 I didn't get the assistant manager job.
5 Are you going away this summer?
6 Do you like detective stories?
7 What are you doing here so early?

38
I've been on a few mystery tours, but the one I did in Prague was probably the best. And I'm not the only person to say so. If you look at reviews, you'll hardly find one negative one. I'm not going to give you too many details because that would spoil the surprise if one day you happened to do it too. What I will tell you is that it started at night and involved a segway, some canoes, a jazz band and a large breakfast. If that hasn't aroused your curiosity, I don't know what will.

39
Now when I was a little chap I had a passion for maps. I would look for hours at South America, or Africa, or Australia, and lose myself in all the glories of exploration. At that time there were many blank spaces on the earth, and when I saw one that looked particularly inviting on a map (but they all look that) I would put my finger on it and say, 'When I grow up I will go there.' The North Pole was one of these places, I remember. Well, I haven't been there yet, and shall not try now. The glamour is gone. Other places were scattered about the hemispheres. I have been in some of them, and ... well, we won't talk about that. But there was one yet – the biggest, the most blank, so to speak – that I had a hankering after.

True, by this time it was not a blank space any more. It had got filled since my boyhood with rivers and lakes and names. It had ceased to be a blank space of delightful mystery – a white patch for a boy to dream gloriously over. It had become a place of darkness. But there was in it one river especially, a mighty big river, that you could see on the map, resembling an immense snake uncoiled, with its head in the sea, its body at rest curving afar over a vast country, and its tail lost in the depths of the land. And as I looked at the map of it in a shop-window, it fascinated me as a snake would a bird – a silly little bird. Then I remembered there was a Company for trade on that river. Dash it all! I thought to myself, they can't trade without using some kind of craft on that lot of fresh water – steamboats! Why shouldn't I try to get charge of one?

I went on along Fleet Street, but could not shake off the idea. The snake had charmed me.

I got my appointment – of course; and I got it very quick. It appears the Company had received news that one of their captains had been killed in a scuffle with the natives. Soon after I left in a French steamer, and she called in every port they have out there. I watched the coast. Watching a coast as it slips by the ship is like thinking about an enigma. There it is before you – smiling or frowning, grand or mean, insipid, or savage, and always mute with an air of whispering, 'Come and find out.' This one was almost featureless, with an aspect of monotonous grimness. The edge of a colossal jungle, so dark-green as to be almost black, fringed with white surf, ran straight, like a ruled line, far, far away along a blue sea.

40

Very few people still hitchhike, these days. We all know that it can be dangerous. And actually, why would you take the risk when there are so many other cheap options available, like Megabus? But if you have the time – and that's important 'cos it's generally not a quick way to travel – if you have the time, you *can* have some amazing experiences. A year ago, a group of us from university had a competition to see who could get to Barcelona the quickest by hitchhiking. We were in pairs and we all set off from different points in London. Amazingly, within about ten minutes of our standing on the slip road to the motorway, we got a lift with a lorry driver who said he was going all the way to the Spanish border. We couldn't believe our luck. Once in France we drove for about six hours and then around midnight, the driver said he had to stop to get some sleep. He pulled over at a resting point, which by chance, happened to have an area for pitching tents. Thinking it would be better not to disturb him, we got out and put up our little tent.

The following morning, we woke up early, ready to get back in the lorry, but to our dismay, it had gone. We sat down and tried to rationalize the situation: he'd probably just had an emergency and couldn't help leaving in a hurry; we'd probably get another lift before too long – if anyone else stopped here – but the place was actually deserted. Feeling pretty miserable, we started to pack up our tent. But just at that moment, we heard a loud horn sounding. It was our driver. He pulled up, jumped out the lorry and produced three cups of coffee and some fresh croissants.

41

Long vowel sound: amazement, annoyance, delight, dismay, frustration, relief, surprise

Short vowel sound: astonishment, embarrassment, horror, regret, shock

42

F = Friend, MA = Model answer
F: So, tell me what happened?
M: Well, a couple of weeks ago I got the train to go and visit my aunt. She lives in Newville.
F: And what went wrong?
M: I was really tired because I had been up late the night before and I started to doze.
F: Did you wake up in time for your stop?
M: No, to my horror, I woke up just as the train was leaving Newville and the next station was fifty kilometres away.
F: Oh no! What did you do?
M: Well, luckily, there was a really nice conductor on the train. And he explained to me the quickest way to get back to my station from the next stop. He also put a note on my ticket saying I didn't need to pay again.

Unit 6

43

In 1968, the Beatles turned up in Rishikesh to study transcendental meditation at Maharishi Mahesh Yogi's ashram. They wrote about forty songs here, many of which ended up on their famous *White Album*. I hadn't come to write music, but to get over chronic back pain – one of my vertebrae being severely out of line – or at least put off the day when I would have to face back surgery.

Perched above the Ganges River, Rishikesh is now a shopping mall for those looking for mental and physical healing, pulling in hundreds of thousands of foreign visitors each year. My chosen retreat was the Parmarth Niketan Ashram, which is less strict than other ashrams and allows guests to come and go as they please. I had also been attracted by the fact that it supports around 200 disadvantaged boys – some orphaned – putting them up in simple accommodation, and providing them with food and a basic education.

At 6.50 a.m. on the first day, I found myself sitting in a plain room with a wooden floor, white walls and a metal roof. We worked on a breathing technique that involved inhaling and exhaling through one nostril at a time. There were no other distractions – no New Age tunes playing, no yoga outfits, no blinding heat, no incense and no attitude; just students and a teacher. Meals were conducted in silence, something which I found odd at first but came to appreciate. During one of the meals, another guest sitting across the 20-centimetre high table broke this silence to comment on how horribly fast I ate. I felt a little taken aback, but thanked him and noted the point.

The yoga carried on in a serene way for two weeks, never causing me even to break sweat. In fact, more than once I wondered how it could be helping me. Yet by the end of my visit, the simple lessons – stretch, breathe, eat more slowly and more healthily, relax – had an effect. I can now touch my toes and even sit cross-legged for thirty minutes through a meal. My back? The persistent pain hasn't entirely gone away, but it has subsided. More importantly, I can now put up with it because I've given up worrying about it.

44

A: The other day I looked up what fitness classes there were available locally and I couldn't believe how many there were.
B: Did you come across any that you liked the look of?
A: Not really. I didn't know what half of them were: Boxercise, Boot camp, Aqua aerobics … and loads based on dance.
B: You mean like Zumba?
A: Yes. I knew Zumba was a craze that had taken off, but there were others: Jazzercise, Bodyjam. I mean, if you go in for dancing, why don't you just sign up for a dance class?
B: And do you? Go in for dancing, that is?
A: Yes, I do. I think that's what I'll do … take up samba or something.

46

I = Interviewer, E = Expert
I: What impact has globalization had on our idea of beauty?
E: Well, I guess the first thing to say is that not necessarily globalization, but general economic growth, has had a huge impact on the amount of time and money people spend on beautification. The global cosmetics and perfume industry is worth around $200 billion. Americans spend over a billion each year on their fingernails alone. And new markets keep being found. Male grooming, which twenty years ago was not a big

I: industry at all, now brings in over $30 billion. But I think the question you're getting at is: Has a globalized world made our ideal of beauty more homogenized?

I: Yes, I suppose what I'm asking is: Is there now a more global view of what beautiful is or means?

E: Well, that's an interesting question and I think the beauty industry is a good example of what has happened more generally in the world over the last 100 years or so. But I think we need to stress that there have been different stages of globalization – not just the most recent one that began in the 1980s. If you go back to the early 20th century and the days of western imperialism, you do find that cosmetics companies were peddling a Western and 'white' ideal of beauty. There was even the promise by some companies that regular washing with soap could help to turn a dark skin whiter.

I: Goodness!

E: Obviously, it was an effective marketing tactic: if people everywhere could aspire to the same notion of beauty, it would be far easier for the companies to mass-produce products. So using the ideals presented by Hollywood film stars and fashion magazines, they persuaded people not only that it was desirable to look a certain way, but that their collection of skin creams and lipsticks and fragrances would help them achieve that.

I: And did that marketing effort really work? Were people convinced by these ideas of beauty?

E: Well, yes and no. Local cultural values were never completely taken over by the global message of the marketers. People aren't stupid and they could see that they were being offered an American ideal. Henry Kissinger was right when he said that globalization in that era was just another name for Americanization. You know, I think generally people are able to differentiate between what they are being asked to aspire to and the reality of their daily lives.

I: And you talked about different eras of globalization. Can you just explain a bit more about that?

E: Sure, well, the more recent era of globalization – the one that began in the 1980s – is one in which companies definitely have to be more conscious of local traditions and values. You only have to look at how a company like McDonald's alters its menu to suit the tastes of each local market to see that. There is an increasing emphasis on diversity. So, as we all seem to get closer in a world of global communications, at the same time we want to celebrate individuality and local differences.

I: So now companies incorporate diversity into the products they make?

E: Definitely. Multinational companies can still accept the universal values of beauty that we all aspire to: a clear skin, healthy-looking hair, a youthful glow, and then they can adapt their products to include local and traditional ingredients: for example, black soap in Africa for skin cleansing, or the Huito fruit in South America – traditionally used for body painting – as an ingredient in hair dye.

47

Speaker 1
On the whole, I really like what the architect's done. But he's put in two lifts, which I think is excessive. A better alternative would be to have just one which can be a service lift and also be used for wheelchair access. That way, people will be obliged to use the stairs – it's only two flights – and that will actually be good for them. It'll help them stay fit. I realize that sometimes people who have heavy things to move or who aren't so mobile will sometimes want to use the lift, but we can easily work around that.

Speaker 2
I think the health problems associated with air conditioning systems are well documented. What you're getting is the same air – and so consequently the same germs and diseases – being recycled around the building. It would be much better just to have straightforward fresh air sucked in from outside, as Giovanni suggests. Admittedly, it wouldn't always be cool air, but it would be a lot healthier – and cheaper.

Speaker 3
I think the idea of a staff canteen is great, but we have to be very careful who we choose to run it. I think what we need to do is to make up our own list of what kind of food we think is acceptable – healthy options and so on – and then invite local companies to bid for the contract. I haven't really thought through who should be responsible for making the list, but I do think it's important to make one.

Speaker 4
I think the idea of forming a partnership with the local fitness and leisure centre is probably the best option. I love the idea of staff being able to do sports together – it'd be very good for morale. I know not everyone will want to join in in that way, but for a lot of people the social element will really be a big attraction.

49

C = Colleague, MA = Model answer

1
C: What do you think of the proposal?
MA: I think it's a great idea. It would really help staff to keep in shape and get exercise during their lunch hour or after work.

2
C: And do you think that staff will really make good use of it?
MA: I don't see why not. Admittedly, there will be some who aren't interested, but I think that they'll be the minority.

3
C: Don't you think that it's quite an expensive way to promote health among the staff?
MA: Well, I realize it's not going to be cheap, but I think that you have to look at all the benefits. Like reducing the number of days of absence and making people more productive.

4
C: And do you see other benefits too?
MA: Well, yes. I think it could help attract people to come and work for us. It's a good advertisement for the company.

Unit 7

50

There's a paradox about technology. It's generally thought to be a positive thing, something that solves problems and helps us to be healthier and live more comfortably. But at the same time, it's also created a lot of problems for our planet: emissions from industrial plants are changing our atmosphere and plastic debris in our oceans is believed to be changing marine ecosystems irreparably as we speak.

So I was fascinated to read the other day about a use of new technology that combines exploration with conservation. An archaeologist called Albert Yu-Min Lin is doing archaeology in a kind of virtual reality way. Working with the California Institute for Telecommunications and Information Technology, Lin has swapped his spade and trowel for an array of digital 3D immersive technologies.

122

Audioscripts

What this allows him to do is to gather, synthesize and visualize data using cutting-edge tools such as satellite imagery and ground-penetrating radar. This means he can make discoveries in areas where physical excavations would be either physically difficult or highly sensitive.

One example is the search for the tomb of Genghis Khan, a quest that is known to have frustrated scientists and historians for centuries. For many Mongolians, the tomb is considered to be an extremely sacred place and it's even said by some that disturbing it could trigger a curse that would end the world.

But most impressive are the labs where all this data is crunched – the Star Cave. The Star Cave is a totally immersive virtual reality room where scientists and historians can navigate, fly and manipulate their way through landscapes. Backlit screens project images on the ground and walls, and special eyewear creates the 3D effect. Virtual explorers zoom over mountains, down slopes. So when Lin learns from an ancient text where a particular mountain or tomb was supposed to have been in the past, he can go into the Star Cave and travel around that region to find evidence of its existence.

At the moment, these new approaches are being used by archaeologists, historians and geologists, but they are expected to benefit all kinds of projects in future, from tracking animal migrations to mapping the brain. The principle of synthesizing information gathered using digital technology and then creating a new 3D world remains the same.

51

I was very aware on my travels across Europe, posting my blog and photos, that Paris was going to present a particular challenge. I didn't want to photograph the obvious sites, like the Eiffel Tower, even though I was keen to visit them all. But as Paris is said to be one of the world's most photogenic cities, instead, I decided to take as few images as possible and come away with some really memorable compositions.

So here they are. They're not supposed to be anything more than a small collection of my memories of this wonderful place: more like postcards than photos. I'll let you decide how successful they are.

52

P = Presenter, A = Amrita Dall

Part 1

P: … and later we'll be talking to Mr Dearman about his ingenious new method for storing wrong-time electricity using cryogenics. But first a report from Amrita Dall, who last week visited the Cleanweb Hackathon in New York City, to learn about some exciting projects in the field of sustainability. Hi, Amrita. Just before we get into the detail of the event you visited, could you just explain to our listeners what a hackathon is?

A: Sure, it's sometimes also called a hack-day or a hackfest, but basically a hackathon is an event where computer programmers and web experts come together to design new software or new apps. They usually take place over a day or a weekend and at the end, the different teams present what they've come up with.

P: Are they competitions?

A: They often are, but they don't have to be. They're generally centred around a particular cause or a particular need, which was the case with the one I visited, the Cleanweb Hackathon in New York.

P: OK, so let's hear about that …

A: Well, I'd just better explain what Cleanweb is then. It's a network of concerned people who are dedicated to finding what are called 'cleantech' solutions to the various grave environmental problems that are facing us in the world today. What does that mean? Well, in the main, it means applying technology – web, mobile, social media technology – to the task of conserving resources, minimizing pollution, creating cleaner fuels, reducing waste, and so on.

P: And can you give an example of how those kinds of digital technology can do that?

A: Sure. One interesting idea I heard was about using social and mobile media to encourage less ownership and more efficient consumption. So, for example, you could set up a local neighbourhood network on the web – a 'resource cloud' as it was called – so that if one neighbour needed a tool, like an electric drill, to do a job, he or she could send that request out to the community and someone would lend one rather than the person having to buy a new one.

Part 2

P: OK. That's interesting. So are they mostly community-based ideas and not for profit?

A: No, Cleanweb definitely backs people who have good business ideas as well. One of the organizers I talked to was clear about the part that business had to play. What he said really rang true: that most people have a kind of blind faith that humanity will innovate its way out of a future environmental crisis. But actually we're in a crisis now, and so according to him, firms and others had better start innovating now.

P: And what about the hackathon itself? Did it seem to be a good environment for serious innovation?

A: Yeah, it was a very dynamic and positive kind of atmosphere. The theme was energy, and it kicked off on Friday evening with some introductions and then sharing ideas for apps to promote energy saving and energy awareness. Then on the Saturday, the various teams got down to the job of designing their apps. Work went on at a really high intensity through to Sunday when each app was submitted to the judges.

P: And who were the winners?

A: Well, one was an app called Econofy and that enabled the user, when shopping, to make comparisons between the energy efficiency of different electrical appliances. I thought that was practical, and some of the sponsors and other companies that were present were clearly very interested in it.

P: And did you get the feeling that Cleanweb could make more than just a marginal difference?

A: Yes, I really think it's an organization that could. Actually it's wrong to call Cleanweb an 'organization'. It's more like a movement … and it's growing very fast: there are plans for hackathons in Italy and Canada, for example.

P: Well, thanks, Amrita. If you're now interested in getting involved in the Cleanweb network, their internet address is cleanweb.com and you …

53
See 52

54
See 52

55
A new study has detected a species of flesh-ripping dinosaur previously unknown to scientists, which is believed to have terrorized North Africa some 95 million years ago.

The species – Sauroniops pachytholus – was identified from a single fossil unearthed in south-eastern Morocco in 2007 by a team of scientists led by Andrea Cau of the Bologna Geological Museum.

The fossil comprises only the upper part of the dinosaur's skull, but from this, Cau has been able to conclude that this was probably a large two-legged meat-eater rather like Tyrannosaurus Rex and perhaps measuring as much as twelve metres in length. The long shape of the skull suggests that Sauroniops had a large jaw with dozens of blade-like teeth.

The fossil also revealed a large bump on Sauroniops's already thick forehead, from which it appears that this dinosaur used its head in fights with other large dinosaurs.

This fossil find reinforces the case that this area of North Africa seems to have been particularly popular with predatory dinosaurs. Such dinosaurs tended to gather where there was an abundance of food, and the warm climate and large river delta would certainly have attracted fish and crocodiles. But whether they fought each other, as the adventure films like to show, is another matter. Arguably, says Cau, they targeted different prey and had no need to compete for food.

57
F = Friend, MA = Model answer
1
F: So what did you find?
MA: It seems to be some kind of old oil lamp.
2
F: How do you know that's what it is?
MA: Well, it looks like the kind of lamps I've seen in museums.
3
F: How old do you think it is?
MA: Well, I couldn't say for sure, but probably it dates back to Roman times.
4
F: Do you know that that kind of object existed then?
MA: Yes, the Romans were believed to have settled in this area, so I think it's quite likely that it is a Roman lamp.
5
F: Do you think it has some historical significance?
MA: Well, there's some writing on the bottom of it which suggests it could be of interest to a museum or historian.

Unit 8

58
NGM = Nat Geo Music, JS = Jake Shimabukuro
NGM: When did you first start playing the ukulele?
JS: We learned the ukulele in school like most kids learned the recorder in school. I remember when my mom first placed it in my hands and taught me my first three chords, and I was just hooked. I would play all the time. The ukulele is synonymous with Hawaii, and if you walk around Waikiki, you'll always see people hanging around playing.
NGM: What kind of music did you enjoy playing growing up in Hawaii?
JS: Up until my early teens, I was playing a lot of traditional Hawaiian music. Once I entered high school, you start meeting all these different cliques and people start introducing you to different styles of music. From classical, to jazz, to rock and of course the popular groups on the radio at that time. So I would try and find the notes on the ukulele. People'd look at me and say, 'You're not supposed to be doing that on a ukulele!' and I remember that feeling of just surprising people with doing different things. I basically created my own technique and ways of playing the instrument. I remember playing 'More Than Words' by Extreme and everyone just freaked out! They never thought a song like that was possible to play on the ukulele.
     I realize that cover songs work so well on the ukulele because it has a very limited range, which allows you to simplify the songs, since you can only play four notes at once. But the audience has such a strong reference of the tune they're filling in the parts that can't be played on the ukulele.
NGM: What has it been like for you touring on a global scale?
JS: People always say 'music is the universal language', but I believe music is the language of the universe; because it communicates raw human emotion. And to me, that's more powerful than anything else. It's a more intimate, deeper connection than just having a conversation with someone.
NGM: You are quoted as saying: 'If everyone played the ukulele, the world would be a better place.' Why?
JS: When you have the opportunity to create music yourself, you feel more connected to the things around you. People shouldn't be intimidated by it, my grandmother just started playing it! She and her friends sit around and play, and have a blast with it. I believe just taking that step to give any kind of instrument a try will bring people immense joy. In this day and age we live in, where technology always expects us to multi-task and give up our contemplative time, we're always expected to respond so quickly; it can be stressful. So coming home after a long day, picking up the ukulele and playing it feels like a yoga session to me! It gives you the chance to let loose and act silly!

59
1 A: Will that work?
   B: Yes, that's just the job!
2 A: Shall we go?
   B: Yes, I'm just coming.
3 A: How are you doing?
   B: Just fine, thanks.
4 A: Can I help you?
   B: No, thanks, I'm just looking.
5 A: Why do you ask?
   B: I'm just curious.
6 A: Is Jaz there?
   B: No, he's just left.

60
Is there a way to learn an instrument fast? What do you think? The answer is almost certainly not, if you want to do it properly. To do anything well takes time and patience. You can take shortcuts to avoid learning each step, but in the end this will catch up with you. You may reach a certain destination faster, but it won't be the one that you're ultimately aiming for. I always advise people to bear in mind the three 'P's: pay attention to your instructor; practice – to improve you need to practise as often as possible; and patience. Progress is always slower at first and ninety per cent of people give up within the first year of taking up an instrument.

61
Ask someone to name a famous blues artist and you'll get some different names: BB King, Ella Fitzgerald, John Lee Hooker, but very seldom will you hear the name of the harmonica, or blues harp, genius, Sonny Boy Williamson II. Yet Sonny Boy was perhaps the first black media star of the American South. His fifteen-minute midday show on KFFA radio in the early 1940s, broadcast when workers took their main meal of the day between long shifts either side, was the most listened to musical event in the Mississippi Delta at the time. It's said that on a warm summer day with the

windows open, you could walk from one side of Helena, Arkansas, to the other through black and white sections of town and never miss a note of Sonny Boy's playing.

Sonny Boy Williamson was born in 1912, the youngest of twenty-one children and the only musician in the family. He started playing the harp at a young age, perhaps as early as five. He became so skilled at it that later he developed a technique where he could put the harmonica in his mouth and play without using his hands. Very little is known about his early life, but we know times were hard for black people in that era, working for little pay in factories and on the plantations, and it's from tales of hard times that the blues draws its name.

Although married, he led a rootless existence. We have accounts of him drifting around the Mississippi Delta in the 1930s captivating people with his music and jamming with other musicians in this golden era of blues music. He took himself where his music led him, up to Detroit, to Tennessee and in the 1950s, to Chicago, where his Chess record label was based and where he made some of his greatest recordings.

What is it that sets Sonny Boy apart? His music is uncomplicated yet powerful, switching from a simple rhythm to an impassioned solo; his lyrics are moody and at the same time witty; his lyrics are delivered in a weary tone but without any sense of negativity. Above all, he's his own man, a figure who, without trying at all, exudes charisma. It's the charisma of a musical genius who is supremely confident in his art.

In the 1960s, he came to Europe to tour and was greeted wherever he went with great acclaim. It was at this time that he met various young British musicians who were influenced by American blues music. One of these was Jimmy Page, later of the rock band Led Zeppelin. Their first encounter in a nightclub says much about Sonny Boy's charisma. After seeing him play, Page approached him and said how much he admired him and enjoyed his music. Would it be all right to have his autograph? Sonny Boy gave him a withering look and told him to 'get lost'. Page says that he would never think of treating a fan like that himself, but there was something about Sonny Boy that made Page respect him even more. In spite of his gruff manner, Sonny Boy loved the respect he was given in Europe. One of his last recordings, made with Jimmy Page on guitar, was entitled 'I'm Trying to Make London My Home'.

Sonny Boy returned home but died in 1965 at the modest age of 53, when he was still at the peak of his powers. Some say he looked closer to 70. He is a legend among those who listen to the blues, and I firmly believe that one day his recordings will be appreciated by more than just a few aficionados.

62
I = Interviewer, A = Aleah
I: So you came from a very musical background. Your father was a musician and your aunt was a famous singer too. Was it obvious to you that you'd go into music as a profession?
A: No, I never really thought about it like that. I think people suppose that I'm part of some musical dynasty – that I was destined to be a musician. But my mother definitely had other ambitions for me. She wanted me to go to college and become a lawyer or a doctor or something.
I: Why?
A: That's a good question. I think she was like a lot of parents who want something stable and secure for their children. I don't think it had anything to do with being married to a musician herself.
I: The settled life she never had, maybe?

A: I honestly don't know. But I don't think so. Actually, she seemed to enjoy that aspect of her life – the lack of a strict routine, the unexpected visitors, late nights staying up playing music and chatting.
I: And you did go to college, but you left after a year. Was it the pull of the music world that made you leave?
A: Mmm, that's difficult to say. I don't think it was as simple as just wanting to get back to singing. I was feeling very restless at college – I wanted to travel and see more of the world.
I: And so you took off to India. Were your parents unhappy about that?
A: Do you know, I couldn't tell you really. They were very laid-back parents. Certainly in the sense that they weren't judgemental, or didn't want to be seen to be being judgemental about the things we did as kids.
I: So your first record …
A: Yes, this dates back to the time when I was travelling in India and it's actually a bit of mass-produced pop. It's what they called *filmi* – songs that are adapted for use in Bollywood movies. It's not musically brilliant or anything, but it always makes me feel happy when I hear it.

64
F = Friend, MA = Model answer
1
F: Did music play a big part in your childhood?
MA: That's a good question. Certainly it was very important at high school. Your circle of friends tended to be influenced a lot by the kind of music that you listened to.
2
F: And was music a big part of family life?
MA: I've never really thought about it like that. Listening to music wasn't really something we did together as a family.
3
F: And what kind of music did your parents like?
MA: I couldn't tell you really. My mother used to listen to the radio a lot: usually pop music from the 1960s and 70s. I don't think my father was that interested in music.
4
F: And is music still very important to you now?
MA: Mmm, I suppose so, yes. It's not the same as when I was a teenager, but I still listen to music a lot. Mostly on my computer when I'm working.
5
F: Who's your favourite singer or band?
MA: That's difficult to say. It varies from month to month. I go through stages of listening to one thing a lot and then I change. At the moment, it's a singer called Jessie Ware.

Unit 9

65
When teacher Bruce Farrer from Regina in Canada asked pupils in his ninth grade class to write letters – ten pages long – to their future selves, most of them imagined that this was just a way of keeping them busy for a few hours and after they'd handed them in, they forgot about them. Little did they realize that twenty years on, the letters would be returned to them.

For the dedicated Farrer, however, this was an assignment with a distinct purpose. Over several decades, he handed out this same task to his fourteen- and fifteen-year-olds, knowing that twenty years later, he would endeavour to track the writers down and post their letters back to them. Although he retired fully from teaching in 2006, Farrer kept all the letters carefully filed and has been continuing since then to return them to their owners one by one. He should finally see the job through in 2026.

Farrer says that the exercise is greatly valued by his past students, partly, he thinks, because letters are nowadays a rarer and more treasured form of communication. In the writing part of the assignment, the aim was to make students think about what they wanted to do in life and whether they were on the right track. Then, when they read them back, at the age of 35 or so, the letters had become interesting historical documents. First and foremost, says Farrer, they are just something to enjoy as you would enjoy any object that you re-discovered from your past.

Finding the students so long after they have left the school has not been a straightforward job – Farrer describes it as 'a lot of detective work'. But the rewards are great. He gets to find out how their lives have actually evolved and, in addition, receives their gratitude for going to the trouble of returning the letters.

Not all the pupils agreed for him to read their letters, but he has kept and is returning these letters too. Most are delighted to receive them; a few are embarrassed because of the immaturity of their letters. But of those who did agree to share what they'd written, he has some interesting stories. He remembers one boy who was a big fan of the Swedish pop group Abba. The boy's dream was to move to Sweden and marry a beautiful girl. Twenty years on, he has fulfilled his wish.

In spite of the profound effect the exercise has had on his former students, Farrer is modest about his own teaching skills, saying that he's just a regular teacher who happened to set a rather unusual assignment.

66

Archaeologists working outside Vienna, Austria, believe they have discovered a huge school for ancient Roman gladiators, rivalling in size the training grounds outside Rome's Colosseum.

The facility includes features never before seen at a Roman gladiators' school, such as a wooden training dummy and outside its gates, the first known gladiators' cemetery.

In addition to a walled field for wild animals, it includes a mini-amphitheatre. Here gladiators, who were mostly foreign slaves, could practise their moves and perform in front of potential purchasers.

67

Eight bells struck. Fletcher Christian, acting mate of His Majesty's Armed Vessel *Bounty*, came on deck to take over the watch. The ship's commander, Lieutenant William Bligh, was asleep in his cabin below.

'I am now unhappily to relate one of the most atrocious acts of piracy ever committed,' Bligh later wrote. 'Just before sun-rise, Mr Christian, with the master at arms, gunner's mate and seaman, Thomas Burkett, came into my cabin while I was asleep, seized me, tied my hands with a cord behind my back and threatened me with instant death if I spoke or made the least noise. The boatswain was ordered to hoist the launch out; and some others of the crew were hurried over the side.

'Christian … then said—"Come Captain Bligh, your officers and men are now in the boat, and you must go with them; if you attempt to make the least resistance you will instantly be put to death" and without any further ceremony, with the cord still tied around my hands and a tribe of armed ruffians about me, I was forced over the side. A few pieces of pork were thrown to us, and some clothes and cutlasses and we were cast adrift in the open ocean.'

So, on 28 April 1789, began one of the greatest sea stories of all time: the mutiny on the *Bounty* and its fantastic train of events.

Bounty had sailed from Spithead in December of 1787, under orders to proceed to Tahiti, there to take on breadfruit for transport to the West Indies. She stayed nearly six months at the island taking on plants and then proceeded to Endeavour Strait by way of Tonga. There, motivated by the attractions of living in this south-sea island paradise, and by the increasing strictness and cruelty of his captain, Bligh, Fletcher Christian led the famous mutiny.

In a boat only 23 feet long, heavily laden with 19 men, Bligh performed the most celebrated open-boat voyage in the chronicles of the sea. In 41 days, he sailed from Tofua to Timor, 3,618 nautical miles, without the loss of a single man. From there he returned to England.

As the launch pulled away from the *Bounty*, the castaways heard the mutineers shout 'Huzza for Tahiti!' Christian and his mates returned to their island paradise, where 16 of them elected to remain ashore. Then, in the night, nine of them including Christian plus six native men and twelve Tahitian women, sailed from Tahiti and vanished from history. Not until the ship *Topaz* of Boston landed at Pitcairn Island, a lonely rock 1,300 miles southeast of Tahiti, eighteen years later, was the mystery solved.

Christian had taken his little band to this uninhabited island, stripped the *Bounty*, then run her ashore and burned her. Christian knew the English Admiralty had a long arm, and that sooner or later they would send a ship to look for him and his fellow mutineers. True to his fears, the frigate *Pandora* arrived in Tahiti a year and a half later and captured all the mutineers there.

At Pitcairn, Christian's little colony lived in peace for about two years until the wife of John Williams, one of the mutineers, died in a fall from a cliff. Williams took the wife of one of the Tahitians, who banded together to take revenge. The Tahitians were already resentful that the mutineers had divided the land on Pitcairn between themselves, and there followed a series of bloody incidents. Fletcher Christian was shot to death as he worked in his field. Ten years after the *Bounty* had landed at Pitcairn, all the Tahitian men were dead, and only one mutineer, Alexander Smith was still alive.

When Captain Mayhew Folger in the ship *Topaz* of Boston called at Pitcairn to look for seals in 1808, he was astonished to see a canoe put out to sea from what he thought was an uninhabited island. In the canoe were three young men, bearing presents of fruit and a pig. The youths took the captain ashore to meet their 'father Aleck' Smith.

To this day, Pitcairn islanders, of whom there are around fifty, are the direct descendants of these mutineers and their Tahitian friends.

68

A: How was your anthropology lecture today?
B: It was fascinating. It was about the history of eating and drinking etiquette.
A: What do you mean by 'etiquette'? Like table manners?
B: Yes, exactly. We started off looking at how people in the Middle Ages behaved at the table. They did sit at a table with a tablecloth like we do, but the cloth was a kind of communal napkin. People would wipe their hands or mouths on it. They drank soup straight from a bowl and when they ate, they used shared knives

Audioscripts

and spoons, and just helped themselves to the meat or bread or whatever else was on the table ...
A: Are you saying that they didn't really have food served up on individual plates ... or pass food around for each other like we do?
B: No, that's right.
A: So, in other words, it was a bit of a free-for-all.
B: Yeah, I guess you could say that. And by today's standards it would seem very rude, but the point is that politeness is a relative thing. They did have *some* standards. For example, if they wanted to spit, they had to do it behind them, not into the table cloth ...
A: Hmm ... great. Am I right in thinking that forks came a bit later?
B: Yes, forks didn't really become widespread until the 17th or even 18th century. And that's when napkins came in too. It's only when you have these individual pieces of tableware that you get the evolution to the type of table manners we're more used to today.
A: So, let me get this straight. You mean that when people started to share less, then their manners started to improve?
B: I think you have to be careful using words like 'improve' in this context, because who's to say what's right and wrong? What I meant was that that's when we can see the beginning of modern table manners.

70
F = Friend, MA = Model answer
1
F: I saw a great programme last night about the making of the modern world.
MA: What do you mean by 'the making of' the modern world?
2
F: It was about how the technology of the 1980s – all the things that were invented then – changed the world we live in radically.
MA: Really? What kind of things are you talking about?
3
F: Well, for example, things like the internet, mobile phones ... and also the whole consumer and shopping boom. It all really started in the 80s.
MA: Umm, correct me if I'm wrong, but didn't the internet come later than that?
4
F: Yeah, you're right. The internet wasn't actually invented 'til 1990. But the point is that the foundations for all these things were laid in the 1980s.
MA: And why's that important? Sorry, perhaps I missed something, but I'm not sure that I really understand the significance of all this.

Unit 10

71
I = Interviewer, N = Naturalist
I: So we've talked a bit about animals that organize themselves efficiently, like ants and bees, and display the greatest collective intelligence, but which are the most social animals? I mean, which animals are the most socially aware? Which species treats other members of its group in a considerate way?
N: Oh, that would have to be the elephant – they're very considerate creatures, although I should qualify that perhaps by saying the female elephant.
I: Why's that? What about the males?
N: Well, elephant society is matriarchal – that's to say, it's the older females who lead a herd. And the older males, or bulls, live a more solitary existence. They either leave voluntarily or are pushed out of the herd when they reach maturity. One way or another they don't remain long in the family group.
I: I see. And can you describe some of the social behaviour of the main herd? What makes them socially intelligent?
N: Well, female elephants seem to form very close relationships with the other female members of the herd. This is well documented. Just to give you one recent example I read about: A young female, barely one year old, became separated from her own family and was wandering around in a disoriented way. Seeing another group nearby, she attempted to join them. This group rejected her – literally pushed her away and injured her in the process. Later she found her own family and the matriarch of this group recognized instantly that the young female had been the victim of some maltreatment. She seemed to put two and two together and marched straight over to the other herd and remonstrated with them. Stranger still, she seemed to know which of the elephants in the other herd had been responsible for the injury to the young female.
I: That's amazing. You'd hardly think that was possible.
N: Another example of socially cooperative behaviour came in a study in Thailand, where female elephants were given a reward task. Two elephants were each given a rope. If they pulled simultaneously on their rope, a table with corn on it appeared before them. However, if one pulled their rope before the other, nothing happened. The elephants, unlike other species which have been given similar tests, learned very fast to coordinate their pulling. And this just backs up what we know about their cooperative behaviour in the wild.

72
1 Research suggests that crows are able to tell the difference between one human being and another from their faces.
2 If one dolphin is ill, another will stay by it and help it to breathe.
3 Meerkats can be very selfless: one will often stand watch while the others are playing or eating.
4 Young Emperor penguins often group together and play together in a kind of nursery.
5 Killer whales in the Northern Pacific live with their mothers all their lives.

74
P = Presenter, S = Sophie Marler
P: This week in our series *People who changed society* we're looking at the work of peace activist Leymah Gbowee. Sophie Marler has the story.
S: In 2011, Leymah Gbowee, along with Ellen Johnson Sirleaf, the first female president in Africa, were awarded the Nobel Peace Prize for their part in bringing peace to the war-torn country of Liberia. Leymah Gbowee's story is not just the story of the power of one individual to effect meaningful change in society, but of the power of collective action. Because although Gbowee started the women's peace movement that led to the end of the civil war in 2003, without the tireless support of thousands of like-minded women, peace would likely not have come.
The problem that faced Gbowee was how to reconcile different parties after years of conflict and how to begin the process of healing among victims, many of them young children. In 1998, Gbowee returned to Liberia, having fled with her three children during the civil war, and without a penny in her pocket, set about this daunting task. She volunteered on a programme called the Trauma Healing and

Reconciliation Program to train as a counsellor and worker helping victims of war to overcome their trauma. Underpinning her philosophy was the following belief – shared by other great advocates of reconciliation like Nelson Mandela – as it is described in her book:

'The person who hurt you … If you are still angry at that person, if you haven't been able to forgive, you are chained to him. When someone offends you and you haven't let go, every time you see him, you grow breathless or your heart skips a beat. Perhaps even you dream of revenge. Above you is the Mountain of Peace and Prosperity where we all want to go. But when you try to climb that hill, the person you haven't forgiven weighs you down. It's a personal choice whether or not to let go. But you can't move forward until you break that chain.'

As she trained and worked with victims of the war, she realized increasingly that this was a man's war and it was to mothers that she could most effectively appeal to end it. So she began to mobilize women across all sections of society to reconcile the different factions and in her own words to 'begin the process of renewing a culture of hope' in a country where ordinary people felt hopeless. The message was that every society's future lies in its children.

In 2000, Gbowee met Thelma Ekiyor of Nigeria, an inspirational lawyer specializing in conflict resolution. Together they formed the Women in Peacebuilding Network (WIPNET) of which Gbowee became the Liberian coordinator. She continued her trauma rehabilitation work by day and by night planned actions for WIPNET. These actions were peaceful and involved groups of women going to markets and other public places and spreading the message: 'Women, wake up – you have a voice in the peace process!' They handed out flyers with these words or drawings for those that could not read.

The movement grew and soon there were mass demonstrations of women in the capital all wearing white and praying for peace. In 2003, Gbowee was granted an audience with the then president and got him to agree to hold peace talks with the opposition. Four months later in August 2003, the war officially came to an end. Gbowee remains a tireless campaigner and believer in the power of communities and particularly women to effect social change. She is now an internationally recognized figure spreading her message of hope around the world.

75

'The person who hurt you … If you are still angry at that person, if you haven't been able to forgive, you are chained to him. When someone offends you and you haven't let go, every time you see him, you grow breathless or your heart skips a beat. Perhaps even you dream of revenge. Above you is the Mountain of Peace and Prosperity where we all want to go. But when you try to climb that hill, the person you haven't forgiven weighs you down. It's a personal choice whether or not to let go. But you can't move forward until you break that chain.'

76

A: What are you doing?
B: Watching a TED talk on my laptop. You know, TED – it stands for Technology, Entertainment and Design.
A: Oh, yes. I've seen a few of those – they can be good. Which one are you looking at?
B: It's a guy called Alain de Botton. He's talking about success and failure. He's a really good speaker actually.

A: Yes, he is, isn't he? I heard him on the radio a few months ago being interviewed about a new book. He was excellent. So what's he saying?
B: Well, he's putting forward quite an interesting idea: that we all think that meritocracy in society is a good thing, because it means that those who deserve to get to the top will get to the top, rather than just the rich or the well-connected.
A: Yeah, well, I'd go along with that.
B: Mmm, me too, but what he's saying is that if you believe that, then you'll also believe that those who get to the bottom, or those who just are at the bottom of society, also deserve to be there – and to stay there.
A: Oh, yes, I suppose so. I hadn't thought about it like that before.
B: No, me neither. It's curious, isn't it? So the idea is that if you fail somehow, you've deserved to fail – it's your own fault. And he's saying that that can be pretty crushing for people.
A: Yes, I see, when in fact it might not be your own fault at all. It might be because of some misfortune or a piece of bad luck.
B: Exactly.
A: So what does he suggest we do about it?
B: Well, that we change our attitudes about people who don't succeed; that we don't make judgments about them, calling them 'losers' and things like that. Shall I send you the link?
A: Yes, do. I'd like to watch it. Is it very long?
B: I haven't got to the end yet, but I doubt it. They're usually only about fifteen minutes or so.
A: Thanks. Anyway, why did I pop by? Ah yes, I wanted to ask you about going to the …

77

1 A: What are you doing?
   B: Watching a TED talk on my laptop.
2 A: He's a really good speaker actually.
   B: Yes, he is, isn't he?
3 B: Yeah, well, I'd go along with that.
   A: Mmm, me too.
4 A: … those who just are at the bottom of society also deserve to be there – and to stay there.
   B: Oh, yes, I suppose so.
5 B: I hadn't thought about it like that before.
   A: No, me neither.
6 A: And he's saying that that can be pretty crushing for people.
   B: Yes, I see.
7 A: Shall I send you the link?
   B: Yes, do.
8 B: Is it very long?
   A: I haven't got to the end yet, but I doubt it.

78

1 Doubt it.
2 'Xpect so.
3 Couldn't tell you, I'm afraid.
4 'Fraid not.
5 S'pose so.
6 S'a good idea, isn't it?

79

F = Friend, MA = Model answer
1
F1: What are you doing this evening?
MA: Staying in, I think.
2
F2: I'm reading a really interesting book at the moment.
MA: Really? What's it about?

3
F1: Two hundred years ago, French wasn't the only language spoken in France.
MA: Wasn't it? What did they speak then?

4
F2: I don't normally read history books.
MA: No, me neither. But your book sounds interesting.

5
F1: Are you going to be free later?
MA: No, I'm afraid not. I've got too much work to do.

Unit 11

80

In Japan, there are estimated to be over half a million young people who have withdrawn from society and sit at home in the safety of their bedrooms, fearing what lies outside. These are the hikikomori. Many feel pity for them, believing that it is a symptom of a dysfunctional society. Others say it is self-indulgent and it's high time that these young people pulled themselves together.

Most hikikomori are male and many come from middle-class families – families who do their best to help them. But their children are locked in a cycle of depression and loss of confidence. Mostly they would rather their parents just left them alone to sit in their rooms and watch television or browse the internet; or just to sit doing nothing in their state of isolation.

The hikikomori condition was first formally recognized by Japanese psychiatrist Tamaki Saito in 1998 in his book *Social Withdrawal: A Never-ending Adolescence* and although there have been some similar cases reported in France and other western countries, it seems to be a particularly Japanese phenomenon.

Some say that it has to do with today's uncertain economic prospects. Thirty years ago, young middle-class Japanese males trod a fairly sure path from high school to university to a job for life in one of Japan's corporations. Anyone who didn't take this route was considered abnormal. Nowadays, more graduates compete for fewer jobs and companies are less inclined to offer long-term employment, anyway. Hence why some wonder why, when they have done everything right, they now find themselves without a good or secure job. They are confused and lost and many end up wishing they had not worked so hard for this empty dream in the first place.

Others blame the parents, high achievers in their own careers, whose success the young hikikomori wish they could emulate. Unable to face the disappointment of their children not finding job security, the parents instead enable them to live this reclusive life. If only the parents would act more firmly, these critics say, instead of shielding them from the outside world, the problem would not exist.

Whatever the true causes, this is both a personal and a social problem that needs to be addressed; somehow these lost souls need to be reintegrated into society and re-socialized.

83

OK, so here's my dilemma. I've been offered a fantastic job in Australia, 6,000 miles away from where I live now. The problem is that my parents are in their eighties and I'm the only one in the family who lives near them still. If I took the job, I wouldn't be able to see them more than once or twice a year. Should anything happen to them while I was in Australia, I'd feel terrible. But at the same time, I don't know if I will ever get an opportunity like this again. Were I to tell them, they'd of course say that I must go, but it's not that simple.

84

Part 1
With the exception of the odd robot dog or pet cat, robotics research has, for the most part, been confined to what robots can do to simulate human activity: driving trains, performing industrial operations, even doing household chores. But a team of engineers at Harvard University, who saw a TV programme called 'Silence of the Bees' about the decline of the honey bee population, were inspired to create 'RoboBee', a miniature flying robot that could replicate the flying skills and behaviour of a real honey bee. The application they had in mind for RoboBee was the important function of pollinating crops that the shortage of honey bees has made a necessity.

The scientists have great ambitions for RoboBee. Rob Wood, Gu-Yeon Wei and Radhika Nagpal hope to create colonies of RoboBees that will be able to work together in much the same way that a real bee colony does. In other words, they would like to simulate the collective intelligence of real bees. In this way the small robots will be able to cooperate on a particular task, share information and adapt to changing conditions. Artificial sensors will help them to react to the movement of objects and other RoboBees around them.

Part 2
However, RoboBee faces several technical challenges before it can get to this stage. The first is flying properly. RoboBee has an intricate computer chip brain that works like a nervous system, telling the bee when to flap its wings, what direction to tilt its body and so on. Real bees are amazing flying machines, zipping from one flower to another and then hovering there while they collect pollen. At the moment, RoboBee crashes a bit too frequently. Another problem is powering the small robot. The fuel source cannot be too heavy or it will impede RoboBee's abilty to fly. A collaborator is working on micro fuel cells that could be used instead of batteries. In the future, the team hopes that they will be able to recreate a real bee hive, which the small robots will use as a refuelling station.

Perhaps the most exciting thing about coordinated robotic insects is the variety of purposes for which they can be used. RoboBees can't make honey like real bees, but they can autonomously pollinate fields of crops. Other proposed applications for RoboBees include: search and rescue missions following natural disasters – for example searching for survivors in collapsed buildings following an earthquake; traffic monitoring – this involves flying over a traffic-congested area and taking pictures to determine the severity and the cause of the jam; weather mapping – again using cameras and other sensors in place of eyes and antennae, RoboBees could relay real-time information about weather conditions in a particular area; evaluating or exploring areas which are dangerous for humans to enter, like a nuclear reactor; and military surveillance.

Part 3
Bees, in fact, are not alone in providing inspiration for roboticists. Flies, fish and lobsters have also been the subject of study as scientists attempt to take lessons from nature and apply them to the robot world. It's believed that in the coming years, such study will open up a wide range of discoveries and practical innovations, helping us to create a new generation of machines that will take advantage of the designs of nature and the principles that animals apply in the complex task of daily survival. The National Science Foundation in the USA is certainly convinced of the potential benefits and is funding such research to the tune of $2 million per year.

🔊 **85**
See 🔊 84 Part 1

🔊 **86**
See 🔊 84 Part 2

🔊 **87**
See 🔊 84 Part 3

🔊 **88**
Conversation 1
A: You look a little taken aback. I didn't mean to offend you during the meeting when I said that I didn't like your ideas for changing the website.
B: No, that's OK. You're perfectly entitled to give your opinion. I was just a bit surprised because yesterday when I showed you my ideas, you said they were good.
A: Yes, they are good ideas, but I don't think they're really appropriate for what we're trying to achieve. Anyway, I'm sorry if that came out wrong at the meeting.
B: I just wish you'd been a bit clearer yesterday before I proposed them to everyone.

Conversation 2
A: You seem worried. Is something bothering you?
B: Yes, it is, actually. You shouldn't have talked to Sarah about my feelings about my new job.
A: Did I say something to upset you?
B: Yes, you told her that I wasn't really happy working in the back office.
A: Well, you aren't, are you?
B: No, I'm not. But I don't want her to think that I'm a moaner or someone who can't put up with a bit of routine paperwork.
A: Oh well, I'm sorry. I really hope I didn't give her that impression.

Conversation 3
A: Sorry, why are you laughing? I don't understand what's so funny.
B: Nothing. It was just the way you said 'no' so sharply to Gary when he asked you if you wanted to go with him to the trade fair.
A: Sorry, perhaps that sounded a bit abrupt.
B: No, it's OK. He's very thick-skinned. I don't think he would have minded. Anyway, everyone knows where you stand now.

🔊 **91**
C = Colleague, MA = Model answer
1
C: Well, I'm a bit surprised that you volunteered me for the project.
MA: Oh, I'm sorry. I hope I didn't upset you. I didn't mean to put you in a difficult situation.
2
C: You look worried. Is everything OK? Was it something I said?
MA: No, don't worry. I'm just feeling a little anxious about all the work I have to do.
3
C: If you don't like Indian food, you don't have to accept my invitation to lunch.
MA: Oh, no, it's not that. Please don't think me rude. It's just that I don't eat lunch normally.
4
C: Ha, ha, that's a good one.
MA: Why are you laughing? I don't understand what's so funny.
5
C: Is that all you have to say: 'No'?
MA: Sorry, perhaps that sounded a bit abrupt. I should have said, 'No, I don't think that's likely to be a good technical solution.'

Unit 12

🔊 **92**
I = Interviewer, J = Journalist
I: You immigrated to the United States as a child. How did your love for the landscape in South America affect your relationship with North America?
J: I grew up in a sugarcane hacienda outside Trujillo, Peru, on the coast of the Pacific Ocean, so as a child, I was always aware of the land and the sea. My earliest memories are of earthquakes – there were over fifteen by the time I reached the age of five.
When I came to North America, I was struck by how much of the land around me was inhabited. I couldn't imagine a place where you could drive for hundreds of miles and human beings always be in evidence.
I: What landscapes in North America do you love?
J: The first memorable impression I had was the smell of cut grass. Having grown up in a kind of desert, I had never seen great fields of grass. I loved that.
I: What is your favourite landscape in South America?
J: Most people don't know this, but Peru has five kinds of landforms: coastal desert, mountain, jungle, islands and prairie. And all of it in close-ish proximity! It always amazes me that you can descend a snow-covered mountain not far from Cuzco and suddenly be in the lush, green jungle. I love it.
I: How did flying with photographer Bobby Haas for this project change your understanding of South America?
J: In all truth, I was taken aback by the growth of the cities. The urban centres have burgeoned as countryfolk sought refuge from earthquakes, famines and floods. Seeing the shanty towns that had sprouted up around the cities in the past thirty years or so was heartbreaking. But on the positive side, I was moved to see the prevailing beauty of the land. I had never imagined it could look like that. The sights from around 1,500 metres in the air were astoundingly beautiful!
I: What was it like to ride in an open-door airplane? Was it a thrill, or just terrifying?
J: I was both thrilled and terrified! Terrified by how vulnerable some small airplane can feel and thrilled by the visual feast below us. But what made the greatest impression on me was the physical aspect: fierce gales rushing through the open door and the cold. It's freezing. How Bobby was able to handle his camera and manipulate stuff under those conditions is still a mystery to me.

🔊 **93**
1 A: Where do you live now?
   B: We've moved to a city in Jordan called Irbid, about 100 kilometres north of the capital.
2 A: Is that near where you work?
   B: It's close-ish. The journey to work at the university takes me thirty minutes or so.
3 A: What's the countryside like around there?
   B: It's farmland mostly, but not very rich. Some people would call it sparse, but I kind of like it.
4 A: Are you near the desert?
   B: The desert is to the east, some distance away, but we haven't visited it yet. I'd love to go some time, but there's so much other stuff to see that we haven't got round to it.

🔊 **95**
As cities grow and natural habitats for animals shrink, one of two things is going to happen: either wild animal

populations will decrease because people won't be able to live *with* them, or people can adapt their ways and try to accommodate animals living among them. In Europe, we seem to have got used to urban foxes, for example.

Now, obviously, some animals are easier to live with than others. I'm a big fan of tigers and I'd be devastated if their numbers grew so small that in the end they only existed in zoos and safari parks. At the same time, much as I love them, I don't really want to live next to a tiger, let alone a lot of them. You'd think the same would probably go for most people. Yet some of the tribes of the Western Ghats mountains have shown that co-existence with tigers is not only possible, it's positively healthy.

Encouragingly, in 2016 the number of tigers in the world actually rose – that was the first time in over 100 years that it had – and now stands at around 4,000. And in the Western Ghats in India, the population has almost doubled in recent years. That's because the local tribes there don't hunt tigers and they don't compete with them for food either, given that most are vegetarian (the people that is, not the tigers). In fact, for farmers of vegetable and cereal crops, the presence of tigers is beneficial, because they keep other crop-eating animals under control. One of the tribes, the Soliga, even worship tigers as gods and claim they've not had any kind of conflict with tigers for years.

But, ironically, a lot of the tribes living in India's western nature reserves are now being evicted and relocated. This is being done in the name of safety *and* conservation of the natural areas and wild animals; some also worry that the indigenous people might be tempted to poach tigers illegally for their valuable skins. Yet the fact remains that these are the very people who have made tiger conservation a success.

We need to recognize that the historic residents of these areas – and probably of similar natural areas all over the world – make the best conservationists. They understand the land, their environmental footprint is very light, and most importantly, they respect other living things that co-habit with them. We need to keep them there – whether by giving aid or just leaving them alone – rather than evicting them. Keeping people in tiger reserves may, on the surface, seem like a cruel thing to do, but actually it's the best chance that the tigers have of survival.

96
H = Harry, C = Cynthia, S = Stefano
H: Hi, Cynthia. Hi, Stefano. Mind if I join you?
C: Oh hi, Harry. No, not at all. We were just discussing the new golf course they're planning to build along the seafront.
H: Oh yes, I'm not at all sure about that.
C: Of course, Stefano thinks it's a great idea because he loves golf and …
S: Sorry, can I just interrupt you there? It's not for selfish reasons. I just happen to think golf courses can be very attractive places. And in this area of coast …
C: Yes, but they're exclusive. Only a few rich people get to use them.
S: Well, that's not true, but can I just finish what I was saying? In this area of coast there are plenty of places – beautiful places – for walkers to enjoy the scenery. But there are very few places where people can play sport. So I don't see why you would oppose the idea of giving people a chance to practise their hobby or sport, because you feel that …
H: No, sorry. I have to stop you there, Stefano. I'm afraid I agree with Cynthia. This is an area of outstanding natural beauty and it's not right to make it exclusive when at the moment it can be enjoyed by everyone.
S: Actually, the land will be much better looked after when it's made into a golf course. The grass will be cut, the area will be landscaped in a much more attractive way and …
C: Can I just say something in answer to that? That misses the point completely. This is an area of natural beauty, not of man-made beauty. This is a kind of environmental vandalism.
S: No, hang on a minute. That's a completely inappropriate description. Golf courses actually protect the landscape against other kinds of development.
H: Well, I wouldn't …
S: Harry, you can make your point in a moment. If you put a golf course here, it's a kind of guarantee that no one else is going to develop the land in some other less environmentally friendly way.
H: They're not actually that environmentally friendly. Do you have any idea how much water it takes to keep a golf course going and how much energy they use?

98
Can I just finish what I was saying?

99
F = Friend, MA = Model answer
1
F: I was very pleased to hear about the new golf course. Weren't you?
MA: No, I wasn't actually. I don't see why they have to build it in a National Park.
2
F: Well, it's not as if they're building a shopping mall or anything. Golf courses are naturally beautiful places with lots of …
MA: Sorry, I have to stop you there. They are not natural. They're man-made and they change the landscape.
3
F: Yes, but not in a bad way. If anything they make it more beautiful to walk around.
MA: Well, they do for a few people who can afford to belong to a golf club. But for most people they are inaccessible.
4
F: Anyway, we need more sports facilities in the area. I imagine it will encourage more people, not less, to visit the area.
MA: Hang on a minute. Lots of people already visit the area: walkers, cyclists, families …
5
F: Can I just finish what I was saying?
MA: Sure, carry on.

IELTS practice test

100
Presenter: In this test you'll hear a number of different recordings and you'll have to answer questions on what you hear. There will be time for you to read the instructions and questions and you will have a chance to check your answers. The recording will be played once only. The test is in four sections.
Now turn to Section 1 on page 100 of your book. You will hear a student called Fiona telling her friend about a research project she is taking part in. First you have some time to look at questions 1 to 3. You will see that there is also an example which has been done for you.

Now we shall begin. You should answer the questions as you listen because you will not hear the recording a second time. Listen carefully and answer questions 1 to 3.

Man: Hi, Fiona. How did the meeting about the research project go?

Fiona: Hi. It was interesting. The project's doing a survey into the attitudes of people who use the downtown shopping district as opposed to suburban shopping centres. I picked up a leaflet about it in the college library, but the meeting was held at the head office building of a big retail chain that's based locally.

Man: So is that where the money for the project's coming from?

Fiona: Well, a number of local companies are involved in that, although the funds are being administered by the local council, which is working in partnership with a large educational charity that's organizing the actual survey I'll be working on. They were running the meeting.

Man: So was it a bit like an interview?

Fiona: No, I'd already applied online and provided a character reference – I got my college tutor to do that – this was more of a briefing meeting. But I did have to take photo ID with me to prove that I was the same person who'd made the application.

Man: Wow – serious stuff then. But you're not getting paid, are you?

Fiona: No, it's voluntary – but because our task is to conduct face-to-face interviews with members of the public, they wanted to check that we didn't hold strong views about shopping malls. You had to declare that in the application, and my tutor told me he was asked to comment on that in the reference. I mean, most of the volunteers are students, and it is useful in terms of seeing how a big public survey is set up.

Presenter: Before you listen to the rest of the conversation, you have some time to read questions 4 to 10.

Now listen and answer questions 4 to 10.

Man: So what exactly will you be doing?

Fiona: A week of interviewing people in the city centre.

Man: And is it, like, all day every day?

Fiona: Well, that's up to me. Each interview takes twenty minutes, but I'm not supposed to work more than six hours in any one twenty-four hour period.

Man: Right. Will you have to dress up smart?

Fiona: No, there's no dress code. As long as you've got your badge on, you can wear what you like.

Man: And have they told you what sort of people to target?

Fiona: There are three groups. Group A is like people of working age, group B is retired people and group C is students. But at least sixty per cent are meant to be in the first group, and the other forty per cent roughly divided between B and C.

Man: So how many do you have to do in a day?

Fiona: I've got a target of thirty-five interviews over the seven days, which works out at five a day, but I can choose which days I work and how many I do each day.

Man: So how do you know where to stand?

Fiona: I go where I'm told. So that you don't have to go into the office or phone up, you're sent a text message each morning. Where they send you depends on how interviews have gone the previous day.

Man: How do they know?

Fiona: 'Cos you have to send in your data online each evening. You've got twelve hours from the time of the interview to do that. There's a secure site you log into.

Man: Is it called Survey Monkey? I used that one once.

Fiona: We're using Survey Host actually – though I have used that one for other things.

Presenter: Now turn to Section 2 on page 101 of your book. You will hear someone giving a talk about opportunities to do voluntary work on a game reserve in southern Africa. First you have some time to look at questions 11 to 14.

Now listen and answer questions 11 to 14.

Woman: Hi there. I've come along today to give you some information about opportunities to work as a volunteer at the Phinda Game Reserve in southern Africa.
The reserve is located between the Indian Ocean and the Lebombo Mountains. Very few reserves in Africa have the biodiversity that Phinda offers. This vast tract of bush, river valley and forest is home to dynamic populations of African mammals, and this is where the help of volunteers proves invaluable. As a volunteer, you can join the research team at Phinda dedicated to the management of this ecosystem. Indeed, the people managing the reserve rely on volunteers to support the research taking place at Phinda.
This research aims to ensure that the various wildlife populations remain in balance and well managed within the reserve. Because although the area was at one time somewhat depleted in major mammal species, large-scale reintroduction programmes have allowed for the development of this stunning reserve, which now has viable populations of elephants, big cats and antelope, as well as both black and white rhino species.
What's more, regular and dedicated research has allowed Phinda to become a partner in essential conservation initiatives of worldwide significance, and the recent release of black rhino into the reserve is evidence of this.
A volunteer joining an experienced research team could well be involved in one of a number of research components. Big cat monitoring is a possibility, and this could even include the chance to record the movements and sightings of lions. Most probably, however, you'll spend some time monitoring the white rhino as over one hundred are now in residence, although there is also research into small mammals for those more interested in those species.

Presenter: Before you hear the rest of the talk, you have some time to look at questions 15 to 20.

Now listen and answer questions 15 to 20.

Woman: So what would a volunteer on one of the research programmes at Phinda expect to do? Firstly, let's talk about white rhino monitoring. Over one hundred rhino now roam the reserve, following the reintroduction of a handful some years ago. Volunteers assist in the building up of a database that has been created to record details of gender, age, territorial information and movements. By putting what are called 'notches' in the animals' ears it is possible to collect this information.

Then there's big cat and predator research. For example, there's cheetah monitoring. This involves finding out about the territory and movements of individuals, which are identified through their eye markings. A unique hunting substrate of the forest is also being investigated as part of this research programme. Alternatively, a volunteer might join the active leopard research project, keeping a note of where they are seen. Or if you're very lucky, you might even get to record movements and sightings of two lion prides. In any case, as a volunteer, you are likely to gain useful experience and acquire key skills, such as tracking and the use of telemetry equipment.

Finally, a word about the facilities for volunteers who come to work at Phinda. In terms of accommodation, a rustic farmhouse on the reserve is set aside for both research staff and volunteers. Running water and electricity can occasionally be intermittent due to the remoteness of the reserve, but volunteers are provided with a weekly food kitty to do their own shopping and cooking is on a rotational basis with the other volunteers. The house is equipped with a fridge, freezer, stove, oven and microwave.

Volunteers generally work a six-day week, with Sundays free, when there might be the chance to go to the beach if you can get a lift with someone. Any excursions, whether to the coast or nearby towns, are at the volunteers' own cost, so bringing some spending money is recommended.

The daily work schedule varies heavily depending on the research objectives at the time. But volunteers do get some time to relax. There is a TV in the house, though only local channels are available, but there is also a DVD player. Volunteers are encouraged to bring some films to watch, as there is not much available to buy locally.

So I hope I've covered everything – does anyone have any questions?

Presenter: Now turn to Section 3 on page 103 of your book. You will hear part of a radio programme about a disease which is affecting a species of tree called the European ash. First you have some time to look at questions 21 to 25.

Now listen and answer questions 21 to 25.

Diana: Hi, I'm Diana Wherry and on today's programme we're talking about trees. A major news story in the UK recently has been the discovery of ash dieback disease, a fungal infection that destroys members of the ash species of trees. To find out more about this threat I'm talking to plant pathologist, Dennis Walkern. First of all, what is this disease that we're calling colloquially 'ash dieback'?

Dennis: It's a fungus which spreads by spores which form on fallen leaves and then infect the leaves of a healthy tree. Once established, it spreads from there into the bark and the other parts of the tree. Eventually, it will kill small trees. In older trees, it kills shoots and maybe branches, and weakens the tree so that it becomes vulnerable to other diseases.

Diana: Is it just ash trees that are vulnerable to this particular infection or can it hop on to other trees and species too?

Dennis: As far as we're aware, it only affects ash trees – and here that means the common European ash, which is the one we have in the UK. It seems to be less of a serious problem on Far Eastern ashes. It seems to exist in a benign form, co-existing fairly happily with certain types of ash tree in Japan and presumably other parts of East Asia.

Diana: So how come it's only relatively recently arrived in the UK?

Dennis: It's happened because sometime in the early 1990s, it migrated from its Japanese home and took up residence somewhere in Eastern Europe, and it's been spreading from there ever since. It moved to Scandinavia, where by 2009, I think, ninety per cent of Danish ash trees had some signs of infection. Then it turned up in France, so this is a big spreading wave of infection. How it got to Europe in the first place, we don't know.

Diana: We're hearing this number of ninety per cent of European ash trees being vulnerable. Is this a reflection on the fact that not all European ashes are made equally? Are there different subtypes?

Dennis: Well, no. It's more that ash trees are quite variable. In studying trees which appear to have been less badly affected in Scandinavia, it's been found that some trees appear to have survived because they're genuinely more resistant to the infection. In looking at the seeds that arise from those trees, there are estimates that maybe one per cent of the population will be able to survive.

Diana: So, is the long-term prospect that we'll end up selecting out the trees that are vulnerable to this, and breed a new strain of trees just naturally, which are naturally resistant to it? So we just have to wait for one generation of ash trees – then we'll have trees that aren't vulnerable and the problem will go away.

Dennis: Probably more than one generation, actually, because you'd have a sort of sputtering epidemic – in other words you'd have some trees which survive the first waves anyway. Otherwise, I think that you're probably correct. The only catch there is to think what the generation time of an ash tree is, because some of the more attractive landscape trees may be over a century old.

Presenter: Before you hear the rest of the programme, you have some time to look at questions 26 to 30.

Now listen and answer questions 26 to 30.

Diana: So we're saying that, for the next decade or two, we'd see perhaps a third of the trees around us disappearing – because ash is an extremely common species in the UK.

Dennis: So much so, actually, that nobody knows exactly how many there are in reality, still less exactly how evenly they're spread across the country. As a mathematical modeller, I'd be interested in establishing such facts and other details about the spread of this disease. We know that immunization of trees isn't possible because they don't have adaptive immune systems, but some management of the disease may be possible. So we need to find out if it's affecting old and young trees equally, whether it's spread to all regions, and whether there are populations of ash trees in areas that can be isolated from the spread of the disease. We also know that the use of fungicides isn't feasible on a large scale because of the sheer number of ash trees out there, and the need for regular re-application. One much loved ash tree in an urban setting might be saved in that way, but not the species at large. But if those other facts can be established then the prospects of managing the disease might be greater.

Presenter: Now turn to Section 4 on page 104 of your book. You will hear a university teacher giving his students some information about internships, and the report that interns have to write as part of the course. First you have some time to look at questions 31 to 37.

Now listen and answer questions 31 to 37.

Man: Hi, there. Today I want to talk about your internship and the report you have to write after you've done it. As you know, as in other subjects like medicine and law, an internship is an integral part of your degree programme in electronic commerce. Put simply, an internship is a period spent working for a company as an unpaid member of staff. But it should provide you with valuable insights into the practical aspects of the subject.
To fulfil the academic requirements of the internship, you have to submit an internship report following the specifications outlined in the Faculty guide. Please consult the programme website for the latest version of this document.
In a nutshell, your internship report must include a number of specific features: Firstly, it should outline the specific business of the company or department in which you perform your internship; secondly it should outline your job description there. These first two components can be brief, and they can be included in the introduction of the report. The major focus of the report should be on the third component, the critical analysis of a specific internship-related topic, which relates academic knowledge to practical experience. However, note that sadly many aspects of your daily work can be practice-oriented rather than academically-oriented and you'll be asked to do routine tasks most of the time. It is, of course, important that you do as you are asked. However, to pass the academic requirements of the internship you must go, if necessary, beyond the following of instructions and demonstrate your ability in logical thinking. Ideally, the report will be of practical benefit to your employer and go beyond your usual duties.

Presenter: Before you hear the rest of the talk, you have some time to look at questions 38 to 40.

Now listen and answer questions 38 to 40.

Man: So, now I'll give you some recommendations for the actual writing of your reports. Once you have gathered your information and planned an outline, you can begin writing. Your report needs to be serious and academic, but bear in mind that your tutors are unlikely to be impressed by the excessive use of technical terms. So don't worry about fancy beginnings or profound ideas – just write! As you work, keep your target audience in mind. Are they going to be familiar with the acronyms used in your work place? If in doubt, leave them out and write the words out in full.
Once you have completed your first draft, put it away and give your mind a rest. When you take it out again, begin revising. Substitute accurate words for ambiguous ones; substitute clear simple sentences for complicated grammatical structures. You may want to rewrite paragraphs or entire sections.
The bottom line is to produce a smoothly written, logical report. Having someone else read your revised draft is a sure test of effective communication. A fellow intern or workmate will tell you if what you've written is understandable. Revise a second time on the basis of this criticism. Your final version should be flawless. If your report includes typos and spelling mistakes, then your readers are likely to be distracted and you risk losing credibility. Although the internship report should conform to the overall structure I've described, there's no strict rule when it comes to length and specific formatting of text. You should be able to present your report in the style most appropriate for your studies. However, a typical internship report consists of three main sections: the preliminaries, the main text and the reference material, all of which are required.

Answer key

Unit 1

1a (pages 4 and 5)

1
1 his book about scientific inventions
2 some rules of life (that he read about 15 years ago in a book by Charles Sykes)

2
1 unjust   2 can't expect   3 more strict   4 a beginning
5 your   6 have to be done by everyone
7 seldom   8 technical expertise

3
1 Currently   2 about fifteen years ago   3 Before that
4 next year   5 Many years ago   6 at the time
7 Over the last twenty years   8 rarely   9 Sooner or later

4
1 am (*or* 'm) taking   2 attended   3 had never been
4 seem   5 have (*or* 've) been wondering   6 will (*or* 'll) have

5
1 said (than) done   2 valuable   3 guiding
4 point   5 from (my) mistakes   6 thumb

6
One of the problems with advice is that people tend to interpret it to suit their own purposes. An example of this is the wisdom of the 18th-century economist, Adam Smith. One of his main ideas was that if you allow people to seek wealth for themselves, they will naturally create jobs and wealth for others. He called this 'the invisible hand'. People trying to improve their own situation also help their neighbour to improve theirs, but without meaning to, as if with an invisible hand. Unfortunately, a lot of people took Smith to mean that it was all right to be greedy and selfish and not to help others directly, which is not at all what he meant.

1b (pages 6 and 7)

1
b

2
1 T   2 T   3 T   4 F   5 F   6 F

3
past perfect continuous: *Had they already been thinking*
present perfect continuous: *have been following*
past continuous: *were looking at*
present continuous: *are continually changing*
future continuous: *will be calling me*

4
1 a) is already b) is becoming, i.e. it's a trend
2 a) statement of fact b) suggests irritation about this situation
3 a) the list is finished b) the list isn't complete – they are still working on it
4 little difference in meaning although b) suggests they thought about it for some time
5 a) I decided after I got married   b) I decided at or around the time of the marriage
6 a) statement of fact b) the speaker expects that they are hoping

5
1 Had you been waiting
2 Has someone been smoking
3 had been playing, fell
4 am working
5 have been living, are repairing *or* have been repairing
6 have heard

6
1 c   2 f   3 e   4 b   5 d   6 a

7
1 peace and quiet   2 as and when   3 short and sweet
4 aches and pains   5 Now and then   6 fun and games
7 First and foremost   8 By and large

9
1 d   2 b   3 f   4 e   5 a   6 c

1c (page 8)

1
1 T   2 T   3 F   4 F   5 T   6 F

2
1 b   2 a   3 a   4 a   5 b   6 a

3
1 b   2 a   3 b   4 a   5 b

4
2 saver   3 walks   4 brings   5 fact   6 story   7 lifelike   8 time

1d (page 9)

1
Conversation 1
Place: conference
Teresa: conference organizer and lecturer in Social Sciences in Toronto
Ana: academic in Social Sciences at Deusto University in San Sebastian, Spain

Conversation 2
Place: bus stop at airport
Jeff: primary school teacher
Khalid: M.Sc. student of Quantum Physics. Has come from Amman in Jordan

2
Conversation 1
1 think of   2 should have   3 Whereabouts   4 fancy
Conversation 2
1 heading   2 by (the) way   3 going, studying   4 impressive

3
1 a   2 a   3 b   4 b   5 b

4a
1 What did you think of   2 Do you fancy
3 What kind of   4 What's it like   5 I should have mentioned
6 How are you finding   7 Shall we go and get a
8 have you been here

5
Students' own answers.

1e (page 10)

1
1 pay grade 6   2 line manager   3 18 months

2
1 weeks   2 that is *or* that is to say   3 months   4 years
5 to be confirmed   6 for example

3
1 approx.   2 re *or* ref   3 incl.   4 etc.   5 10 a.m.   6 hrs
7 NB   8 pc *or* %   9 2nd *or* sec (time)   10 p.w.

4
Jeff rang at eleven o'clock (this morning). He wants you to go to London to discuss the contract details, i.e. commission, quantities, etc. The time of the meeting is to be confirmed. Note that he isn't in the office until Thursday.
(Note that *i.e.* and *etc.* are perfectly acceptable in writing.)

5
New policy
no limits on how much/little holiday staff can take
try policy out for limited period, i.e. 6 mths
not entirely sure if going to work, but pretty confident
Reasons for policy
much better to be adult and responsible – all have busy working lives + busy lives outside work
given a little freedom, organize time better
Employee responsibilities
NB not an excuse to take as much time off work as possible
can't organize completely independently – negotiate with colleagues to avoid disruptions
also still have work targets to reach
Details
start date tbc – 2nd half of this year
policy applies to every employee incl. part-time staff
reviewed after approx. 4 mths

Wordbuilding / Learning skills / Check! (page 11)

1
1 or 2 or 3 and 4 and 5 but 6 and 7 and 8 or 9 and 10 to

2
1 back to front 2 give and take 3 wear and tear
4 more or less, out and about 5 sink or swim
6 cut and dried, take it or leave it
7 slowly but surely, live and learn

3
1 You can sound more natural, impress your audience and create more vivid images to support your arguments.
2 It can sound ridiculous.
3 a T b F Putting a correct idiom in an otherwise incorrect sentence could sound odd. c T d F Use idioms that have widespread and established use. e F Slang is very informal language that is usually spoken rather than written.

4
1 no 2 yes

6
1 a sit b work c yourself d blind
2 a dreamer b joker c outgoing
3 a nowadays, generally b so far, recently
c sooner or later d prior to that

Unit 2

2a (pages 12 and 13)

1
1 in Tibet
2 a small fungus (called *yartsa gunbu*), because it is highly valued
3 herding yaks and/or sheep

2
1 searching 2 fungus 3 medicinal 4 caterpillar 5 stalk
6 energy 7 soared 8 yaks 9 overpicking

3
1 get by 2 get out of 3 get back 4 gets over
5 getting at 6 get round to

4
1 has dropped 2 are looking for 3 has been known
4 had been searching, found 5 have prescribed 6 started
7 has grown 8 are thriving 9 will have disappeared
10 will be searching
(Note that 4 *had searched* and 8 *thrive* are also possible.)

5
1 has shown (*or* shows) 2 helps 3 have criticized (*or* criticize)
4 is based 5 showed 6 had used 7 has not exploited
8 has been 9 will be developed 10 is

6
1 livelihood 2 task 3 trade 4 vocation 5 living

7
/ɪ/
me<u>di</u>cinal
spe<u>ci</u>men
spe<u>ci</u>fic
<u>ca</u>terpillar
art<u>i</u>st

/iː/
pr<u>e</u>vious
<u>ki</u>lo
v<u>i</u>sa

/aɪ/
pr<u>i</u>vate
uns<u>ci</u>entific
surv<u>i</u>ve
presc<u>ri</u>be
t<u>i</u>ny
rev<u>i</u>talize
f<u>i</u>nancial

8
1 I've been travelling in this region for many years and I'd seen this phenomenon before but never paid it much attention.
2 Well, often you'll visit a place with a particular story in mind. Then, while you're researching it, you find something else catches your interest.
3 I was very struck by how well off people in the village seemed compared to when I'd last visited.
4 So I decided to investigate and got this amazing story of the golden worm.

2b (pages 14 and 15)

1
1 They swim very fast; they are difficult to find (because of overfishing and the use of seine nets which has reduced the numbers by 80 per cent); they weigh in excess of 300 kilos and so are difficult to land.
2 (deep-sea) line fishing

2
1 T 2 F 3 F 4 N 5 F 6 F

3
1 d 2 f 3 a 4 h 5 b 6 g 7 e 8 c

4
1 be on the safe side 2 wrap (your children) in cotton wool
3 second nature 4 cut corners 5 follow the correct procedure/do things by the book

5
1 The trip had been organized by my friend, Troy.
2 Once the fish have been found, that's only the beginning of your task.
3 In 'purse seine' fishing, big circular nets are used to trap the tuna.
4 The Atlantic tuna population has been devastated by 'purse seine' fishing in the last thirty years.
5 Troy jumped on the rod so that the line could be kept tight.
6 The fish started to get tired of being chased.

6
1 was (*or* got) called 2 being told 3 could/might get injured
4 being (*or* to be) driven 5 don't get paid
6 Have you been invited

Answer key

7
1 active better, but passive also possible
2 passive
3 passive better, but active also possible
4 active
5 passive better, but active also possible
6 active

2c (page 16)

1
c

2
1 a missing cat   2 a geography teacher   3 memorizing dots on a map   4 outdoor   5 adventures   6 reality of the city   7 by walking   8 think at a high level   9 how friendly the community is   10 creative and innovative

3
1 a   2 b   3 b   4 a

4
1 a   2 c   3 d   4 b

5
1 She got off on the wrong foot, but relations with her colleagues are much better now.
2 I hope I didn't put my foot in it when I told her how like her sister she was.
3 I've never been good at dancing – I have two left feet.
4 She really shot herself in the foot by not taking the promotion when she was offered it.
5 People often ask me why I didn't follow in my father's footsteps and become a doctor like him.
6 Hannah found her feet very quickly at university and made some good friends.
7 I'm now working for Google. I was very lucky to get my foot in the door because so many people want to work there.
8 She was going to jump from the ten metre board but she got cold feet.

2d (page 17)

1
1 conscientious   2 reliable   3 enthusiastic   4 motivated   5 focused   6 flexible   7 well-organized   8 resourceful

2
1 infrastructure projects   2 He spent one year working on a transport and metro hub, where he helped to design (or adapted) the programme for planning work schedules for staff.

3
1 conscientious – got a commendation for his previous work
2 well-organized – he says he's good at planning and organization
3 resourceful – he had to adapt a computer programme
4 enthusiastic and motivated – he's keen to work for an
5 international company and says he is enthusiastic about learning

4a
1 experience   2 commendation   3 infrastructure   4 authorities   5 suitability   6 particular   7 relevant   8 important   9 enthusiastic

5
Students' own answers.

2e (page 18)

1a
a attracts or attracted   b available   c response   d Currently   e As, suitable   f attached   g taking, consider   h requirements

1b
1 c   2 f   3 d   4 e   5 a   6 h   7 g   8 b

2
The missing elements are:
1 when it was advertised
3 your present situation
4 why you are suited to the job
and 9 (possibly) give a personal touch

3
Example answers:
… in response to your advertisement on the Jobsonline website (1) this week … and relevant experience. …
(3) I am currently working in a temporary position for a local charity making calls to potential donors. (9) It is interesting and worthwhile work but desk-based and I am someone who likes to get out and meet people.
The job attracted me because … world of work again. (4) As someone who understands the education sector and has experience of fundraising, I think I am a suitable candidate.

Wordbuilding / Learning skills / Check! (page 19)

2
1 e   2 j   3 f   4 i   5 b   6 h   7 a   8 d   9 g   10 c

4
Possible answers:
1 a to inform   b specific information   c When will it be available to buy? How much will it cost?
2 a to inform, to persuade   b gist   c What is different about this book? Have attitudes to childhood changed?
3 a to inform, to give opinions   b gist and specific information   c What is the film? Would they recommend it?

5
1 a eagle hunter   b Moken   c smokejumper
2 a wait a long time   b see well   c keep fit and healthy
3 back, later   b get
4 a not, contact   b my, in   c I, hearing, you,   d job, male
Name: Jimmy Chin

Unit 3

3a (pages 20 and 21)

1
Possible answers:

	Glastonbury	Ghent
Location	west of England	Belgium
Size of town	small (but growing)	large, like a city
Type of town	market town. now with mix of residents – older and more conservative vs younger and alternative, wacky	university town, historic town, port, industrial
Reasons for liking	NM	lively and friendly, open-minded people, masses to do – good music scene, interesting museums and galleries, beautiful architecture, nice parks

2
1 b   2 a   3 b   4 b   5 c   6 a

3
1 g   2 a   3 d   4 f   5 h   6 b   7 e   8 c

4
1 ghost   2 quaint   3 shanty   4 sprawling   5 scruffy
6 characterless   7 sleepy   8 resort   9 run-down

5
1 fairly   2 quite a sleepy   3 rather   4 a bit (*quite* is also correct)
5 quite like it   6 cheating slightly   7 quite   8 particularly
9 pretty   10 a bit

6
1 very   2 particularly *or* very   3 quite *or* fairly   4 quite
5 fairly *or* pretty *or* rather   6 quite *or* rather

7
1, 5 and 6 mean 'but probably not enough'.

8
A: How was your trip to Russia?
B: Great, thanks. We had quite a packed schedule, but it was very interesting. We started in Moscow and saw the sights around Red Square. Strangely, the thing I loved most was the metro. Each station is like a work of art in itself. The service is pretty efficient too.
A: And how did it compare to St Petersburg?
B: Very different. St Petersburg is a very grand and gracious city. Actually, it feels a bit closer in atmosphere to other cities in central Europe, whereas Moscow doesn't feel particularly European. But that's the thing about Russia. You don't realize what an enormous and diverse country it is until you travel there.

3b (pages 22 and 23)

1
1 Geography: Mustang is a former kingdom in north-central Nepal; Climate: the climate is incredibly inhospitable; (wind-savaged)
2 10,000 (conservatively estimated)
3 It was a centre of scholarship and art, and a key place on the salt trade route from Tibet to India.
4 most showed signs of domestic habitation; in others there were stunning treasures: in one cave, a 26-foot-long mural; in another, 8,000 calligraphed manuscripts; many seemed to be elaborate tombs full of amazing riches
5 burial chambers
6 For safety. Because the territory was frequently fought over, they placed safety over convenience and took refuge in the caves.

2
1 ~~absolutely~~   2 ~~extremely~~   3 ~~completely~~   4 ~~absolutely~~
5 ~~absolutely~~   6 utterly   7 ~~very~~   8 ~~incredibly~~

3
1 incredibly *or* really *or* very   2 absolutely *or* completely *or* totally   3 absolutely *or* quite   4 incredibly *or* really *or* very   5 absolutely *or* really   6 incredibly *or* really *or* very   7 completely *or* totally   8 quite

4a
1 I'm utterly exhausted.
2 I'd really appreciate that.
3 It's so hot today.
4 It's OK. I quite understand.
5 You're absolutely right.
6 It's very difficult to say.

5
1 f   2 i   3 h   4 a   5 g   6 c   7 e   8 j   9 b   10 d

6
1 wildly optimistic   2 vaguely familiar   3 patently obvious
4 perfectly reasonable   5 deadly serious   6 painfully slow

7
a a garage/workshop, a walk-in wardrobe
b a gym, a sauna
c a conservatory, a roof garden
d a games room, a home cinema, a library
e en suite bathrooms, a state-of-the-art kitchen

3c (page 24)

1
1 It means copying good design from nature and applying it to things that are man-made.
2 the architect Gaudi took inspiration from nature in his design of the Sagrada Familia and the materials he used; the Swiss Re Tower is built in a shape taken from nature; the chimneys in the Eastgate Centre in Harare imitate the heating and cooling system in a termite mound

2
1 a   2 c   3 b   4 b   5 b   6 c

3
1 a   2 b   3 b   4 b   5 a

4
1 keeps (his) feet   2 Stand   3 grounds   4 new, in
5 get off   6 covered

3d (page 25)

1
For: 1) people won't have to waste time going down to the canteen to get their coffee; 2) it will encourage employee interaction
Against: staff might spend too much time there away from productive work

2
1 all, basically   2 recommend   3 have to   4 disagree with
5 shouldn't underestimate   6 mean
7 much, favour, given   8 by (the) way, touch

3a
1 d   2 y   3 r   4 t   5 w   6 w

3b
1 first‿of‿all
2 with‿a‿bit‿of‿luck
3 as‿a‿matter‿of‿fact
4 as‿far‿as‿I'm‿aware
5 between‿you‿w‿and‿me
6 let's‿be‿j‿honest
7 at‿the‿j‿end‿of‿the‿day
8 I've‿no‿w‿idea, I'm‿afraid

4
Students' own answers.

3e (page 26)

1
a 4   b 3

2
against
the benefits of high-rise building to the wider environment are great; it's not possible to keep expanding our cities outwards

3
1 b   2 e   3 d   4 f   5 a   6 c

Wordbuilding / Learning skills / Check! (page 27)

1
1 rent   2 studio   3 lets   4 furnished   5 share   6 move
7 budget   8 bills   9 charges   10 properties

Answer key

11 commission   12 tenant   13 landlord   14 deposit
15 advance   16 references

4
1 There are only <u>two</u> interesting <u>bu</u>ildings in the <u>a</u>rea around <u>New</u>port.
2 The <u>green</u> belt should <u>definitely</u> be pro<u>tec</u>ted from de<u>ve</u>lopers.

6
Across: 5 deprived   8 time   9 rich   10 compact   11 en suite
Down: 1 modern   2 a bit   3 seem   4 spacious   6 vibrant
7 debate

Unit 4

4a (pages 28 and 29)

1
Possible answers:
It's a play on words. *Boring* also means 'making deep holes'. In this case, it refers to making deep underground tunnels below cities to serve as a new transport system.

2
1 To go round it, over it or under it.
2 Building channels around sandcastles. (They fill up as soon as you build them.)
3 Accidents in the air could also impact those below.
4 It's expensive.
5 On sleds in underground tunnels.
6 By using single-lane tunnels and more efficient tunnelling machines.
7 By having everyone travelling in the same direction.
8 Vacuum.
9 900 km an hour.

3
1 ring   2 debris   3 pull   4 venture   5 hold   6 tried

4
1 likely   2 might (*could* also possible)   3 could (*might* also possible)   4 good chance   5 should   6 possibly

5
1 Such solutions will probably never work / probably won't work because …
2 Rather than removing the problem, the chances are you are just moving it somewhere else.
3 It's possible that collisions or accidents in the air (might/could) have an impact on those below.
4 Given his amazing record, he may well pull this off.
5 Musk's idea is that his techniques are likely to reduce the cost enormously.
6 In his mind is the idea that in future, the tunnels could use vacuum technology.

6
1 may well
2 will almost certainly come up with
3 probably will be
4 are likely to be driving (*or* are likely to drive)
5 should have
6 will probably be
7 is unlikely to change
8 the likelihood of that happening
9 is

7
1 doable, desirable   2 non-negotiable   3 unimaginable
4 irreplaceable   5 insurmountable   6 intolerable

8
1 returnable   2 unbreakable   3 drinkable   4 walkable
5 non-washable   6 contactable

4b (pages 30 and 31)

1
1 d   2 b   3 a   4 c

2
1 scientists   2 day   3 problem   4 money
5 afford   6 tests

3
1 a   2 b   3 b   4 b   5 a   6 b

4
1 d   2 a   3 f   4 e   5 c   6 b

5
1 I must have ridden   2 I should have taken   3 I didn't need to   4 I could have wheeled   5 I had to be   6 I had to find
7 I needn't have worried   8 Someone might have dropped

6a
1 have   2 have   3 have   4 to   5 have   6 to

7
1 about   2 across   3 up   4 up   5 down

4c (page 32)

1
1 internet and mobile communications
2 they are actively involved in spending their money (more 'hands on') whereas past philanthropists set up long-term foundations and scholarships for future generations; they want to see a quick return on investment as they would in business

2
1 T   2 T   3 F   4 T   5 F   6 F

3
1 self-made   2 counterparts   3 return   4 seed money
5 bring about   6 no strings   7 self-confessed   8 ethos

4
1 ethos   2 seed money   3 return   4 bring about
5 self-made   6 counterpart   7 self-confessed   8 no strings

5
1 all *or* best   2 thought *or* consideration
3 break *or* chance   4 go *or* try   5 ahead   6 time

4d (page 33)

1
1 (school) children   2 It's a bag that also functions as a desk.
3 Not all children have a desk at school or even a table at home.
4 It has compartments for notebooks, pens and a water holder.

2
1 so original, ask   2 would, want, that
3 how, people, be able

3
1 The bag also functions as a desk.
2 Not all children have a desk at school or even a table at home.
3 The price is a little higher in Europe to help lower the cost of a bag for a family in a developing country.

4
Possible answers:
1 So how does it work?
2 Isn't that rather expensive, you ask?
3 So why would I need one?
4 So, what's our ambition for this?

5
1 <u>Clear</u>ly   2 <u>Fi</u>nancially   3 <u>E</u>ssentially   4 <u>Prac</u>tically
5 Of <u>course</u>   6 <u>Ho</u>nestly   7 <u>Ob</u>viously   8 To be <u>ho</u>nest
9 <u>Ba</u>sically

6
Students' own answers.

4e (page 34)

1
1 Yes, but only in theory.
2 A scheduled discussion between colleagues every two to four weeks; the opportunity to visit other organizations.
3 Giving employees a structure; rewarding employees for good ideas; giving innovation and creativity a more formal role.

2
1 To tell the reader what the report is about.
2 Using bullet points and sequencing words – *first of all, secondly,* etc.
3 *In summary*

3
1 are   2 should   3 giving   4 have   5 should visit

Wordbuilding / Learning skills / Check! (page 35)

1
1 drop   2 stroke   3 bit   4 bit   5 gust   6 hint   7 plot
8 word   9 shred   10 bite

2
a a drop of water
b a hint of disappointment
c a shred of evidence

3
2 2

6
1 necessity   2 foldable   3 bionic   4 elevator pitch
5 social entrepreneur

7
1 thought   2 off   3 must   4 shrink
Name of company: TOMS

Unit 5

5a (pages 36 and 37)

1
1 Being with knowledgeable guides
3 Meeting fellow travellers
5 No planning – everything is arranged for you
7 Optional free time

2
1 b   2 b   3 c   4 c   5 b   6 a

3
1 sheep   2 million   3 wrong   4 nothing   5 out   6 of

4
1 by   2 and   3 to   4 in   5 from, to   6 to

5
1 What I want from travel is a bit of independence and freedom.
2 The thing that changed my mind was a guided tour I took.
3 I do like visiting museums.
4 It did make me reassess my whole attitude to organized tours.
5 What surprised me was how knowledgeable and interesting some of the other travellers were.
6 … particularly if it's a more remote or not-so-safe place you're visiting.

6
1 The thing I remember best about/from my childhood is how amazing family holidays were.
2 It was enough to have a rough idea of where we were going.
3 We did stop when we saw things that interested us.
4 It wasn't money that was the issue.
5 What I loved was the lack of any kind of routine.
6 I do like sleeping in the afternoon.
7 When I have children, what I'm going to do is (to) recreate a similar experience for them.

7
1 do   2 did   3 do   4 does

8
Across: 1 cosy   4 slow   7 romantic
Down: 2 officious   3 elegant   5 wary   6 grand

5b (pages 38 and 39)

1
1 to educate the rest of the world about Africa
2 the football World Cup in South Africa in 2010
3 They aim to reveal Africa as seen by Africans themselves rather than through the eyes of an outsider.
4 presenting a one-dimensional, stereotyped view of Africa

2
a haphazardly   b seize   c conspicuous   d turbulent
e (her) portrait   f stereotyped   g decree

3
1 a Chinua Achebe Centre for African Writers and Artists   b writer
2 a (The fact that) many things are already familiar to them   b observing the details
3 a Africa   b series of travel books   c travel books
4 a be   b author(s)/writer(s)

4
1 one   2 (omit underlined words)   3 do (so)   4 others *or* other ones   5 This *or* That   6 one   7 to   8 so *or* it is

5a
1 B: <u>Yes</u>, I'd <u>love</u> to.
2 B: <u>No</u>, I've <u>got</u> one, <u>thanks</u>.
3 B: <u>No</u>, I'm <u>afraid not</u>.
4 B: <u>Oh</u>, I'm <u>sorry</u> to <u>hear</u> that.
5 B: I <u>hope so</u>.
6 B: Oh, <u>yes</u>. I <u>love</u> a good <u>thriller</u>.
7 B: <u>Catching</u> up on <u>emails</u>.

6
I've been on a few mystery tours, but the one I did in Prague was probably the best. And I'm not the only person to say so. If you look at reviews, you'll hardly find one negative one. I'm not going to give you too many details because that would spoil the surprise if one day you happened to do it too. What I will tell you is that it started at night and involved a segway, some canoes, a jazz band and a large breakfast. If that hasn't aroused your curiosity, I don't know what will.

5c (page 40)

1
1 He dreamed about exploring.
2 It had ceased to be a mystery. *or* It had become a place of darkness.
3 He got a job as a ship's captain aboard a steamboat.

2
1 blank spaces   2 rivers, lakes and names   3 an immense, uncoiled snake   4 It was used for trading.   5 He had been killed ('in a scuffle with the natives').   6 It was featureless, monotonous and grim.

3
1 positive   2 No, they haven't.   3 It is curled up/asleep.
4 b   5 a   6 cannot speak *or* not speaking

4
1 laughing   2 mind   3 course   4 principle   5 way   6 that

5d (page 41)

1
1 To Barcelona. It was a competition amongst a group of university friends.
2 A lorry driver going all the way to the Spanish border picked them up within ten minutes.
3 In the morning, they couldn't see the lorry driver and they thought he'd had to leave in a hurry. The lorry driver returned with coffee and croissants.

2
1 these days   2 We all know that   3 A year ago
4 Amazingly,   5 believe   6 by chance, happened
7 The following morning   8 our dismay
9 Feeling pretty miserable   10 just at that moment

3
a by chance   b Just at that moment,   c Feeling pretty miserable   d these days   e Amazingly,   f A year ago
g The following morning   h To our dismay

4a
Long vowel sound: am_a_zement, ann_o_yance, delight, dism_a_y frustr_a_tion, rel_ie_f, surpr_i_se
Short vowel sound: ast_o_nishment, emb_a_rrassment, h_o_rror, regr_e_t, sh_o_ck

5
Students' own answers.

5e (page 42)

1
³ It is 1857 and the British Empire in India is facing severe unrest from the indigenous population. For the ruling British class in the northern town of Krishnapur, life is calm and polite until the sepoys at a nearby military fort rise in mutiny and the British are forced to retreat into the British Residency. Food and other supplies become short, disease sets in and the inhabitants' resources are tested to the limit.

This is the first part of J.G. Farrell's empire trilogy, ¹ an examination of the British Empire in its decline. *The Siege of Krishnapur* serves as a metaphor for this decline as each character is forced to examine their own view of the world.

Although the situation is desperate, ⁴ Farrell describes it with great elegance and humour, conveying the ridiculousness of the British position. Some would argue that in not describing the hardship and injustice suffered by the local Indian population, Farrell has done them a great injustice. ² But I do not think that was his aim. What he has done is to write both a gripping story and a thought-provoking study of colonial life.

2
d

3
1 provoking   2 going   3 uneventful   4 fetched
5 convincing   6 wrenching   7 uninspiring   8 poorly

Wordbuilding / Learning skills / Check! (page 43)

1
1 spot   2 managed   3 ruined   4 tough   5 coped   6 courage
7 expectations   8 make (it) out   9 set off   10 thrilling

4
1 officious   2 sustainable, expectations   3 magical, unknown
4 graphic   5 cartoonist   6 relief, worryingly
7 thought-provoking   8 transformative

Unit 6

6a (pages 44 and 45)

1
1 Rishikesh (India)   2 chronic back pain   3 yes – because he's given up worrying about his bad back

2
1 the Beatles arrived in Rishikesh to study transcendental meditation at Maharishi Mahesh Yogi's ashram
2 songs the Beatles wrote in Rishikesh
3 foreign visitors who go to Rishikesh each year
4 disadvantaged boys that the Parmarth Niketan Ashram supports
5 the man started his exercise regime on the first day
6 the table at which they ate their meals
7 the man's visit to the ashram
8 the man can sit cross-legged through a meal

3
1 a   2 b   3 b   4 a   5 a   6 a

4
1 intransitive   2 intransitive   3 chronic back pain
4 the day   5 mental and physical healing   6 hundreds of thousands of foreign visitors   7 them (the disadvantaged boys)   8 a breathing technique   9 intransitive   10 it (the pain)   11 worrying

5
1 put up   2 put up with   3 separable: pull in, put off, give up   inseparable: get over, look for, work on

6
1 The pain is quite bad, but I've learned to put up with it.
2 I got the injury playing football and it took me a long time to get over it.
3 If you think going to yoga classes will help, then there's no point putting it off.
4 I used to ski a lot, but I gave it up.
5 Reducing the cost of the course for students really pulled them in.
6 Can you put me up for the night on Tuesday when I'm in town?
7 I'm not as supple as I used to be, but I put that down to my age.
8 I can't touch my toes yet, but I'm working on it.

7
1 come across   2 set aside   3 take up   4 put someone off   5 go in for   6 takes off   7 get out of   8 carry out
9 comes about   10 fall back on

8
1 keep   2 do   3 out   4 shape   5 on   6 am *or* keep
7 watch   8 for

9
A: The other day I looked up what fitness classes there were available locally and I couldn't believe how many there were.
B: Did you come across any that you liked the look of?
A: Not really. I didn't know what half of them were: Boxercise, Boot camp, Aqua aerobics … and loads based on dance.
B: You mean like Zumba?
A: Yes. I knew Zumba was a craze that had taken off, but there were others: Jazzercise, Bodyjam. I mean, if you go in for dancing, why don't you just sign up for a dance class?
B: And do you? Go in for dancing, that is?
A: Yes, I do. I think that's what I'll do … take up samba or something.

6b (pages 46 and 47)

1
1 Simply put, cross-training means practising other sports or forms of exercise to improve, indirectly, your abilities in your main or target sport. (para 1)
2 Finally, and most importantly, it prevents athletes from getting the kind of repetitive strain injuries that they often suffer if they only practise the same activities day in, day out. (para 2)
3 The lesson of cross-training is that the body reacts well to new experiences. (para 4)

2
1 c   2 c   3 a   4 b   5 a   6 c

3
1 help (more generally) to increase, tend(s) to be, learn to deal with
2 require(s) you to control, enable them to continue (playing)
3 let(s) you build, recommend everyone incorporate
4 mean(s) practising
5 succeed in performing
6 prevent(s) athletes from getting

4
1 to warm up   2 to do   3 doing   4 exercise, (to) see
5 playing   6 about getting   7 for getting   8 to be
9 playing *or* to play   10 playing, training

5
1 grazed   2 stubbed   3 bumped   4 chipped   5 bruised
6 lost   7 sprained   8 pulled

6
1 passed <u>out</u>   2 <u>on</u> the mend   3 run <u>down</u>   4 shaken <u>up</u>
5 <u>off</u> colour   6 <u>in</u> a bad way

7a
They all have the stress on the second syllable apart from *practise* and *welcome*.

7b
All the verbs with stress on the second syllable have common prefixes, e.g. *pre-, post-, de-, ex-*.

6c (page 48)

1
b

2
1 a is worth around $200 billion
   b spend over a billion each year on their fingernails alone
2 Male grooming (now)
3 regular washing with soap could help to turn a dark skin whiter
4 McDonald's alters its menu to suit the tastes of each local market
5 a black soap in Africa   b in South America as an ingredient in hair dye

3
Possible answers:
1 similar   2 selling   3 idea   4 changes   5 shine

4
1 long   2 straight   3 brave   4 it   5 lose   6 music

6d (page 49)

1
1 b   2 d   3 e   4 f

2
1 lift   2 air conditioning   3 staff canteen
4 staff to do sports together

3
1 sometimes people who have heavy things to move or who aren't so mobile will want to use a lift   2 fresh air from outside wouldn't always be cool   3 who should be responsible for making the list   4 not everyone will want to join in with doing sports with other staff

4
1 alternative, be   2 realize, easily (work) around
3 would (be) much   4 Admittedly, but   5 through
6 know (not) everyone

5a
1 I'm not <u>very</u> much in <u>favour</u> of the proposal.
2 It's not <u>exactly</u> what I had in <u>mind</u>.
3 It's not a <u>particularly</u> <u>cheap</u> option.
4 It hasn't proved to be <u>so</u> <u>successful</u>.
5 I'm not <u>entirely</u> <u>convinced</u>.

6
Students' own answers.

6e (page 50)

1
1 There is concern that children in the school are not eating healthily enough, and this is affecting both their general health and their academic performance.
2 Most children are not getting a balanced diet.
3 That school meals should be compulsory for all pupils and that they are given the choice of different meals, but not a choice of different elements within each meal.

2
1 In view of this   2 Overall   3 However
4 Accordingly   5 apparently   6 specifically

3a
1 pupils   2 lunches   3 good variety of foods
4 what packed lunches should include   5 choices
6 We (also) suggest

3b
Possible answers:
serving the meals
majority of the pupils
benefit children

Wordbuilding / Learning skills / Check! (page 51)

1
1 flashbacks   2 turnout   3 breakthrough   4 follow-up
5 catch-up   6 breakdown   7 lookout   8 faraway
9 break-in   10 showdown

2
a getaway   b cutback   c clampdown   d show-off
e turn-up   f break-up

4
1 a, c, d   2 a, b   3 b, c   4 c, d

5
1 jogging, swimming   2 Japan   3 India   4 very long
5 necks   6 only skin   7 calories   8 insurance

Unit 7

7a (pages 52 and 53)

1
using 3D glasses

2
1 an archaeologist; he does archaeology using virtual reality with technologies such as satellite imagery and radar
2 a totally immersive virtual reality room

Answer key

4
1 laughing 2 mind 3 course 4 principle 5 way 6 that

5d (page 41)

1
1 To Barcelona. It was a competition amongst a group of university friends.
2 A lorry driver going all the way to the Spanish border picked them up within ten minutes.
3 In the morning, they couldn't see the lorry driver and they thought he'd had to leave in a hurry. The lorry driver returned with coffee and croissants.

2
1 these days   2 We all know that   3 A year ago
4 Amazingly,   5 believe   6 by chance, happened
7 The following morning   8 our dismay
9 Feeling pretty miserable   10 just at that moment

3
a by chance   b Just at that moment,   c Feeling pretty miserable   d these days   e Amazingly,   f A year ago   g The following morning   h To our dismay

4a
Long vowel sound: am**a**zement, ann**o**yance, delight, dism**a**y frustr**a**tion, rel**ie**f, surpr**i**se
Short vowel sound: ast**o**nishment, emb**a**rrassment, h**o**rror, regr**e**t, sh**o**ck

5
Students' own answers.

5e (page 42)

1
³ It is 1857 and the British Empire in India is facing severe unrest from the indigenous population. For the ruling British class in the northern town of Krishnapur, life is calm and polite until the sepoys at a nearby military fort rise in mutiny and the British are forced to retreat into the British Residency. Food and other supplies become short, disease sets in and the inhabitants' resources are tested to the limit.

This is the first part of J.G. Farrell's empire trilogy, ¹ an examination of the British Empire in its decline. *The Siege of Krishnapur* serves as a metaphor for this decline as each character is forced to examine their own view of the world.

Although the situation is desperate, ⁴ Farrell describes it with great elegance and humour, conveying the ridiculousness of the British position. Some would argue that in not describing the hardship and injustice suffered by the local Indian population, Farrell has done them a great injustice. ² But I do not think that was his aim. What he has done is to write both a gripping story and a thought-provoking study of colonial life.

2
d

3
1 provoking   2 going   3 uneventful   4 fetched
5 convincing   6 wrenching   7 uninspiring   8 poorly

Wordbuilding / Learning skills / Check! (page 43)

1
1 spot   2 managed   3 ruined   4 tough   5 coped   6 courage
7 expectations   8 make (it) out   9 set off   10 thrilling

4
1 officious   2 sustainable, expectations   3 magical, unknown
4 graphic   5 cartoonist   6 relief, worryingly
7 thought-provoking   8 transformative

Unit 6

6a (pages 44 and 45)

1
1 Rishikesh (India)   2 chronic back pain   3 yes – because he's given up worrying about his bad back

2
1 the Beatles arrived in Rishikesh to study transcendental meditation at Maharishi Mahesh Yogi's ashram
2 songs the Beatles wrote in Rishikesh
3 foreign visitors who go to Rishikesh each year
4 disadvantaged boys that the Parmarth Niketan Ashram supports
5 the man started his exercise regime on the first day
6 the table at which they ate their meals
7 the man's visit to the ashram
8 the man can sit cross-legged through a meal

3
1 a   2 b   3 b   4 a   5 a   6 a

4
1 intransitive   2 intransitive   3 chronic back pain
4 the day   5 mental and physical healing   6 hundreds of thousands of foreign visitors   7 them (the disadvantaged boys)   8 a breathing technique   9 intransitive   10 it (the pain)   11 worrying

5
1 put up   2 put up with   3 separable: pull in, put off, give up   inseparable: get over, look for, work on

6
1 The pain is quite bad, but I've learned to put up with it.
2 I got the injury playing football and it took me a long time to get over it.
3 If you think going to yoga classes will help, then there's no point putting it off.
4 I used to ski a lot, but I gave it up.
5 Reducing the cost of the course for students really pulled them in.
6 Can you put me up for the night on Tuesday when I'm in town?
7 I'm not as supple as I used to be, but I put that down to my age.
8 I can't touch my toes yet, but I'm working on it.

7
1 come across   2 set aside   3 take up   4 put someone off   5 go in for   6 takes off   7 get out of   8 carry out
9 comes about   10 fall back on

8
1 keep   2 do   3 out   4 shape   5 on   6 am *or* keep
7 watch   8 for

9
A: The other day I looked up what fitness classes there were available locally and I couldn't believe how many there were.
B: Did you come across any that you liked the look of?
A: Not really. I didn't know what half of them were: Boxercise, Boot camp, Aqua aerobics … and loads based on dance.
B: You mean like Zumba?
A: Yes. I knew Zumba was a craze that had taken off, but there were others: Jazzercise, Bodyjam. I mean, if you go in for dancing, why don't you just sign up for a dance class?
B: And do you? Go in for dancing, that is?
A: Yes, I do. I think that's what I'll do … take up samba or something.

141

6b (pages 46 and 47)

1
1 Simply put, cross-training means practising other sports or forms of exercise to improve, indirectly, your abilities in your main or target sport. (para 1)
2 Finally, and most importantly, it prevents athletes from getting the kind of repetitive strain injuries that they often suffer if they only practise the same activities day in, day out. (para 2)
3 The lesson of cross-training is that the body reacts well to new experiences. (para 4)

2
1 c 2 c 3 a 4 b 5 a 6 c

3
1 help (more generally) to increase, tend(s) to be, learn to deal with
2 require(s) you to control, enable them to continue (playing)
3 let(s) you build, recommend everyone incorporate
4 mean(s) practising
5 succeed in performing
6 prevent(s) athletes from getting

4
1 to warm up 2 to do 3 doing 4 exercise, (to) see
5 playing 6 about getting 7 for getting 8 to be
9 playing *or* to play 10 playing, training

5
1 grazed 2 stubbed 3 bumped 4 chipped 5 bruised
6 lost 7 sprained 8 pulled

6
1 passed out 2 on the mend 3 run down 4 shaken up
5 off colour 6 in a bad way

7a
They all have the stress on the second syllable apart from *practise* and *welcome*.

7b
All the verbs with stress on the second syllable have common prefixes, e.g. *pre-, post-, de-, ex-*.

6c (page 48)

1
b

2
1 a is worth around $200 billion
  b spend over a billion each year on their fingernails alone
2 Male grooming (now)
3 regular washing with soap could help to turn a dark skin whiter
4 McDonald's alters its menu to suit the tastes of each local market
5 a black soap in Africa b in South America as an ingredient in hair dye

3
Possible answers:
1 similar 2 selling 3 idea 4 changes 5 shine

4
1 long 2 straight 3 brave 4 it 5 lose 6 music

6d (page 49)

1
1 b 2 d 3 e 4 f

2
1 lift 2 air conditioning 3 staff canteen
4 staff to do sports together

3
1 sometimes people who have heavy things to move or who aren't so mobile will want to use a lift   2 fresh air from outside wouldn't always be cool   3 who should be responsible for making the list   4 not everyone will want to join in with doing sports with other staff

4
1 alternative, be 2 realize, easily (work) around
3 would (be) much 4 Admittedly, but 5 through
6 know (not) everyone

5a
1 I'm not very much in favour of the proposal.
2 It's not exactly what I had in mind.
3 It's not a particularly cheap option.
4 It hasn't proved to be so successful.
5 I'm not entirely convinced.

6
Students' own answers.

6e (page 50)

1
1 There is concern that children in the school are not eating healthily enough, and this is affecting both their general health and their academic performance.
2 Most children are not getting a balanced diet.
3 That school meals should be compulsory for all pupils and that they are given the choice of different meals, but not a choice of different elements within each meal.

2
1 In view of this 2 Overall 3 However
4 Accordingly 5 apparently 6 specifically

3a
1 pupils 2 lunches 3 good variety of foods
4 what packed lunches should include 5 choices
6 We (also) suggest

3b
Possible answers:
serving the meals
majority of the pupils
benefit children

Wordbuilding / Learning skills / Check! (page 51)

1
1 flashbacks 2 turnout 3 breakthrough 4 follow-up
5 catch-up 6 breakdown 7 lookout 8 faraway
9 break-in 10 showdown

2
a getaway b cutback c clampdown d show-off
e turn-up f break-up

4
1 a, c, d 2 a, b 3 b, c 4 c, d

5
1 jogging, swimming 2 Japan 3 India 4 very long
5 necks 6 only skin 7 calories 8 insurance

Unit 7

7a (pages 52 and 53)

1
using 3D glasses

2
1 an archaeologist; he does archaeology using virtual reality with technologies such as satellite imagery and radar
2 a totally immersive virtual reality room

Answer key

3
1 a   2 b   3 b   4 b   5 c

4
1 repair   2 shirts   3 a knife   4 holy
5 a burglars   b only bad luck   6 to process

5
1 Technology is generally thought to be a positive thing.
2 Plastic debris in our oceans is believed to be changing marine ecosystems irreparably as we speak.
3 The quest is known to have frustrated scientists and historians for centuries.
4 The tomb is considered to be an extremely sacred place.
5 Lin learns from an ancient text where a particular mountain was supposed to have been in the past.
6 These new approaches are expected to benefit all kinds of projects in the future.

6
1 Lin is thought to be unusual because of his varied interests.
2 Lin is said to have been inspired by an art historian who uses digital imaging.
3 Genghis Khan is known to have died far from his homeland.
4 It is also known that he wanted to be buried in some mountains in the north.
5 He was reported at the time to have asked to be buried in an unmarked tomb.
6 His tomb isn't expected to be found any time soon.

7
1 ~~upload~~   2 ~~blog~~   3 ~~network~~   4 ~~tweet~~   5 ~~posted~~   6 ~~blogged~~

8
I was very aware on my travels across Europe, posting my blog and photos, that Paris was going to present a particular challenge. I didn't want to photograph the obvious sites, like the Eiffel Tower, even though I was keen to visit them all. But as Paris is said to be one of the world's most photogenic cities, instead, I decided to take as few images as possible and come away with some really memorable compositions. So here they are. They're not supposed to be anything more than a small collection of my memories of this wonderful place: more like postcards than photos. I'll let you decide how successful they are.

7b (pages 54 and 55)

1
1 F (there are so many different channels to choose from - Youtube, Instagram, Linkedin and Twitter to name just a few - each with a different user profile)
2 T (If you use social media incorrectly, it can actually put customers off)
3 T (yet not using it is not really an option any longer, since it has become a key area in which companies compete with each other for customers' attention.)
4 T (there are various analytic software tools available at a relatively low cost that monitor both customer traffic and the reaction of those who see your campaign).
5 T (an equal mix of promotional material, new ideas and engaging or relatable content)
6 F (Remember that it is not how many people you reach but whether you reach people with a message that appeals to them.)

2
1 a   2 b   3 a   4 b

3
1 Having such a wide choice of different channels to choose from makes it difficult to know where to begin.
2 Incorrect use of social media can actually put customers off.
3 There are, however, some simple principles you can follow to ensure success.
4 Thirdly, it is important to keep the strength of your brand identity and the coherence of your message.
5 Remember that it is not the number of people you reach that matters but the appeal of your message.
6 Their aim was to raise awareness of the millions of children in the world who walk barefoot.

4
1 concern, cost of the work, speed
2 effect of the, popularity, launch
3 little interest, sales suddenly
4 The number of, late arrival

5
1 ballpark   2 loop   3 win   4 rocket   5 practice   6 page   7 box   8 reality

6
1 problems   2 contact *or* talk to   3 exploit / use to one's advantage   4 completely obvious

7c (page 56)

1 and 2
A hackathon is an event where computer programmers and web experts come together to design new software or new apps.
The focus was on applying technology to serious environmental problems.

3
1 hack-day, hackfest   2 a day or a weekend
3 web, mobile, social media   4 conserving resources, minimizing pollution, creating cleaner fuels, reducing waste   5 less ownership and more efficient consumption
6 a tool, e.g. an electric drill

4
1 start innovating now
2 dynamic and positive
3 to make comparisons between the energy efficiency of different electrical appliances
4 some of the sponsors and other companies that were present were clearly very interested in their app
5 a movement

5
1 bank   2 news   3 habit   4 in   5 ice
6 back   7 even

7d (page 57)

1

What is it?	a flesh-ripping dinosaur
Where was it found?	south-eastern Morocco
Who found it?	a team of scientists led by Andrea Cau of the Bologna Geological Museum
What does the discovery tell us about this part of Africa?	this area of North Africa seems to have been particularly popular with predatory dinosaurs

2
1 is believed   2 probably   3 perhaps   4 suggests that   5 appears that   6 seems to   7 tended to   8 Arguably

4
Students' own answers.

143

7e (page 58)

1
1 David Attenborough and German zoologists
2 They found an even smaller species, *Brookesia micra*.
3 On one of the smaller islands off the coast of Madagascar.
4 The German team used a different method to find *Brookesia*: searching with torches at night when the tiny chameleons climb into the trees and are said to be easier to spot.
5 In 2012
6 Because it seems to suggest that in certain circumstances, such as being confined to an island, some animals grow smaller in order to adapt to a restricted habitat.

2a
a it seems to suggest
b are said to be easier to spot
c almost
d generally
e likely (para 1), certainly (para 3)

2b
1 David Attenborough is probably one of the world's best-known nature documentary makers.
2 Attenborough seems to have found his pygmy chameleon by looking on the forest floor.
3 Apparently, German zoologists have found an even smaller species.
4 The German team appear to have used a different method to find *Brookesia*.
5 Some animals are believed to grow smaller in order to adapt to a restricted habitat.

3
Example answer:
We already know that some species of snake can fly and it is believed that some can glide up to 100 metres. But up to now no one has been able to understand how they are able to do this. Now a new study from Virginia Tech shows that scientists may have found the answer.
It seems that snakes can flatten their bodies to make a wing shape. In flight, they usually hold their heads up and their tails down, enabling them to glide.
It is not thought likely that this discovery will have any significance for aeroplane or military technology, but it is certainly true that it will change our view of what snakes are capable of.

Wordbuilding / Learning skills / Check! (page 59)

1
1 under   2 out   3 over   4 out   5 out   6 under   7 over
8 over   9 out   10 under   11 out   12 out

2
all three

3
1 main verb = implies, subject = the evidence, object = an increase
2 subject = the evidence that Jenkins has supplied, object = an increase in the number of people under fifty suffering from memory loss
3 extra information = whether you agree with Jenkins's methods of collecting data or not

5
1 social   2 even   3 languages   4 flag   5 invisible   6 emoji
Word: selfie

Unit 8

8a (pages 60 and 61)

1
1 in school   2 Hawaii   3 traditional Hawaiian music
4 a variety of styles; cover songs of more popular music
5 Because music can give great pleasure; you can feel more connected to things around you; it can be relaxing.

2
1 hooked   2 synonymous with Hawaii   3 cliques
4 created his own technique   5 freaked out   6 raw human emotion   7 have a blast   8 contemplative time

3
1 age   2 up   3 stressful   4 picking   5 yoga   6 silly

4
1 d   2 e   3 a   4 c   5 b

5
1 We just got back from holiday.
2 The new museum is just stunning.
3 That's just what I think.
4 We just use bicycles; we don't own a car.
5 There are just under three million people living in the city.
6 Hang on. I'm just trying to call the bank before it closes.

6
One of the song titles on Shimabukuro's album *Peace, Love and Ukulele* consists of just three numbers: 143. Shimabukuro says that the song was written for his fiancée at the time and that the significance is that in those days they just had pagers, not mobile phones. 143 means 'I love you' in numeric code. So he used to page her with that code, in just the same way that some people now text the letters *ILY*. Even after pagers were replaced with mobile phones, they still used the code, because it was just something they both understood. So the song is just a piece of nostalgia, really.

7
1 c   2 a   3 a   4 c   5 c   6 b   7 b   8 c   9 a   10 b

8a
1 d   2 e   3 f   4 a   5 b   6 c

9 and 10
Genres of music: folk, classical
Moods of music: upbeat, expressive, romantic
Musicians: busker, composer
Ways of singing: hum
Tastes in music: eclectic, conservative
Attributes of a musician: naturally-gifted, accomplished

8b (pages 62 and 63)

1
The article mentions neurological disorders such as: Alzheimer's, dementia, multiple sclerosis and Parkinson's.

2
1 F   2 T   3 T   4 F   5 T   6 T

3
1 is so simplified
2 so as to use
3 to prevent the subject feeling
4 such a lot of research that
5 to improve
6 because it lifts
7 so as not to be

4
1 d He left his job at the bank to concentrate on playing music.
2 a We perform live sometimes, but just for fun.
3 e Please turn any phones or music devices off so as not to / in order not to disturb other passengers.
4 c You have to practise to / in order to / so as to get better.
5 b Singers drink a lot of water to avoid getting throat problems.

5
1 play   2 dance   3 tune   4 ears   5 trumpet   6 chord
7 score   8 face

Answer key

6
Is there a way to learn an instrument fast? What do you think? The answer is almost certainly not, if you want to do it properly. To do anything well takes time and patience. You can take shortcuts to avoid learning each step, but in the end this will catch up with you. You may reach a certain destination faster, but it won't be the one that you're ultimately aiming for. I always advise people to bear in mind the three 'P's: pay attention to your instructor; practice – to improve you need to practise as often as possible; and patience. Progress is always slower at first and ninety per cent of people give up within the first year of taking up an instrument.

8c (page 64)

1
1 the harmonica *or* blues harp
2 charismatic and 'his own man' (i.e. confident and not easily influenced by others)
3 as a legend

2
1 a   2 c   3 b   4 a   5 c   6 a

3
1 star   2 radio *or* midday   3 hard   4 five *or* young
5 hands   6 wandering *or* drifting *or* travelling
7 jamming *or* playing   8 simple   9 negativity
10 charisma   11 Europe   12 influenced   13 respect
14 legend

4
1 nail   2 miss   3 nerve   4 note   5 record

8d (page 65)

1
1 musical: father a musician, aunt a singer
2 a singer
3 They wanted her to be a doctor or lawyer initially, but in the end, let her find her own way.

2
1 really thought about it like   2 good question
3 honestly don't   4 that's difficult to   5 tell you really

3a
Sentences 1, 3, 4 and 6 use wavering intonation.

4
Students' own answers.

8e (page 66)

1
1 Indian pop stars, in Bollywood films; everywhere
2 Yes. It's joyous, infectious, feel-good music.

2
1 vibrant, deafening
2 like a throng of happy voices
3 the already hectic nature of Indian city life, an environment which threatens to overwhelm your senses
4 The music is … joyous and infectious. You can't help tapping your foot along to the rhythm.
5 I'd be surprised if you weren't carried along in its happy wake.
6 match the prettiest faces on screen with the best voices around; It's not great music, it's feel-good music.

3
Possible answers:
1 friendly faces
2 in modern styles *or* in western styles
3 are infectious dance songs
4 and its modern side

5 performing dance routines, acting
6 focuses almost entirely on musicals

Wordbuilding / Learning skills / Check! (page 67)

1
1 beep the horn   2 bump your head   3 clap your hands
4 gulp down a drink   5 mumble the words   6 pop a balloon
7 sigh with relief   8 sniff the air   9 strum a guitar
10 tap on the window   11 tut-tut in disapproval
12 yawn with boredom

2
1 sighed   2 tut-tutted   3 sniffed   4 mumbling   5 tapped
6 yawned

4
1 <u>reg</u>gae   2 <u>coun</u>try   3 ca<u>lyp</u>so   4 experi<u>men</u>tal   5 <u>fu</u>sion
6 <u>op</u>era

5
1 a solo artist b band   2 a trumpet b chord
3 a Fado b face   4 electric; eclectic   5 love

Unit 9

9a (pages 68 and 69)

1
1 Bruce Farrer's ninth grade students.
2 The students' thoughts about what they wanted to do in life and whether they were on the right track.
3 Because the students don't see them again for another twenty years (after they'd forgotten about them).

2
1 They saw it as just something to keep them busy while he did something else.
2 He filed it carefully. And twenty years later he posted it back to the student who had written it.
3 He is retired.
4 He wants them to enjoy them, like any object you find years later.
5 Finding out how their lives have evolved and gratitude from the students for returning the letters.
6 That he wouldn't read it if they didn't want him to.
7 Because he was a big fan of the Swedish band ABBA.
8 dedicated, hard-working, caring, committed

3
1 distinct   2 see (the job) through   3 be (on the right) track
4 straightforward   5 fulfil   6 profound

4
later

5
1 In   2 From   3 at   4 In   5 Back   6 To

6
1 e   2 c   3 d   4 a   5 f   6 b

7
1 They handed them in and subsequently forgot about them.
2 In spite of retiring fully from teaching in 2006, Farrer kept all the letters carefully filed.
3 Following his retirement, he continued posting the letters back to his former pupils.
4 The exercise is greatly valued by his past students, partly owing to the fact that letters are rarer and more precious nowadays.
5 As well as getting to find out how their lives have actually evolved, he receives their gratitude for going to the trouble of returning the letters.
6 Not all the pupils agreed for him to read their letters. Nevertheless, he has kept and is returning these letters too.

8
Possible answers:
1 Some pupils were too embarrassed to make their letters public **because** their letters were immature.
 or **owing to** the immaturity of their letters
2 The exercise has had a profound effect on the students. **However**, Farrer remains modest about his part in its success.
 or **Although** the exercise ..., Farrer remains modest ...
 or **In spite of** the profound effect that the exercise has had ..., Farrer remains modest ...
3 Farrer thought the idea would inspire his students to write more. **In addition**, he hoped they would think more about the importance of education in their lives.
 or **As well as** thinking that the idea would ..., Farrer (also) hoped that ...
4 Another student wrote that he wanted to go to college and play football. **Nevertheless, / In spite of this,** having graduated from high school, he **then/subsequently** went to work in a steel mill.

9
1 uncovered 2 determined 3 evidence 4 indicated
5 clues 6 deduced

10
Archaeologists working outside Vienna, Austria, <u>believe</u> they have discovered a huge school for ancient Roman gladiators, rivalling in size the training grounds outside Rome's Colosseum.
The facility includes features never before seen at a Roman gladiators' school, such as a wooden training dummy and outside <u>its</u> gates, the first known gladiators' <u>cemetery</u>.
In addition to a walled field for wild animals, it includes a mini-amphitheatre. Here gladiators, who were mostly <u>foreign</u> slaves, could <u>practise</u> their moves and perform in front of potential purchasers.

9b (pages 70 and 71)

1
William Thompson crime: small-time fraudster
punishment: sent to prison
Natwarlal crimes: con man, forger, fraudster
punishment: sentenced to 113 years in prison
Ferdinand Demara crimes: impostor, impersonator
punishment: none

2
1 He looked and sounded like a gentleman, but he was a criminal.
2 have confidence in
3 an expert at pretending to look like someone else
4 He died before he could be found again.
5 He chose roles that didn't threaten other people's positions in an organization and he wasn't interested in money.
6 He became too well-known.

3
1 b 2 b 3 a 4 b 5 a

4
2 Believing: they (upper-class citizens); same
3 Considering: (= if we consider) we; different
4 having given: he (Natwarlal); same
5 compared to he (Demara): same
6 Having published: Demara, same
7 Making: (=which made) the fact that he became a well-known figure; different

5
1 Having gained 2 Provided 3 Using 4 Given
5 Assuming 6 Seen 7 having read 8 Considering

6
1 Having tried a few times, she gave up.
2 I stood in front of the White House, amazed at how much smaller it is compared to how it looks on TV.
3 Given that he's so young, it's not fair to ask him to practise the piano for four hours a day.
4 Fearing that she would be the first to arrive, she walked around the block a couple of times.
5 Assuming you're happy with the arrangements, I'll send out the invitations.

7
1 court 2 charged 3 dangerous 4 guilty 5 brought
6 found 7 fine 8 against

9c (page 72)

1
1 28 April 1789, off Tofua (in the Pacific Ocean)
2 Christian and his mates were attracted by the idea of living on an island paradise and had had enough of Captain Bligh's strictness and cruelty.
3 for Captain Bligh, yes (he sailed to Timor and then returned to England)
 for Fletcher Christian and the other mutineers, no (only one mutineer was still alive ten years after they arrived at Pitcairn Island)

2
1 to transport breadfruit from Tahiti to the West Indies
2 They were tied up, forced into the launch (a small boat) and cast adrift in the open ocean. From Tofua they sailed to Timor and then returned to England without losing a single man.
3 eight other crew members, six native men and twelve Tahitian women
4 He stripped her, ran her ashore and burned her. (Note that ships are sometimes referred to as *she*.)
5 They were captured a year and a half later when the frigate *Pandora* arrived in Tahiti.
6 One the mutineers, John Williams, took the wife of one of the Tahitians. (They were already resentful that the mutineers had divided the land on Pitcairn between them.)
7 He was shot to death as he worked in his field.

3
1 terrible 2 loaded 3 everything that could be used or sold
4 that the English Admiralty would find him

4
1 sailed 2 breadfruit 3 mutiny 4 commander *or* captain
5 launch *or* boat 6 ocean *or* sea 7 returned
8 Tahitians 9 Pitcairn 10 uninhabited
11 stripped *or* burned 12 mutineers 13 Tahitians 14 one

5
1 drawing board 2 across 3 take 4 above 5 overboard

9d (page 73)

1
1 F 2 T 3 T 4 T 5 F

2
1 mean by 2 Are, saying 3 other words 4 the point
5 right in 6 let, get, straight 7 What, meant

3
a What do you mean by ...? Are you saying ...? Am I right in thinking ...? let me get this straight
b In other words, the point is, What I meant was ...

4a
i<u>s</u>land salmon <u>w</u>hoever
han<u>d</u>kerchief cas<u>t</u>le <u>w</u>rap
foreign sub<u>t</u>le <u>p</u>sychiatrist
<u>h</u>onour g<u>u</u>esthouse Wed<u>n</u>esday

5
Students' own answers.

Answer key

9e (page 74)

1
1 400 British cavalrymen were killed
2 by quoting Bosquet who said it was madness

2
a some hours earlier   b The following day

3
1 at the time   2 In those days *or* At the time   3 a few days earlier
4 Up to/until then   5 the following day
6 The previous year

4
Example answer:
On the morning of 6 May 1937, the Hindenburg airship passed over Boston, having left Germany three days earlier. Bad weather had delayed its landing at Lakehurst, New Jersey. Cabin boy Werner Franz was working in the kitchen on board the Hindenburg. He planned to visit New York before the Hindenburg returned to Germany the following day.
The captain was trying to steer the airship next to a docking tower when there was a loud bang and Werner saw a big ball of flame. The skin of the ship had broken and the hydrogen inside had ignited.
The ship crashed to the ground. Horrified onlookers ran for their lives. Franz opened the kitchen hatch where food was pulled up into the kitchen, jumped and then ran to safety. Ten minutes after the fire had started, there was nothing left of the airship.

Wordbuilding / Learning skills / Check! (page 75)

1
1 on: base, count
2 for: account, long
3 to: adjust, subscribe
4 in: result, specialize
5 from: benefit, resign

2
1 count on   2 adjust to   3 account for   4 resign from
5 long for   6 result in   7 insist on   8 recover from

5
1 find, out, evidence, clues
2 rights, afterwards, from, in
3 impostor, claim, of, found
4 gold/ivory, spices
   sank, coast

Unit 10

10a (pages 76 and 77)

1
The adjectives that match the description of female elephant behaviour are: considerate, intelligent, protective, cooperative.

2
1 b   2 c   3 b   4 a   5 c   6 a

3
1 socially aware (b)
2 in a considerate way (d)
3 (leave) voluntarily (a)
4 long (c)

4
1 Elephants normally eat around 200 kilos of food a day.
2 Although they walk faster than us (approx. seven km/h), elephants still move around in a leisurely way.
3 However, they can move fast if they need to at speeds of up to forty kilometres per hour.
4 Technically, elephants do not 'run' (*or* Elephants do not technically 'run') because they do not lift all feet off the ground at the same time.
5 In spite of their thick skin, elephants are extremely sensitive to touch and can feel a fly if it lands on them.
6 Typically, male elephants leave the herd when they become 'teenagers'.
7 Elephants undoubtedly have excellent memories, which they use to remember the whereabouts of food and water.
8 Around fifty elephants are killed illegally (*or* illegally killed) every day for their ivory.

5
1 What makes them socially intelligent?
2 This is well documented.
3 She was wandering around in a disoriented way.
4 This group rejected her – they literally pushed her away.
5 She marched straight over to the other herd.
6 Strangely, she seemed to know which of the elephants in the other herd had been responsible.
7 If they pulled simultaneously on their rope, a table with corn on it appeared before them.
8 The elephants learned fast to coordinate their pulling.

6
1 play   2 do   3 have   4 show   5 lend   6 take

7
1 Research suggests that crows are able to tell the difference between one human being and another from their faces.
2 If one dolphin is ill, another will stay by it and help it to breathe.
3 Meerkats can be very selfless: one will often stand watch while the others are playing or eating.
4 Young Emperor penguins often group together and play together in a kind of nursery.
5 Killer whales in the Northern Pacific live with their mothers all their lives.

10b (pages 78 and 79)

1
Many of our most important innovations have their origins in human beings just having a bit of fun.
'We find the future wherever people are having the most fun.'

2
1 industrialization and mechanization
2 the Jacquard loom *or* the computer
3 augmented reality

3
1 Technological progress is one of the benefits of play (rather than play being a benefit of technological progress).
2 a period (in the past) when something was at its most successful
3 They caused big changes.
4 a machine that you could give instructions to and then leave to work
5 only something found in the past

4
1
a Not only were
b Little did anyone realize
c in no way is this
2
To add emphasis or for dramatic effect.
3
a These engineering feats were not only ahead of their time …
b Nobody really/fully realized at the time the huge implications this …
c Johnson says that this phenomenon is in no way / not in any way confined to the past.

5
1 will (*or* do)   2 hardly (*or* scarcely *or* barely)   3 than
4 does (*or* will)   5 else   6 rarely (*or* seldom)
7 Hardly (*or* Scarcely)   8 is, also

6
1 Under no circumstances should you drink water from the tap.
2 Only very rarely does the Queen attend public functions these days. She's very elderly now.
3 No sooner did the news break than hundreds of journalists gathered at the presidential palace to get more details.
4 Only when you have been in the country for five years can you apply for a working visa.
5 Never have I heard such nonsense.
6 Barely had I had time to put on my waterproof jacket when the most torrential rain started.

7
1 Under <u>no</u> circumstances should you <u>open</u> it.
2 We <u>barely</u> <u>speak</u> anymore.
3 Not <u>only</u> did he win; he won <u>convincingly</u>.
4 It's <u>hardly</u> a <u>success</u>, is it?

8
1 It takes the fun out of it.
2 have such a laugh about things
3 pit his wits against the
4 making a play on words
5 play a joke on
6 see the funny side of it

10c (page 80)

1
1 For bringing peace to Liberia.
2 She appealed to women to play their part in bringing an end to the war.
3 She spreads her message of hope around the world and continues to campaign tirelessly for social change.

2
1 female president in Africa   2 civil war   3 women's peace
4 counsellor   5 forgive   6 a culture of hope   7 public places *or* markets   8 the end of the civil war

3
1 hurt   2 chained   3 offends   4 skips   5 dream of
6 move forward

4
1 d   2 a   3 e   4 f   5 b   6 c

5
1 spirit   2 lunch   3 scot   4 feel   5 rein

10d (page 81)

1
1 It was about success and failure.
2 He criticized the idea of meritocracy, because it suggests that those who are at the bottom deserve to be there.
3 He suggests that we change our attitudes about people who don't suceed; that we don't make judgements about them.

2
a, c, d (the listener did all three)

3
1 Watching   2 isn't he   3 too   4 suppose so   5 neither
6 see   7 do   8 doubt it

4a
1 <u>I</u> doubt it.
2 <u>I</u> expect so.
3 <u>I</u> couldn't tell you, I'm afraid.
4 <u>I'm</u> <u>a</u>fraid not.
5 <u>I</u> suppose so.
6 <u>It's</u> a good idea, isn't it?

5
Students' own answers.

10e (page 82)

1
Possible answers:
He worked hard; he was very ambitious; he'd already had a good educational foundation; his parents were high achievers; he came from a comfortable background; he was intelligent/gifted; he had a natural business instinct; he had the skills and knowledge required to start his own business.

2
1 An ability to manage relationships is a key factor in career success.
2 A survey of commercial and non-commercial organizations in Singapore found that what employers value most highly in employees is the ability to listen, to work with colleagues and to persuade others.

3a
suggests, implies

3b
1 This example illustrates how/that people with good skills go further in life *or* how/that social skills help people go further in life.
2 We can infer from this example that people with good social skills are likely to go further in life.
3 This proves that the workplace is changing.
4 This example points to there being a big difference between those with good social skills and those without.

Wordbuilding / Learning skills / Check! (page 83)

1
Possible answers
A beaver is a large rodent with sharp teeth, which lives partly in the water. It is known for building dams (walls made of sticks and earth) across rivers.
Beavering away means to work hard for a long time.

2
1 duck   2 monkey   3 swan   4 wolf   5 hound   6 ram
7 parrot

3
Possible answers:
1 Never mind. Thanks anyway.
2 Chocolates? That's very kind of you, but you shouldn't have!
3 Do say 'hello' from me. *or* Give them my best wishes.
4 I'm so sorry, I didn't realize.
5 Have you come far? *or* Have you seen this speaker before?
6 I'd love to, but I can't. *or* but I'm afraid I've got too much work on.

4
Possible situations:
You've arrived late at a meeting or lecture; you've met someone and you can't remember their name; someone sneezes; someone's just had their hair cut; you need to interrupt someone who's working to ask them a question; someone tells you they can't join you for dinner; someone offers to help you with a heavy bag; someone asks if you mind if they smoke.

5
1 b and g   2 a and d   3 c and f   4 e and h

Answer key

Unit 11

11a (pages 84 and 85)

1
1 shut away in their bedrooms at home
2 young males from middle-class families
3 a more insecure economy; misguided parents who over-protect them

2
1 b   2 a   3 b   4 a   5 a   6 c

3
1 pulled   2 locked   3 trod   4 inclined   5 lost

4
1 c   2 e   3 b   4 a   5 d

5
1 c   2 b   3 d   4 e   5 a

6
1 were, would you do   2 had left, wouldn't have got
3 told, tell   4 lived, would be (or had lived, would have been)   5 stopped, realized   6 would just talk

7
1 He wrote the letter without thinking about the consequences it might have.
2 I'm not against meeting them face to face, but skyping would be easier.
3 Before deciding, shall we ask Naomi what she thinks about it?
4 I was able to log onto the computer by using your old password.
5 I think I got the injury from using a mouse all day.

8
1 e   2 a   3 b   4 c   5 d

9
1 d   2 h   3 a   4 f   5 c   6 e   7 g   8 b

10
Possible answers:
1 cross or a bit down or miserable or fed up
2 optimistic or upbeat
3 taken aback or astonished
4 done in or exhausted
5 livid or cross
6 content
7 nervous or scared or on edge or petrified
8 all over the place

11b (pages 86 and 87)

1
Students' own answers.

2
1 PT   2 JT, CL   3 CL   4 JT   5 CL   6 AB

3
1 let the decision be taken out of my hands.
2 gut feeling
3 go round and round in circles
4 torturing yourself
5 forced
6 is kidding themselves

4
1 But were there still some left, then I'd buy them.
2 Had I stayed where I was, I'd probably have been much happier.
3 Should you be thinking about whether to take a new job or not, then make a list of advantages and disadvantages.

5
1 take   2 hadn't left, would still   3 would be, spent   4 doubt
5 didn't have (or hadn't had), would have moved
6 had known

6
1 Were I to take the job, it would probably lead to other opportunities.
2 Had I not left when I did, I think I would still be there now.
3 Life would be easier if people were to spend more time on simple decisions and less time on complicated ones.
4 Should you doubt what I say, read Jonah Lehrer's bestselling book, *How we decide*.
5 Were it not for (or Had it not been for) my husband's well-paid job in London, we would have moved out to the countryside years ago.
6 Things would be very different had I known what I know now.

7a
1 /ɒt/   2 /eɪt/   3 /ɒt/   4 /eɪt/   5 /eɪt/

7b
For the noun form, the stress falls on the first syllable.
For the verb form, it falls on the second syllable.

8
OK, so here's my dilemma. I've been offered a fantastic job in Australia, 6,000 miles away from where I live now. The problem is that my parents are in their eighties and I'm the only one in the family who lives near them still. If I took the job, I wouldn't be able to see them more than once or twice a year. Should anything happen to them while I was in Australia, I'd feel terrible. But at the same time, I don't know if I will ever get an opportunity like this again. Were I to tell them, they'd of course say that I must go, but it's not that simple.

11c (page 88)

1
1 to get it flying properly; powering the robot / using an appropriate fuel source which isn't too heavy
2 Examples given in the text: pollinating crops; search and rescue missions following natural disasters; traffic monitoring; weather mapping; evaluating or exploring areas which are dangerous for humans to enter; military surveillance

2
1 robot dogs and cats
2 a TV programme about the decline of the honey bee population
3 to pollinate crops where there is a shortage of honey bees
4 They would like to create colonies of RoboBees that will work cooperatively and collectively.
5 artificial sensors

3
1 nervous system
2 crashes frequently
3 refuelling station
4 honey, pollinate crops
5 eyes and antennae

4
1 inspired   2 lobsters   3 nature   4 principles   5 Science
6 $2 million

5
1 perform   2 adapt to   3 face   4 flap
5 determine   6 take

6
1 recognition   2 a joke   3 me   4 doubt   5 duty   6 means

149

11d (page 89)

1
Conversation 1: c   Conversation 2: a   Conversation 3: d

2
1 Because the first speaker hadn't been clear about their opinion before the second speaker proposed their ideas to everyone at the meeting.
2 That she moans (complains) about routine paperwork.
3 No, because he's thick-skinned.

3
1 look, little, offend   2 came out   3 seem
4 say, upset   5 so funny   6 sounded

4a
1 /t/   2 /d/   3 /d/   4 /d/   5 /d/   6 /ɪd/   7 /d/
8 /t/   9 /ɪd/   10 /t/

4c
/aɪd/

5
Students' own answers.

11e (page 90)

1
1 I'm joking of course!
2 Many thanks for getting back to me so quickly.
3 Please don't take this the wrong way. We do really appreciate your offer.
4 Don't worry – I'm not offended in any way. It just took me rather by surprise.

2
5 b   6 d   7 c   8 a

3
Example answers:
5
Thank you for your long and thoughtful answer. I do appreciate all your work on this. I will reply to you when I have time to read it properly.
6
Great to hear from you! Your spelling hasn't improved much since we were at school. I had to re-read your email three times before I could understand it. I'm joking, of course! Your idea of meeting up on 8th December sounds perfect. Let me know where you'd like to meet.
7
I sent you a quotation as promised a week ago, but you have not replied. I don't want to pressure you, but are we to suppose that you are not interested?
8
I received your email saying that you don't want to take up my offer of advice about the design of your website. It took me rather by surprise, but I'm not offended in any way. I hope the person you have found to help you with this does a good job.

Wordbuilding / Learning skills / Check! (page 91)

1
1 f   2 b   3 h   4 g   5 d   6 e   7 a   8 c

2
1 wound (v) /waʊnd/ wrapped around
2 tear (v) /teə(r)/ rip or split
3 row (n) /raʊ/ argument or dispute
4 minute (adj) /maɪˈnjuːt/ very small, tiny
5 alternate (adj) /ɔːlˈtɜːnət/ one of every two
6 sewers (n pl) /ˈsuːə(r)z/ underground pipes which take away waste water
7 refuse (n) /ˈrefjuːs/ rubbish or waste
8 delegate (v) /ˈdeləgeɪt/ pass on or give responsibility to someone junior to you

5
Across: 1 emotional   5 bits   6 look   7 low   9 irrational
Down: 2 micro   3 and 8 if only   4 Nobel   6 livid   10 A.I.

Unit 12

12a (pages 92 and 93)

1
North America: fields of grass; photo 3
South America: mountain, jungle, prairie, coastal desert and islands; photos 1, 2 and 4

2
1 snow-covered   2 lush, jungle   3 fields   4 shanty

3
1 b   2 c   3 b   4 b   5 c   6 a

4
1 a   2 a   3 b   4 a   5 a   6 b

5
1 over fifteen   2 hundreds of miles   3 a kind of desert
4 close-ish   5 thirty years or so   6 around 1,500 metres
7 stuff

6
1 120-odd years   2 roughly 300   3 kind of small
4 in the next year or two   5 some ambition
6 dozens of ideas   7 help out with stuff

7
1 wooded   2 cloudless   3 rich   4 lush   5 dramatic
6 sparse   7 rugged   8 snow-capped   9 monotonous
10 a blot

8
1 We've moved to a city in Jordan called Irbid, about 100 kilometres north of the capital.
2 It's close-ish. The journey to work at the university takes me thirty minutes or so.
3 It's farmland mostly, but not very rich. Some people would call it sparse, but I kind of like it.
4 The desert is to the east, some distance away, but we haven't visited it yet. I'd love to go some time, but there's so much other stuff to see that we haven't got round to it.

12b (pages 94 and 95)

1
Students' own answers.

2
1 red tides
2 Aurora Borealis
3 red tides, ice circles
4 sailing stones
5 Aurora Borealis, ice circles
6 Aurora Borealis, red tides, ice circles

3
1 dew   2 the poles   3 toxic   4 scorched   5 spinning

4
a 4   b 5   c 7   d 2

5
1 Would you do   2 Would you take   3 would be really nice
4 the car wouldn't start   5 would go   6 would have got
7 'd imagine/expect   8 we would stay   9 I wouldn't put

Answer key

7
1 sopping 2 brand 3 fast 4 rock 5 pitch 5 freezing
7 lightning 8 sick 9 wide 10 stiff

8
a bored stiff   b dirt cheap, bored stiff, filthy rich

12c (page 96)

1
By looking at how the societies who have traditionally co-existed with these animals have managed to do this.

2
1 b 2 c 3 a 4 b 5 a 6 b 7 b 8 a

3
1 Much 2 co-exist (*or* co-habit) 3 compete 4 healthy
5 growing 6 evicted 7 ironic(al) 8 survival

4
1 on 2 on 3 in 4 around
5 off 6 to 7 out 8 over

12d (page 97)

1a
2 just 3 finish 4 there 5 in 6 on 7 moment 8 make

1b
Interrupting: 1, 2, 4, 5, 6
Preventing interruptions: 3, 7, 8

2
a golf courses are attractive; they provide a facility to play sport; the land will be better looked after; they protect against other development
b golf courses are exclusive, they are not environmentally friendly

3
Phrases 1, 2, 3, 4, 5, 6 and 8 are used.

4a
They are all said with a polite and firm intonation, except number 3.

5
Students' own answers.

12e (page 98)

1
1 The (cheering) fact that wildlife is thriving in our cities.
2 The (worrying) fact that so many animals are killed on the roads.
3 Drivers should be more attentive to animals on the roads and also take action if they hit an animal.

2a
1 I am a vet
2 injury from road accidents is the most common reason animals are brought to our clinic
3 What I cannot accept
4 So, be animal aware.
5 We all know how upsetting it is to hit an animal in your car.
6 But taking steps to lessen any negative consequences will make you – and the animal – feel a whole lot better.

2b
1 a – It's a stronger claim, a more direct statement.
2 b – It gives a clear statistic.
3 a – 'Careless attitude' is a more emotive expression.
4 a – 'Inexcusable' is a stronger, more emotive word.

3
Students' own answers.

Wordbuilding / Learning skills / Check! (page 99)

1
1 visually 2 socially 3 industrially 4 physically
5 geographically 6 culturally 7 internationally
8 emotionally 9 environmentally 10 ethnically

4
1 worth spending 2 In the end 3 I have had
4 is made up of 5 beyond a joke

5
1 cloudless 2 geo-literacy 3 Basho 4 seventeen
5 Angeles 6 blot 7 air 8 editor
Vegetable: cabbages

IELTS practice test

Listening
1 A   a number of local companies are involved in that
2 B   I did have to take photo ID with me
3 C   they wanted to check that we didn't hold strong views about shopping malls
4 6/six (hours)   I'm not supposed to work more than six hours in any one twenty-four hour period
5 (a/your) badge   As long as you've got your badge on, you can wear what you like.
6 60/sixty   But at least sixty per cent are meant to be in the first group (A)
7 35/thirty-five   I've got a target of thirty-five interviews over the seven days
8 text (message)   you're sent a text message each morning
9 12/twelve hours   You've got twelve hours from the time of the interview to do that.
10 Survey Host   We're using Survey Host actually
11 C   Very few reserves in Africa have the biodiversity that Phinda offers.
12 A   although the area was at one time somewhat depleted in major mammal species
13 A   worldwide significance, and the recent release of black rhino into the reserve is evidence of this
14 B   Most probably, however, you'll spend some time monitoring the white rhino
15 database   Volunteers assist in the building up of a database
16 eye(s)   individuals, which are identified through their eye markings
17 leopard   leopard research project, keeping a note of where they are seen
18 B   volunteers are provided with a weekly food kitty to do their own shopping
19 C   The house is equipped with a fridge, freezer, stove, oven and microwave.
20 F   there is also a DVD player
21 B   spores which form on fallen leaves and then infect the leaves of a healthy tree
22 B   It seems to be less of a serious problem on Far Eastern ashes.
23 C   it migrated from its Japanese home and took up residence somewhere in Eastern Europe
24 A   Diana: Are there different subtypes? Dennis: Well, no.
25 A   Probably more than one generation, actually
26 A   nobody knows exactly how many there are in reality
27 C   still less exactly how evenly they're spread across the country
28 D   we need to find out if it's affecting old and young trees equally
29 F   whether it's spread to all regions
30 G   whether there are populations of ash trees in areas that can be isolated from the spread of the disease
31 electronic commerce   an internship is an integral part of your degree programme in electronic commerce

32 unpaid   working for a company as an unpaid member of staff
33 faculty guide   following the specifications outlined in the Faculty guide
34 job (description)   secondly it should outline your job description there
35 critical analysis   on the third component, the critical analysis of a specific internship-related topic
36 routine tasks   you'll be asked to do routine tasks most of the time
37 logical thinking   and demonstrate your ability in logical thinking
38 B   acronyms used in your work place? If in doubt, leave them out
39 E   If your report includes typos and spelling mistakes, then your readers are likely to be distracted and you risk losing credibility.
40 F   A fellow intern or workmate will tell you if what you've written is understandable.

Reading
1 Texas   moving North Dakota into second place among US states, ahead of Alaska ... output could eventually close in on that of Texas – at two million barrels.
2 14 million barrels   By the time the frenzy ends, perhaps 20 years from now, as many as 14 billion barrels
3 pipelines   Until more pipelines are built ... most of the oil and water will be transported by truck
4 farms/farming   But how does a region of farms weather the human onslaught?
5 sand   fracking, by which large amounts of fresh water combine with sand and smaller amounts of other substances
6 dirty water   How will the dirty water that's pumped out be prevented from contaminating groundwater ...?
7 TRUE   The extraction technology refined in the Bakken is in effect a skeleton key that can be used to open other fossil fuel treasure chests.
8 FALSE   North Dakota has boomed before, in the 1950s and 1980s.
9 FALSE   in south-western Montana, where they still live
10 FALSE   Earlier in her career, the Delaware native had driven a commercial bus ... also an airport transit bus ...
11 NOT GIVEN   (We only know that she did the special training course – not how she found it.)
12 TRUE   'It was a big gamble,' she says, referring less to the likely availability of work than to the reception she would almost certainly get in such a male-dominated environment.
13 FALSE   waiting out the 'umpteenth blizzard' of the season ... the owner of a small water-hauling company ... he cold-called and offered her a job next day.
14 iv   The overwhelming evidence is that the wildcat is going to be extinct very soon.
15 x   That is certainly a more encouraging figure, but the future of this ... animal is worryingly uncertain
16 v   the answer ... stems from recent studies into the origins of wildcats
17 viii   Soon the cats adapted to life with humans, who in turn came to rely on them as a means of pest control. As farming spread westwards, the cats came too.
18 ii   Its population had already been drastically reduced by loss of habitat in historic times. ... Wildcats disappeared in lowland England around 1800. Then they vanished ... 1860.
19 vii   it is not the loss of habitat that is causing the imminent extinction of the species. It is the spread of the domestic cat.
20 ix   domestic cats can survive there in such numbers ... their ever-growing population
21 B   *Felis silvestris lybica* is the Middle Eastern wildcat, which has now become feral in Scotland.
22 A   *Felis silvestris silvestris* is the European wildcat, which disappeared from England in the 19th century.
23 B   *Felis silvestris lybica* is the Middle Eastern wildcat, which was domesticated about ten thousand years ago.
24 C   *Felis silvestris cafra* is not mentioned in relation to Scotland.
25 neutering   almost certainly involves the widescale neutering ... of feral cats.
26 rescue project   its prospects have been transformed by a rescue project
27 snares   persuaded local hunters ... to stop ... laying down snares in lynx territory
28 relocating   conservationists have since been capturing animals and relocating young adult lynxes in protected territory
29 captive breeding   Captive breeding centres have also been established ... thanks to those programmes.
30 disproportionate   Some would consider that disproportionate, whilst others would think it money well spent.
31 B   the revolution in the field of genetics is sometimes taken for granted
32 D   Many people believe ... while this is an appealing idea, it's wrong ... In reality, ... Similarly, for years it was accepted that ... However, recently, researchers found that ... This raises the radical possibility that ...
33 FALSE   Epidemiologists ... receiving the majority of funding
34 TRUE   ... these ('tea, coffee, sunshine and exercise'] can explain or predict less than 5% of most diseases, the only exception being smoking, which has repeatedly been identified as a direct cause of disease
35 NOT GIVEN   (Doctors are often misinformed about how many genes we have, but the text doesn't say that they believe nature to be more important than nurture)
36 TRUE   The study appeared to show that the brothers shared an extraordinary number of similarities in later life ... However, closer analysis revealed ... the brothers' environments were still quite similar and many pronounced differences in their lives were not revealed to the public.
37 FALSE   Obesity can be addressed, according to Professor Jones, by changing that environment
38 FALSE   whether in the form of ... superior nutrition ... remains an open question
39 NOT GIVEN   (the text talks about the athletic performance of Kenyan runners but doesn't mention them participating in research)
40 TRUE   the two terms should not be seen as separate or exclusive. Instead, they are parts of the same process